Praise for
The Man Who Listens to Horses

"*The Man Who Listens to Horses* will first break, then mend your heart.... [It is] easy to read and hard to put down."
—*The New York Times Book Review*

"Here is a man who is a real, live horse whisperer.... From those cold nights and blazing days in the desert, he would build a life anchored by his love and understanding of the horse."
—*The Washington Post Book World*

"Monty Roberts has become [the] world's most famous horse trainer and the best-known writer reared in Salinas since John Steinbeck."
—*San Francisco Examiner*

"Utterly engrossing ... For those who have ridden the high plains country, wide open, atop a horse in the full, mature glory of its strength, the only honest reaction after reading the book is to smile in warm agreement."
—*The Globe and Mail* (Canada)

"[A] surprisingly complex and lively memoir of a successful and influential horse trainer who helped pioneer nonviolent methods of breaking horses in ... Roberts's surpassing love for horses [is] captured here in his evocations of the horses he has trained over a career spanning four decades."
—*Kirkus Reviews*

"A riveting read ... [It] could change your life."
—*Horse and Hound*

The Man
Who Listens
to Horses

Monty Roberts

BALLANTINE BOOKS

NEW YORK

2009 Ballantine Books Trade Paperback Edition

Copyright © 1996 by Monty Roberts

New chapter and Afterword copyright © 2009 by Monty Roberts

Published in the United States by Ballantine Books,
an imprint of The Random House Publishing Group,
a division of Random House, Inc., New York.

BALLANTINE and colophon are registered trademarks of Random House, Inc.

Originally published in hardcover in the United States by Random House,
an imprint of The Random House Publishing Group, a division of
Random House, Inc., in 1997.

This work was originally published, in different form, in Great Britain by
Hutchinson, a division of Random House UK, London, in 1996.

Library of Congress Cataloging-in-Publication Data
Roberts, Monty
The man who listens to horses/Monty Roberts
p. cm.
ISBN 978-0-345-51045-7
1. Roberts, Monty.   2. Horses—Behavior.   3. Horses—
Training.   4. Human-animal communication.   5. Horse trainers—
California—Biography.   I. Title.
SF284.52.R635A3   1997
636.1'0835'092—dc21
[B]   97-17318

Printed in the United States of America

www.ballantinebooks.com

10 12 14 16 18 19 17 15 13 11

Book design by J. K. Lambert

DEDICATION

I could think of no other choice than to dedicate this book to *Equus: The Flight Animal.* It is my opinion that we owe this species an apology for causing it to endure our lack of understanding for thousands of years. Equus has been my teacher, my friend, and my provider.

WITH WARM AND LOVING APPRECIATION

It must be said with utter sincerity that the partnership with my wife, Pat, has been the strongest contributor in the advancement of my career. Her hard work in the management of our operation allowed me travel time and the time to study my art. Her sacrifices have been monumental.

Pat, along with our children—Deborah, Laurel, and Marty—deserve my deepest thanks for their love, patience, tolerance, and incredible work load.

THANK YOU TO MY TEACHERS

While Equus has been my greatest teacher, Marguerite Parsons, Sister Agnes Patricia, Bill Dorrance, Don Dodge, and Dr. Bob Miller must take a lot of credit for creating an environment in which I could learn.

AND A WORD TO MY READERS

While horses are friendly animals, mistreatment and fear can render them hostile, and caution should be used if you are unsure of a horse's temperament.

Acknowledgments

A debt of gratitude is owed to many who made a great deal of effort in helping me with the creation of the original *The Man Who Listens to Horses* and also the tenth-anniversary edition. First and foremost, without the encouragement of Her Majesty Queen Elizabeth II, I would never have had the courage to write my story. The Queen opened the door for me and was persistent in the belief that "there must be a book."

Larry Scanlan traveled from Canada to spend time with us and worked brilliantly to edit copious pages and still have them read in my vernacular for the U.S. edition. Sam North traveled from England and helped with the editing of the U.K. edition.

Jane Turnbull has been and still is my enthusiastic and totally supportive literary agent, who believed in me from the very beginning. Judy Sternlight, editor at The Random House Publishing Group, and her staff, including Rebecca Shapiro, have done a superlative job of pulling this revised edition together in a miraculously short period of time. Thank you, Judy.

I am grateful to the instructors who have gone through my training program and taken what they learned to further spread my concepts throughout the world. Thankfully they are numerous enough now that I can't list them all, but they know who they are and how much I appreciate their support in carrying my message.

Without the "home" support, it would be impossible to continue to travel year round in pursuit of my goal: to leave the world a better place than I found it, for horses and for people, too. Daughter, Debbie

Loucks; assistant, Guilia Orth; instructors and staff on the farm; and my wife, Pat, who is a 24–7 full-time support staff in herself—they all keep the balls in the air. Other organizations would need ten times the number to accomplish what these few people manage so admirably.

Monty Roberts
June 2008

Contents

The Man
Who Listens
to Horses

CHAPTER 1

The Call of the Wild Horses

It all dates from those summers alone in the high desert, me lying on my belly and watching wild horses with my binoculars for hours at a time. Straining to see in the moonlight, striving to fathom mustang ways, I knew instinctively I had chanced upon something important but could not know that it would shape my life. In 1948 I was a boy of thirteen learning the language of horses.

In the wilderness of Nevada, the soil is silky and cool to the touch at dawn, and at midday will burn your skin. My summer vigils were marked off by the heat of the day and the cold of the night and a profound sense of solitude. It felt right to be there under those vast skies on that dove-gray moonscape in the company of wild and wary horses. I remember, especially, a dun mare with a dark stripe along her back and zebra stripes above her knees. Clearly the matriarch of the herd, she was disciplining an unruly young colt who had been roughing up foals and mares. I vividly recall how she squared up to him, her eyes on his eyes, her spine rigid, her head pointed arrowlike at the adolescent. No longer full of himself, he knew exactly what she meant. Three hundred yards from the herd, the outcast would know by her body position when he could return to the fold.

If she faced him, he could not. If she showed him part of her body's long axis, he could begin to consider it. Before her act of forgiveness had to come signs of his penitence. The signals he gave back to her—the seeking of forgiveness—would later be fundamental to a technique I would develop to introduce young horses gently to saddle and rider. It was the mustangs who taught me their silent body grammar, and the dun mare was my first teacher.

I grew up in Salinas, California, where wild horses were annually put to other uses. In 1948, the Wild Horse Race was a featured part of the Salinas Rodeo. And because I lived in a house on the rodeo grounds (or "competition grounds," as I called it) where my parents ran a riding school, rodeo was part of our lives. Normally, wild horses were cheap and plentiful. Doc Leach, a short, bespectacled man who was our dentist and also president of the association that governed the competition grounds, would have called the usual people and said, in effect, "Come on, folks, I need a hundred and fifty mustangs to be delivered to Salinas by July the first"—and it would happen. But with horsemeat used so extensively during the war, mustang numbers had dwindled significantly, and by 1947 the herds in northern California, Nevada, and southern Oregon had diminished by as much as two-thirds, with the horses now located almost exclusively in Nevada. That year Doc Leach's calls had fallen on deaf ears. "What mustangs?" the Nevada ranchers had countered. "You come up here and see if you can get them yourself." The wild horse race was usually no race at all but a kind of maniacal musical chairs played with mustangs, but that year the Salinas Rodeo Association had to scrape together what they could find, and so it was a fairly tame wild horse race, with too few horses and too many old ones to put on the show required.

The following year I saw an opportunity to provide Doc Leach with a service that would both salvage the reputation of the wild horse race and save the lives of a hundred or more horses. I was only thirteen; he might not listen. But I was driven by both a fierce young entrepreneurial spirit and my love of the horses. In previous years, after the rodeo, the mustangs were sent to Crow's Landing to be slaughtered for dog food. If I could somehow make them worth more than that...

"What if," I proposed to Doc Leach, "I go to Nevada and get the mustangs?"

Doc Leach's eyebrows popped up above his glasses. "How you going to do that, walk?"

"No, I've made a lot of friends from trips to horse shows there. I know I can ask for help from the Campbell Ranch." Bill Dorrance, a remarkable horseman in his mid-fifties who would become my mentor, had contacts at the ranch and would make the arrangements. Ralph and Vivian Carter, good horse people and friends of the family, had business to conduct near there and had agreed to help. Finally, I had a truck driver lined up.

"Good for you," Doc Leach came back, a hint of mockery in his voice. I was, after all, little more than a boy.

"I'd ride up to the ranges with some of the day hands from the Campbell Ranch, and I bet I could secure one hundred and fifty head."

"Head of what? Chickens or horses?" He had a sophisticated sense of humour.

"Strong and healthy mustangs, Dr. Leach." I explained to him that my younger brother, Larry, and I could care for them at the competition grounds until the rodeo was held. "They'll be ready on the spot, with the pair of us on hand to see they're all right." Doc Leach shifted his pipe from one corner of his mouth to the other and blinked a couple of times. That meant he was cogitating.

Finally he asked, "What's in it for you?"

"I was thinking, sir, that after the rodeo Larry and I could break in the mustangs and maybe have an auction sale, so they'd be worth more than Crow's bait." That was the euphemism for animals taken to Crow's Landing for slaughter.

This year, I told him, he would not have to send any animals to the abattoir. "There'd definitely be more than a few that would go through the sale ring ridden by my brother or myself and maybe provide someone with a useful mount, sir."

He was still cogitating, so I went on.

"And perhaps the rodeo association could show a profit at the end of the day, more than the slaughter value anyway." Doc Leach weighed the arrangement, turning it over in his mind. He was like the buyer of a used car, kicking the tires and looking for the hidden defect. When he could find none, he agreed.

He offered to call up Irvin Bray and contract him to provide me with transport for the return journey. Finally, we agreed that the net proceeds of any sales were to be divided equally between the rodeo association and the Roberts brothers.

I was on my way to Nevada to gather 150 head of mustangs. It would prove to be the most important opportunity of my life: to study horses in their natural groups, in the wild. For the next three years I would be crossing the Sierra Nevada to the high desert beyond, to live alongside wild herds for several weeks at a time. From that experience I would begin to learn a language, a silent language which I have subsequently termed "Equus." With that as a spring-board, I would assemble a framework of ideas and principles that would guide my life's work with horses. I would have none of this were it not for my time as a teenager spent in the company of mus-tangs.

In June 1948, Ralph and Vivian Carter and I put our horses and our equipment in the van and headed off. The Carters were an odd cou-ple. Older than Ralph by fifteen years, short, stocky and strong, Vivian had been an exceptional rider as a teenager and very successful in the showring, but in her late twenties a horse bucked her into the trunk of a tree. She would still ride well, but walk with a decided limp for the rest of her life. Nevertheless, the smile on her face was constant and spoke of her inner beauty. She was far and away a better horse person than Ralph was, and I learned to listen more to her than to him. Ralph had the appearance of an all-American/Scandinavian cross: blond hair and eyebrows, blue eyes, tall and handsome, broad at the shoul-ders, narrow at the hips.

The van carrying us weaved back and forth around the foothills be-fore climbing the Sierra Nevada, following roads cut by our fore-fathers into the stern, harsh landscape 400 miles north and west of Salinas. North beyond Battle Mountain lay the high desert and the Campbell Ranch, and the vast, empty tract of federal land owned by the Bureau of Land Management.

What I noticed first as the door of the truck swung open was the air, how thin it was. Climbing down from the cab, I knew already that this landscape would be like nothing I had ever encountered. The horizons, the sky, stretched endlessly. I had the sense of being on a different planet. The lunar landscape was covered in sage and rough grasses and cut by deep barrancas (ravines) overgrown with stunted trees. Somewhere in this vast natural wilderness were wild horses.

Indian day hands at the Campbell Ranch were detailed to help us. I was half expecting them to recommend the same trick my Cherokee ancestors had apparently used—before driving the mustangs toward the trap, push them in the opposite direction for a day or so. The horses' tendency is to press back against the control inflicted on them. The day hands, though, had another plan.

Some fifty miles from the homestead, they had built a corral about a quarter of a mile long. They had searched for a heavily traveled canyon and set the corral at the bottom end. From the air it bore the shape of a keyhole, with two sides angled into a narrow gap and a circular area beyond. The posts and fencing were camouflaged with sage and brushwood.

It was a two-day ride to reach this makeshift structure, and when we got there the day hands walked us around and explained how the mustangs should be driven into the wedge at the bottom and funneled through the narrowest part into the circular area, where they would slow up and be forced to turn. Riders, meanwhile, would come down the wings and close the gate across the narrowest part of the keyhole. Familiar with this canyon, the horses would not have seen a vehicle, a building, or even a fence post to scare them off.

But where were the horses?

They were not to be seen by any casual scanning of the earth's surface, a large part of which seemed to lie spread in front of us, a fissured plateau baking in the sun. The Indians pointed here and there. The whereabouts of the wild-horse herds could not be guessed accurately, and the ranch hands were happy to allow the Carters and me to head off and start bringing them back ourselves. They had work to do, but they would help us complete the job.

For this undertaking I had two saddle horses and two packhorses.

The latter were piled high with blankets and utensils. Brownie was my number-one saddle horse, but in addition I had Sergeant and Burgundy as well as a second packhorse, Oriel. The going was stoney and rough; the barrancas, in particular, made for precarious riding, so I would be leading Brownie on foot much of the time. He was precious to me, and I wanted to save him from too much wear and tear if I could.

I was anticipating the adventure of a lifetime, and Brownie caught my excitement and shared it, or perhaps it came from deep inside him. When he took his first steps into this cracked and thirsty land, this son of a mustang was heading home.

Brownie was always a steady and well-mannered horse, but the conviction with which he carried me into his home territory hinted that he knew something I did not.

Ralph, Vivian, and I broke camp at dawn and hurried to stamp out the remains of the fire and bury it, kicking at the loose earth, enjoying the burst of activity if only to warm ourselves in the chill air. We wore yesterday's clothes, and as we mounted our horses and started to peel the oranges that my mother insisted I eat every day, the sun rose like a golden disk, watery at first but then burning with increasing strength as the morning wore on.

Things began to go wrong, or so I thought, as soon as we saw the first herd of fifty or so wild horses.

Brownie caught their scent as we traversed a barranca. Large stones littered its slopes where stunted trees struggled to suck enough water and take advantage of the shelter. Though it was dangerous, you could ride the bottoms of these canyons, along natural paths formed by the scouring action of flash floods. As we descended, Brownie's heels dragged behind him when he tried to load more weight onto his hocks to take the strain.

At one point he stopped dead, concentrating on something I could not see or hear. I knew from his lack of agitation—and the fact that he was keen to move on in the same direction as his ears were pointing— that he had scented this herd of his brothers and sisters, the mustangs of northern Nevada.

But when we caught up with them—and they were already moving away, fully aware of our presence—Ralph and I had different ideas on how to proceed. The Carters, not unreasonably, wanted to press on and simply drive the horses back toward the ranch. Because we had to cover fifty or sixty miles of ground on the return journey, we would have to go relatively fast to stick to our schedule.

I, on the other hand, wanted to stop and simply observe the horses. There was something compelling about seeing them as a family, the alpha male or breeding stallion circling and lifting his tail, stepping out with a high, proud action, and acknowledging our presence. It made me want to melt into the background and see what could be seen, without subjecting them to our interference. It was almost as if I wanted to be a horse myself, so thoroughly had I taken their side. These horses were not only Brownie's brothers and sisters, they were mine, too. I wanted to understand them, and I was more than ever certain that I knew less than I thought I did.

This unspoken conflict of interest between the Carters and me generated an unspoken compromise. They hurried me along, and I slowed them down. We none of us got what we wanted.

As we pressed the mustangs ahead of us, we saw the signals that would be obvious to anyone with experience of horses. A pair of forward ears shows interest in something anterior or in front. Forward ears with head high denotes interest in something in front but far off. Forward ears with the head held low indicates interest in something up close, near the ground.

The mustangs we pursued held their heads in normal position but with a "split ear," one forward and one back, signifying interest in something in front, but also concern for anything to the rear—us. The ears were like beacons that told us the direction of their focus. If their ears were hanging relaxed and the horses stood with one hind leg bent and resting, we could assume we were unobserved. At that moment, the signals said, these horses had no concern for their safety.

If a horse pins his ears back on his neck, he is angry. We watched one mustang, ears pinned, maneuvering to position his rear legs and take action against another animal. He was angry, aggressive, and dangerous.

Once or twice we saw the stallion pin his ears back and stick his nose straight out as far as he could reach; he had his head lowered to just below wither height, so that from the shoulder forward the neck and head looked like an arrow; his eyes were steely, and he was moving forward in a stalking mode. He must have possessed very active testicles, for this stance is exclusive to the full-grown adult male. Only as the male reaches potential for supremacy within the family group are you likely to see this particular display.

As Ralph and Vivian and I circled this first group, turning them this way and that to point them back toward the trap set for them, I learned that a horse's field of vision is nearly 360 degrees, with only a slim cut of land right behind him, which he cannot see, and an even slimmer cut directly in front.

Watching the stallion badger the mares in his defensive role, we could confirm that when he switched his tail—other than when clearing insects off his body—he was not content. This we knew already. A trainer who puts too much pressure on a horse with spurs or whip will create what is called "a switch-tail horse," and in Western competition significant points are lost if a horse switches his tail while performing.

Perhaps the most important piece of knowledge that my first foray into the high desert of Nevada indelibly engraved on my mind was this tenet: there are two types of animal, the *fight* animal and the *flight* animal. It bears repeating that the horse is a flight animal. If I knew it before, I understand it now in a more profound way.

It sounds obvious, but it is critical to remember that given the slightest excuse a horse will say, "I don't want to be near you. I feel there is danger if I stay!" The flight animal wants only to reproduce and survive; fear is the tool that allows him to survive. This has to be respected in any dealings with a horse, or he will be misunderstood.

Humankind, however, is a fight animal. Our preoccupation is with the chase, and having dominion over other creatures in order to eat them or use them for our own ends. The horse, then, sits at the far end of the flight animal spectrum, while humankind, the supreme fight animal, is his clear opposite.

In order to gain a horse's trust and willing cooperation, both parties must meet in the middle. However, it is totally the responsibility of the human to achieve this. The only way is to earn the trust of the horse and never abuse his status as a flight animal.

If I learned anything on that first trip, it was that I needed a much longer time if I was to get what I was looking for: a true understanding of how horses behave in the wild.

My frustration was that it could not happen under these conditions. When we got back to the trap in the barranca, we merely jammed a bunch of horses into the circular pen, brought up the hired transport, and carted them off. We did not select suitable animals, grade them by age or sex. Along with the more suitable, younger adolescent colts came older animals and even lactating mares—meaning that somewhere behind was a foal facing certain death.

In short, we were distressingly insensitive. At least I knew what I wanted to do next time.

———

With our convoy of trucks hauling 150 mustangs—all of them banging and kicking in the trailers—we arrived back at the competition gounds in Salinas. When we dropped down the trailer ramps, the horses scooted into their new home, a huge stock corral near the track. The horses were seeing, for the first time, barns and other buildings, and the arena where they would be racing in just a month's time before thousands of people. The mustangs snorted and blew and ran round the perimeter of the corral, astonished at their new circumstances.

I rushed into the house, proud to tell my parents what we had done. "And," I said, "I'm going to take more time next year, and then I can see what those horses are all about. They're barely going to know I'm there."

My mother was receptive and listened intently. "What do you think you'll find out?"

"I don't know, but something. The way they communicate as a family. That's what I hope."

My father was not pleased at all. "About all you'll find out is it's cold at night and hot in the day. You'll find out those mustangs don't want to have much to do with you or your fancy notions." Horses understood one thing only, my father barked, and that was fear. If you did not hurt them first, they would hurt you.

As for the 150 mustangs, we—that is to say, humankind—were going to hurt them quite badly in the wild horse race. But it was not until later that I realized how responsible I was for that. For all my entrepreneurial spirit, I was, in the end, a child, with much to learn.

Some 20,000 spectators came to watch this popular part of the rodeo each of the four days. Larry and I were in among a crush of people pressed against the fence. Waiting on the track were a number of teams of three men each, all of them dressed in full cowboy regalia. They were as likely to get hurt as the horses were, and you could tell they were nervous by the way they fidgeted. The teams milled about some distance apart from one another, waiting to have their wild horse delivered to them, each team with a Western saddle parked ready on the ground nearby.

Riders would come onto the track on their saddle horses, each one literally dragging a wild mustang on the end of a fifteen-foot lead rope connected to the horn of his saddle. At the sight of this, the crowd started to holler and cheer and stamp their feet. Behind the mustangs and pushing them forward were more riders.

Wild with terror, the mustangs were bucking and running, diving and pulling on the ends of their ropes. I imagine the Roman circus generated something like the same hysteria; convinced they were coming to a savage end, the horses raged as they were dragged in. The crowd was whooping.

The riders then handed the lead rope of each mustang to the first member of each team, called "the anchor"—the biggest and heaviest of the three men. The anchors dug in their heels and set about trying to keep these 900-pound wild animals as much as possible in one place.

The second man is called "the mugger," and his is probably the most dangerous job. The mugger travels down the lead rope, hand over hand, turning this way and that to follow the line as the mustang fights and plunges like the wild animal he is. As fast as he can, the mugger has to grasp the horse around his neck, try to put him into a headlock, and pinch his top lips. The idea is to hold him still long enough for another man to put a saddle on him.

My heart was in my mouth as the battle began. Some of the men were thrown off the ropes before they reached the horses; others had better luck and were already hanging in there, wrestling with these animals like they were in a barroom brawl. The third member of the teams, "the rider," began to dart in, carrying a saddle on his arm, trying to throw it on and cinch it down.

Imagine the noise and the confusion. My nerves were screwed to the highest pitch, just watching. Several men limped off, too injured to continue, while others ran forward to take their places. One man was dragged out unconscious from under the feet of a horse and carried off.

By now, some riders had managed to tighten the cinch and were jumping up and aiming to stay on long enough to be handed the lead rope, which is their only method of guidance. It was a scene of utter chaos, with horses bolting in all directions, some with riders on board, some without. Riders who had managed to get mounted were attempting to race each other once around a half-mile track, and were using whatever methods of hazing they could. They were shouting and spurring their horses and pulling at the rope to try to turn them the right way.

I lived the excitement as would any thirteen-year-old raised in the culture of rodeo, but at the same time I recoiled against the mad cruelty. There were some crashing falls, and I felt the impact of each and every one of them as though it was happening to me. One horse, I learned later, had broken his jaw. An excited voice exclaimed behind me each time there was a horse writhing on the ground—"Crow's bait, Crow's bait!"

By the time some riders were up in the saddle and racing around the track, the roar of the crowd doubled in volume and the horses were running for their lives, their heads held low and ears pinned back to their necks. They raced once around the half-mile track and the winner threw one hand in the air and continued sailing around until his horse had slowed enough for him to leap down and take his applause. He would stand to face the audience, his expression one of utmost excitement and triumph.

The wild horse race causes several deaths among horses every year in Salinas, and it is the same at forty or so other rodeos around the country. I believe it should be abolished.

———

The task now was to make the mustangs worth more alive than dead. Larry and I had just sixty days, August and September, to break as many of them as possible. A schooled mustang might fetch a buyer at the October auction; an unbroken one was destined for Crow's Landing. Their lives, and our hopes for a profitable arrangement with Doc Leach, were in our own hands.

Owing to injuries and deaths in the race, only 130 of the mustangs were left to us. We turned them out in the corrals, where they were no doubt glad to relax after the trauma. Their rest would be brief. My brother and I agreed that I would take roughly two-thirds of them, to his third.

My first concern, though, was to hide my new ways of thinking from my father, who broke horses the traditional, violent way. Happily, a pair of barns ran down either side of the pen where I would school the mustangs, so I was sequestered from his view. Despite the impending deadline, I wanted to continue experimenting with the communication skills that so intrigued me. My aim was to refine a technique that used the horse's respect and cooperation, not the one that forced its servitude.

I believed it was important to concentrate on this, in part *because* of the deadline; I was sure my way would be quicker. But I also felt in my bones that I had chanced upon something new that would change the way human beings relate to horses. Although my technique would improve dramatically after the following year's expedition to Nevada, even at this stage I had come to think of my process as entirely different from that of "breaking" horses. That word has connotations of violence and domination.

I changed the nomenclature. From that day on, I called my method "starting" horses. If traditional breaking was designed to generate fear in the horse, I wanted to create trust. If the old way involved ropes and tying horses' heads and legs, I wanted no part of that either. A significant moment came when I realized I could cause trust in a horse without pain or restraint.

In short, instead of telling young horses "You must," I wanted to ask them "Will you?"

I knew from the very beginning that engaging the horse's trust would work. My technique was still haphazard and unrefined, but I got there. After the starting process, I recruited from our riding school four or five of my top students and so brought on to a good standard about eighty of my one hundred mustangs. The students were willing volunteers, and together we learned a great deal from every horse.

On the day of the sale, my eighty horses were ridden through the ring and my brother's were ridden as well. Altogether, the sale took in just under $6,000.

Doc Leach was happy with the results. He got back his $5,000 investment in the herd and made a small profit. This was unprecedented; acquiring mustangs for the wild horse race traditionally meant a substantial loss.

My brother and I were less happy, at least financially speaking. For two months' work, our share of the profit amounted to $250 each. Even in those days, this was not a wage to brag about. It was more like a nod and a thank-you. But given what I had started to learn about wild horses in those first few months, I had an even better feeling of time well spent. This was just the beginning.

———

The following summer was perhaps the finest of my life. I would spend much of it alone in the high desert, in what I came to see as an outdoor university. I was a freshman at Mustang U. But first I had to make some new arrangements with Doc Leach.

"What can I do for you, son?"

"I have an idea how to improve the wild horse race this year."

"You didn't do so badly for us last time."

"How about we reduce the number of mustangs we haul back here?"

"And that's to improve the race, is it?"

"Well," I explained, "I noticed that you didn't use all hundred-and-fifty head. You picked out the best two-thirds of them."

"That's right, we did."

"What if we choose the best two-thirds of them up there in Nevada instead of down here in Salinas? Then we'd only be transporting a hundred head instead of one-fifty, and we could lower the overhead."

Even at fourteen, I had a pretty firm grasp of cost.

Doc Leach looked down at me. "Who's going to judge the best one hundred head—you?"

"That's right, sir. Then we can avoid bringing the lactating mares and the older animals in the first place."

Doc Leach smiled. "You've got a point, I have to admit."

I recommended that we gather 500 head and select the best 100 adolescent colts and fillies. ("Adolescent" in mustang terms means an animal three to five years old, since the limited nutrition and harsh desert environment delay their maturity. Mustangs cover vast territories to feed, and the saying is that they can graze—at twenty miles an hour.)

I paid a trucker to transport myself, Brownie, Sergeant, and Oriel up to the Campbell Ranch. Ralph and Vivian Carter agreed to join me later on this adventure; the helpers and truck convoy would come up with them. But for three weeks I would be alone in the Nevada desert with the mustangs. I would have the time to move slowly and observe them without interfering in any way. The Campbell Ranch had prior information on the location of family groups, which were sometimes ten miles apart. I intended to bring each family group toward the trap in the barranca one by one, very slowly, observing them as I went.

Once again, I was glad to have Brownie as one of my saddle horses for this all-important experience. I patted his neck as we rode out over the high desert ground. Oriel and Sergeant walked along behind, and in addition I had our black-and-white stock dog, called Bobby, three pairs of binoculars (two spares, for I would have been lost without them), a handgun and a rifle.

When we reached the first horizon I twisted around in my saddle and watched the outbuildings of the Campbell Ranch disappear from sight as we moved down the opposite side of the slope. We were on our own.

It felt good to be riding across this open ground again, with its rocky barrancas where the cottonwood and aspen trees grew. I would have to be extra vigilant for rattlesnakes. Worse were the invisible crevices: you might be galloping across what looked like a flat, unbroken expanse of desert in pursuit of a herd when, suddenly, a six-foot crevice yawned at your horse's feet. The mustangs, who usually spotted you before you spotted them, used these depressions cleverly. They would travel in them at the slightest suspicion of danger, and from my vantage a mile away it seemed that the horses in my sights had suddenly vanished.

My father was right, at least, about the weather: the days were hot, the nights cold. Occasionally, rainstorms would lash me and the horses for an hour. Big, billowy, high-desert clouds would give rise to electrical storms. I was living on a diet mostly of jerky—a cured meat—plus pancake mix and salami, as well as oranges.

To find the first family group of horses, I had to consider their food source. The mustangs would eat the sage and the chamise if they were desperate, but they preferred the gramma, brome, and rye grasses.

When I caught up with my first group, my aim was to integrate with the herd as closely as I could. Either they would accept me as no threat, which meant staying more than a mile distant, or I could try to get closer without their knowing I was there. The latter option quickly evaporated. The horses caught my scent from a mile away and began to move off. They were little more than dots on the plateau, and already they were going away.

I left Oriel, my bay packhorse, behind because he was proving rather clumsy and often stumbled over stones, the noise of which carried over vast distances—not that he cared. I was beginning to wonder about this Oriel character. His ears were always at half-mast, neither forward nor backward. He was either a deep thinker or a little dumb, maybe both.

After lightly hobbling him and leaving Sergeant to keep him company, I continued on foot, leading Brownie. We used the barrancas as cover and stayed downwind, moving quietly. Given the time to move slowly and think about what was happening, I was surprised by how hypersensitive the herd was to our presence. If Brownie just scuffed a rock, I could see their ears flick in our direction.

I could get within a quarter mile of the herd, but no closer. I was running out of cover and even though I was downwind of them, they would cede us no more ground. Brownie and I settled down by a cottonwood tree and I counted the horses, trying to log their markings so I could distinguish one from another.

My binoculars were key. When I see young people today strapping on virtual reality helmets, entranced by the world they enter, I am reminded of how I felt when I looked through binoculars at that herd of wild horses. They seemed close enough to touch. I could see subtle shifts of the eyes, ears, tongue. These were pure movements, untainted by human intervention. That day I would watch for eight continuous hours.

I noticed, in particular, the dun mare. Older than most of the others, with a heavier belly that hinted at many pregnancies, she seemed to issue a lot of commands. She ordered her group to move off. She started, the others followed. She stopped, they did likewise. It seemed she was the wisest, and they knew it.

What I was observing, in fact, was the dominant mare. Many people likely still think that the stallion runs the show. The breeding or dominant stallion, sometimes called the alpha male or lead male, will skirt the herd and defend it from marauders. His motivation is to prevent anyone or anything from stealing his harem. But it was the dun mare who was in charge of the day-to-day running of this group. There was no mistaking it.

And then I saw an extraordinary sequence of events. A light bay colt was behaving badly. He was about twenty months old, I guessed, with a vast amount of feathering around his fetlocks and down the backs of his legs, and a mane running down well below his neckline. He took a run at a filly and gave her a kick. The filly cowered and hobbled off, and the colt looked pleased with himself. He was only about 550 pounds in weight, but very aware of the fact that he owned a pair of testicles.

Then he committed another crime. A little foal approached him, moving his mouth in a suckling action to indicate he was no threat but subservient. Just a foal. That cut no ice with this colt; he launched himself at his younger cousin and took a bite out of the foal's backside. The bay colt was a terrorist. Immediately after the attack, he pretended nothing had happened; he went neutral, as though trying to avoid blame.

Each time he behaved badly, the dun mare—the matriarch—weaved a little closer to him. I became certain that she was watching for any more of this behavior. She showed no apparent sign of interest, but she had left her station and was edging closer to him all the time.

The mare witnessed about four such episodes before she finally made her move. Now she stood within twenty yards. Still, the cream-colored colt could not help himself: he launched at a grown mare, grabbed the nape of her neck, and bit down hard.

The dun mare did not hesitate. In an instant she went from neutral to full-blown anger; she pinned her ears back and ran at him, knocking him down. As he struggled to his feet, she whirled and knocked him down again. While this chastisement unfolded, the other members apparently took no notice.

The dun mare ended by driving the colt 300 yards from the herd and left him there, alone. Amazed, I tried to fathom what I was seeing. The mare took up a position on the edge of the herd to keep him in exile. She kept her eyes on his and faced up to him. She was freezing him out.

It terrified the colt to be left alone. For a flight animal, this was tantamount to a death sentence; the predators will get any horse long separated from the group. He walked back and forth, his head close to the ground, several times executing this strange, uncomfortable gait. It looked like a sign of obedience, similar to a human's bow.

Then the colt made his way around to the other side of the herd and attempted to sneak back in that way, but the dun mare had followed his circle. Again she drove him out, running at him until he had fled another 300 yards. Returning to her post on the edge of the herd, she kept her body square on his, and never once took her eye off him.

He stood there, and I noticed a lot of licking and chewing going on, although with all this drama he had eaten nothing. I remembered the foal and how he had snapped his mouth in an obvious signal of humility, as though he were saying, "I'm not a threat to you." Was this colt now saying the same thing to his matriarch?

By this time, it was getting dark, and I would have to get back to the other horses. I wanted the moon bright that night; I wanted desperately to see how the tale would end. I scooped up Brownie's reins and rode back to where Sergeant and Oriel were waiting. My intention was to camp there and continue observing the dialogue between mare and colt.

When I got back, Oriel was standing with his nose in a bush. Then he lifted his head sharply, his whole body tense with surprise. A cloud of bees surrounded his head. This was an emergency, for the horse was clearly being stung. Oriel took a few paces backward and then tried a couple more sideways. He tried it with his head held low and then jerked it up again.

No luck.

Then he shook himself like a dog emerging from water. The bees still hovered, a cloud hooked on a mountaintop. This was a puzzle, and Oriel had nearly run out of tricks. There was only one left: he tossed his head up and down, evidently figuring that if he did this long enough the bees would get bored and leave, which is what they did.

Oriel did not seem unduly perturbed by the experience. It was one of life's many mysteries: the one and only time I ever saw a bee swarm take such a shine to a horse's head.

Oriel was an accident-prone, affable character who always got into trouble but somehow made it seem funny. Once he spiked himself by walking into a shard of wood. I am unsure how he did it—and only he could have done it—but a two-foot-long splinter was driven through his nose and the roof of his mouth. It was a painful sight: not at all amusing, but this was Oriel we were dealing with. He was most apologetic and sorry for himself and allowed me to perform the grisly task of pulling out the splinter. He was then left with a hole in his nose the size of my thumb, blood pouring from the wound.

I took off the bright red bandanna I customarily wore around my neck and used it to plug the hole and stem the bleeding. There stood Oriel with a red flag flying in the middle of his face, and every time he took a drink the cloth would soak up the water. Then it would drip, like tears. It was a sorry sight, but I had to laugh.

The sun now sank surprisingly fast down the western slope of the sky, as though itself desiring rest from a hard day's work. I made camp and hurried to settle Brownie, Sergeant, and Oriel with their feed.

From its place in that vast sky, the moon cast the landscape in a new and surprisingly generous light. I picked up my binoculars and found I could see clearly for quite a distance. I did not realize it then, but my night vision was likely helped by the fact that I am totally color-blind. I know that the color of the high desert is dove-gray only because others have told me. Mine is a rare condition, quite separate from the more common one in which an individual cannot properly distinguish colors.

When I was young, no one believed that I could see only in black and white, but I have subsequently learned that I see in a way very different from normally sighted people.

Oliver Sacks, in his study of "The Case of the Colorblind Painter," describes how his subject had a car accident that caused him to lose all perception of color. But along with that terrible loss came an unexpected gift: "People's figures might be visible and recognizable half a mile off... his vision had become much sharper, 'that of an eagle.' " Distressed by his condition, the artist became nocturnal and at night his extraordinary vision allowed him to identify a license plate four blocks away.

Using the binoculars, I caught sight of my herd. To my astonishment, the dun mare was now grooming the troublesome colt. She was giving him little scrapes on his neck and hindquarters with her teeth, and generally fussing over him. She had let him back in; now she was keeping him close by and giving him a lot of attention. She worked away at the root of his tail, hips, and withers.

Purgatory was behind him. This was heaven.

As it turned out, night was a better time to watch the wild herds. Mustangs fear attacks from predators mostly at dawn and dusk; at night they relax and their social interaction is more marked. It became a habit to watch them by the light of the moon, and I would usually sleep from about one-thirty A.M. until five-thirty A.M.

For the next two summers, I would round up mustangs for the Salinas rodeo, and nothing I saw ever matched the exchange between the dun mare and that light bay colt. It was educational to watch the matriarch disciplining young, adolescent horses because so much happened. The youthful energy and inexperience of the gang of adolescents drove them to make mistakes, much like the young of any species.

Often, like a child, the colt would reoffend immediately after being let back in, to test the disciplinary system and to gain back lost ground. He might fight another colt or bother the fillies. The dun mare came right back and disciplined him again. Each time he sinned she drove him out and kept him out before letting him back in and welcoming him into the group with extensive grooming. The third time he sinned, he practically owned up and exited by himself, grumbling about it but accepting his fate.

Then, finally, his teenage rebellion ceased. Now cloyingly sweet, he had become a positive nuisance, wandering about and asking every horse, "Do you need any grooming?" when all they wanted was to be left alone to eat. For four days the dun mare had made the education of this awful brat her number-one priority, and it had paid off.

As I watched the mare's training procedures with this adolescent and others, I began to understand the language she used, and it was exciting to recognize the exact sequence of signals that would pass between her and the younger horses. It really was a language—predictable, discernible, and effective.

The silent aspect of her commands is worth dwelling on because we often underrate a language that uses a different medium from our own. As I was to learn much later, the most common form of communication on this planet takes place silently—in the dark of the deep sea, where animals use intricate lighting systems called bioluminescence to attract mates, ward off predators, attract prey, and otherwise convey all the signals necessary for their existence.

Body language is not confined to humans or horses; it constitutes the most common form of communication between all animate objects.

In the desert, the dun mare constantly schooled the foals and yearlings, and they responded to her, without a sound. The stallion's security system required near absolute silence, and his investigations of mating potential were also conducted soundlessly. The mustangs were happy with one another, upset with one another, guided and advised one another—all in silence.

I learned that in the equine universe, every degree of a horse's movement has a reason. Nothing is trivial, nothing is to be dismissed. A horse raised alone, I now know, will still speak Equus: genetics imparts much of the language. But the lone horse's communication is dull, less defined. A mustang raised in the wild in a herd, on the other hand, displays as pure a form of the equine tongue as I could have hoped to find anywhere.

I would learn, much later, while starting horses in a round pen, a rich code of signs and subsigns. Keeping my mouth closed invited the horse's discomfort, opening it slightly was fine. Opening a fist on the side of my body away from the horse drew him in, while opening a fist close to him sent him away. Fingers open stirred one response, fingers closed another. Hands above my head with fingers splayed provoked true panic (perhaps it triggers primordial memories of cat claws). Whether I am moving, standing still, facing the horse, or away: all this matters as the horse reads my body language and I read his. I can now enumerate about one hundred or more signs the horse will respond to, and the vocabulary is still growing.

The key ingredient in the equine language is the positioning of the body and its direction of travel. The attitude of the body relative to the long axis of the spine and the short axis: this is critical to their vocabulary. It *is* their vocabulary.

When the dun mare squared up and faced the colt, she was holding up a Keep Out sign. If she showed him part of her long axis, he could begin to consider returning to the herd. But before she would say, "I forgive you," he had to say, "I'm sorry." If the colt paced with his nose close to the ground, then he was asking for a chance to end his isolation and to renegotiate his position with her. He was saying, "I am obedient, and I'm willing to listen." If he showed her the long axis of his body, then he was offering vulnerable areas to her and asking to be forgiven.

Their eye contact also spoke volumes. When she was holding him out there, she always kept one eye directly on his, sometimes for uncomfortably long periods of time. When her eye slid a short distance off his, he knew he might be allowed back in. I came to realize how subtle was this reading of eye contact. Even when I was unfamiliar to this herd, I could cause a horse to alter his direction and pace of movement by changing which part of his body I looked at—even from a distance.

When the colt trotted out to suffer his exile, he would throw his nose out in a circular motion. Translation: "I didn't intend to do that. I'm sorry. It wasn't my idea. It just happened. It was the other guy's fault." The dun mare had to judge whether or not to believe him. I could see her thinking about it. Sometimes she bought it, sometimes not. The licking and chewing action of the colt's mouth was a signal of penitence. He was saying to her, "Look, I'm a herbivore. I'm no threat to you. I'm eating over here."

Observing all this, I could make sense of the "yo-yo effect" once described by my Uncle Ray. Cherokee hunters had for centuries exploited the tendency of prey animals, once chased, to circle back and "hunt" the hunter. Press the young horse away, and his instinct is to return. The dun mare advanced on him, then retreated. When I made this connection between the mare's discipline and Uncle Ray's story, it was as if synapses in my brain all fired simultaneously. A term sprang to my mind—"Advance and Retreat."

In time, I would grasp just how exact a language it was. There were precise messages, whole phrases and sentences that always meant the same thing, always had the same effect.

Perhaps, it occurred to me, I could use the same silent system of communication myself. If I understood how to do it, I could effectively cross over the boundary between human (the ultimate fight animal) and horse (the flight animal). Using their language, their system of communication, I could create a strong bond of trust. I would achieve cross-species communication.

"Advance and Retreat" also offered a psychological explanation for why horses are "into pressure" animals. In my twenties, during a short career riding bucking horses, I once waited in the chute on a horse who was leaning hard on one side, pinching my leg against the boards. Six cowboys were pushing against the horse's body trying to move him over, but the harder they pushed, the more the horse leaned.

Finally, one wise old horseman chanced by and put one finger against the horse's *other* side, as if pushing against it. Instantly, the horse moved into that little bit of pressure and my pinched leg was just as instantly grateful.

Horses, as a natural response, do not move away from pressure, they move into it—particularly if the pressure is applied to their flanks. The wild dogs that prey on horses on every continent attack the horse's belly, aiming to tear a hole in the stomach wall so the intestines will drop out. The dogs can then fall back and track the horse, confident that a meal is imminent.

Once flight is no longer a clear option, the horse's best defense is not to run but to turn into the onslaught and kick: if they run from a bite, their skin will more likely tear. I am convinced that this explains a phenomenon recognized by all good trainers: poke a forefinger into a horse's side and he will move against the pressure rather than away from it. It is perhaps the single most important thing to remember in training horses. *Horses are into pressure animals.*

Go into pain, nature told the horse. And the horse heeded the message. Over the years I would expand my Equus vocabulary, but even the more refined signs would exist within this all-important umbrella concept of Advance and Retreat that I learned at the age of thirteen.

———

Later that same summer I witnessed a fight between two stallions.

Water was in short supply that year, and I watched, fascinated, as the matriarchs made frantic efforts to get their families watered and fed. The different family groups were lining up at a water hole like airliners in a holding pattern. The groups had to keep their distance because the stallions would not tolerate it otherwise. Their territorial instincts were in conflict with those of the matriarchs, and this made all the horses edgy.

Among them was a bachelor group—young males who had left their family groups and were now scrimmaging among themselves, honing their fighting skills for the day when they would make a challenge for a herd of their own. Then the inevitable happened. A bachelor clashed with the alpha male of a family group waiting in line for water. A stallion fight is one of the few times you will hear sounds from a mustang.

I found the noise of battle chilling, but the mares took no notice of the terrible squealing and screaming at the perimeter of their group. This was a contest that one horse would win; a draw was not in the cards. The two males reared and pawed each other with their hooves, plunged and kicked and bit. It continued for five or six hours, well into the night, and though my eyelids were drooping, I had to watch.

Just when it seemed the stallion had won and the bachelor was about to hobble off, the latter redoubled his attack, though his leg was torn and bleeding from the teeth raking his hide. Limping toward the stallion, practically carrying his hind leg, the bachelor waded in again.

When the younger stallion finally left, he did not return. Before long the predators would gather round him and he would be their meal for the next day or two. The bachelor knew it, too. A vanquished male will often commit a kind of suicide, deliberately seeking the areas where the cats are, almost offering himself.

Even the victor, on this occasion, was a sorry sight. He was left battered and limping, and he walked as if he was a century old for the next day or two. Another challenger would have finished him, but none came and he nursed himself back to strength.

———

It took Brownie and me about three weeks to gather the different family groups. When we were five miles from the trap in the barranca with one group, a team of six day hands from the Campbell Ranch would ride out, circle the mustangs, and help drive them into the enclosures where a feed of alfalfa awaited them. They would then tell me where the second group had been last sighted, and take Brownie, Oriel, and me in the van as close as dirt roads would allow, maybe fifteen to twenty miles. When they left us and were driving back, they would drop a trail of alfalfa every mile or two back to the trap, as bait for the horses.

At the end of the three-week period, we had about 500 mustangs corralled. We culled lactating mares, obviously pregnant fillies, breeding stallions, and older animals, then loaded about one hundred young colts and fillies into the trucks and drove them back to Salinas as before.

That year, they had a much better wild horse race. The horses were suitable for the task at hand, and fewer were injured. Once again I watched from the grandstand, but took no pleasure in it. I vowed to train myself as quickly as possible to communicate with horses; I was beginning to realize that there was a lot of apologizing to be done to the equine species.

Euphoric from my time in the desert and bursting with what I thought were critical insights about horses, I looked forward to telling my mother and brother about my discoveries. My mother was a quiet, competent rider who genuinely liked her horses, and she was naturally intrigued by my tales. But the one person who understood better than anyone my sense of excitement, if not precisely what I was saying, was Bill Dorrance, who had helped me connect with the Campbell Ranch.

Bill was born in 1903. He was a slim six-footer, and always wore round glasses. Were you to see him in a three-piece suit and hear him talk, you might take the straight, stiff man for a banker or an accountant, certainly an educated man. In fact, like his brother, Tom, he had little formal schooling, but there was a remarkable brightness about them both.

Now in his mid-nineties, Bill is still a fine rider and roper but as a young man he was nervous when he competed under pressure in the showring. Bill Dorrance was all about careful calculation. In terms of the psychology of a horse, the study of the horse's mind, he was light-years ahead of his time. He was the only one who believed in me, and when I was seventeen my father finally forbade me to see him. "Bill Dorrance will destroy you," he predicted one memorable day in Salinas. Bill was a progressive man with new ideas, ideas I shared and understood. When I got back from the desert, I went right to him. He was like a grandfather to me, an armchair philosopher of horsemanship. He was ridiculed for some of the things he said, but I now see how far ahead of his time he really was.

"You have to cause your horse to be mellow," he once told me, "to be in unison with you, not against you." It was a breathtaking notion for someone of his generation. I owe Bill a great deal. What we shared was a keen awareness of the possibilities between horses and humans, a sense that we had barely scratched the surface of that ancient connection. "I'm discovering things about horses," he once told me, "and I don't want to die before I pass them on. You're young and talented, and I want to pass them on to you."

I felt I did possess a special affinity with horses. Now that I was beginning to understand their silent language, I could turn a great corner. My ambition was immense: change the way humans relate to horses.

The one hundred mustangs at the competition grounds would be the ideal test of my theory: how to form a natural bond with a wild horse; how to convince the horse you are an ally, not a predator; how to cast myself as the dominant matriarch and speak her language.

I would have to work fast, and with one eye on the whereabouts of my father, because I did not want him to interfere—although, underneath it all, I still sought his acceptance and approval.

As it happened, in the course of starting the mustangs, I discovered something so exciting that I began to believe I could persuade even my tradition-bound father to see things my way. I had identified a phenomenon that I called "join-up." As I lay in bed at night I could hardly sleep, so convinced was I that I had stumbled on something that truly would change the way we operate with horses.

Surely, I reasoned, my father would see it. He was too experienced a horseman not to. But I knew better than to go to him and show him directly. Instead, I settled on showing Ray Hackworth, hoping that he could prevail upon my father because he had my father's respect.

Ray Hackworth leased facilities at the competition grounds where we lived. Soft-spoken but also a disciplinarian, he was a noted trainer and a gentleman: I asked him to come and watch what I could do. I told him I had discovered a phenomenon that I could explain only in terms of the horse's own language. I promised him that I could dissolve the natural barrier between horse and man, flight animal and fight animal.

He reminded me that my father had often warned me over the years that my ideas could be dangerous and I should stick to the conventional ways of doing things. But I continued to implore that he come and see for himself what I could do. If I could please Ray, I could surely please my father....

Eventually he agreed.

When we arrived at the round pen, Ray strolled up the ramp on to the viewing deck and leaned against the fence. "OK," he said, tipping his hat to the back of his head. "Let's see it."

I stood in the middle of the pen, together with a three-year-old colt not long past the trauma of the wild horse race. The colt wore no halter, rope, or restraint of any type. The door to the round pen was closed; it was he and I.

From practicing this a hundred times over, I knew what to do. I confidently waited a moment or two to let this unnamed mustang get accustomed to the round pen. He was too nervous to take a single step toward me, although his attention was on me as the main threat currently confronting him. "What I'm going to do," I said, "is use the same language as the dominant mare in his family group." The silence from the viewing deck told me Ray was not going to ask questions, so I continued. "That language is a silent language, a body language, and the first thing I'm going to ask him is to go away from me, to flee. I'm only doing this because then I will ask him to come back and join up with me."

I moved, quite abruptly, toward the colt. I squared my shoulders and fixed my eye on his eye. Straight away, he went into flight, taking off in a canter around the perimeter, staying as close to the wall as he could—and as far from me as possible.

I continued to press him into flight, in the same way that I had observed the matriarch driving away the adolescents in the wild. I remained square on to him, I maintained direct eye contact. For Ray's benefit, I continued to explain what I was doing. "In his own language I'm saying to him, 'Go ahead and flee, but I don't want you to go away a little. I want you to go away a lot. For now, I'll call the shots, until we can form a partnership. You see, I speak your language.' "

I had a light sash line, and I pitched it at the colt—not to hit him, but to encourage him to flee. Which he did. As he cantered around the pen I used the line and my body posture to keep him in flight; my shoulders were parallel to his long axis. I was facing directly toward his head and, with my body, pressing him away. My eyes were locked on his.

This continued for several minutes. I was watching for the signals—the same signals I had observed in the wild, when the adolescents would ask the dominant mare to be released from their enforced exile. Meanwhile, as a test, I allowed my eyes to drop back to his neck. When I did, he slowed.

I let my eyes drop back farther, to his shoulder... and he slowed a bit more; his head started to come off the rail a bit to look over at me. When I let my eyes drop back to his hip, I saw a further reduction in speed, and he began to angle off the wall even more.

Then I took my eyes back to his eyes, and his speed increased immediately; he moved back toward the wall and was in full flight again. He was reading me. He knew we were dealing with each other in *his* language.

I called to Ray, "I'm waiting for his ear to open onto me, for him to start licking and chewing, and then for him to duck his head and run along holding it a few inches off the ground." It was important that Ray realize I could *predict* what would happen.

"Here's the first one, now!" I called. "See?"

The colt's inside ear had opened toward me and stayed fixed in that position. The outside ear was tuned to the surrounding areas, flicking forward and back. The colt was saying, "I don't really know what this is all about, but I'll pay attention to you and we'll see where it goes from here."

The colt had made approximately eight revolutions of the round pen before the ear closest to me was adequately locked on. At this point, I pitched the line in front of the colt and stepped a bit to the front of his action, keeping my eyes locked on his to prevent his coming off the wall toward me. Quickly, he reversed field and fled in the opposite direction. In a moment or two, the ear closest to me was locked onto me as before. It was going according to pattern.

Since Ray could not know what to look for down in that pen between the kid and the colt, it was important that I explain my actions and expectations, but I suddenly sensed this might all be a mistake. A fourteen-year-old explaining things to an older man? It might be seen as arrogant. Still, I hoped, the value of what I was doing would coun-teract that.

I began to take the pressure off the colt. First, I reduced the num-ber of times I cast the line at him. Then I coiled the line and held it in my hand, slapping my leg with it to encourage him to continue. The colt came back to a trot. By this time he had made twelve revolutions of the round pen.

The next signal came right on time. He started to lick and chew. His tongue actually came through his teeth and outside his mouth, then he pulled his tongue back and chewed with his teeth. There was a ripple effect across the large mandibles.

"There!" I called to Ray. "You see that chewing action with his mouth? That's exactly what I saw them doing out on the range. It means he's ready to discuss this situation. He's gone away and I've pressed him away farther. He's recognized my desire to communicate with him, and now he'd like the chance to renegotiate. This licking and chewing action of the colt is a message to me, it's saying some-thing like, 'I am a herbivore; I am a grazer, and I'm making this eating action with my mouth now because I'm considering whether or not to trust you. Help me out with that decision, can you, please?' "

Then came the final signal I was looking for. As the colt trotted around, he dropped his head so his nose was traveling only an inch or so above ground level.

"And there you go!" I called to Ray. "His head's dropped. I can't tell you the times I've seen this out there in the desert, and it always means the same thing—it means 'Let me back in, I don't want to flee any more.' "

It was time for me—like the dun mare—to turn passive, to let this colt come and join up with me. I allowed my eyes to travel to a point maybe fifteen to twenty feet in front of him. I moved my shoulders around to follow my eyes until they were on a forty-five-degree angle to his long body axis. I was avoiding eye contact and showing him my flanks, as it were.

Immediately, he stopped. He came off the wall and faced me. I maintained my position, my body and my eyeline at forty-five degrees to his. He took a step or two toward me. I waited.

Then he walked right up to me, not stopping until his nose was inches from my shoulder. I could not speak. I wanted to shout to Ray, "Look, this is what I mean. How *about* this? Isn't it fantastic?" But I could not afford to break the spell. It was indeed magic: this colt trusted me. No longer a predator, I was his safety zone. The moment of acceptance, or join-up, is what I had discovered, and I felt a shudder of heartfelt emotion. I have felt the same thrill with every one of the 10,000 or more horses I have started this way. I fervently hoped that Ray felt the same way.

To test the strength of the join-up, I took a slow right turn. The colt followed me into the circle, his nose to my shoulder. Then I took a left turn. He hesitated, and looked to be going the other way.

Immediately I knew to return to a dominant stance, and I began to drive him away. He did not like that, and before he had completed one circuit of the round pen he was flicking his nose out and apologizing, asking to be let back in.

I allowed him back, soothed him and talked to him, and gave him a good stroke between the eyes. It is not essential to use the area between the eyes as the stroking point, but it seems to be more effective to touch the horse here than any other part of the body. There is general consensus that for a horse to let you into a part of his anatomy that he cannot see is the ultimate expression of trust.

Now I had the colt walking comfortably behind me and I knew Ray would be amazed. I imagined him saying to my father, "I tell you, Marvin, that boy of yours had a wild horse walking along behind him like it was his best friend after only twenty-five minutes. He's on to something. Come down and see for yourself."

I called out to Ray, as quietly as possible now that the colt was standing next to me, "Ray, you know, now that he's joined up with me and we're on the same side, it's pretty much of a formality." When I was confident the colt fully trusted me, I brought in another long-line, a saddle, bridle, and a saddle pad, as well as a long stirrup leather—all of which I put on the ground in the middle of the pen. With the click of the gate, the colt's stance changed. He saw something different—a pile of equipment—and became frightened. He had justification for being skeptical, so I waited. I allowed him to choose between me and the equipment. He chose me and calmed down. He stood still while I carefully lifted the saddle pad and the saddle onto his back. He let me fix the girth—slowly, smoothly. After taking a step or two away, he steadied and let me continue.

Before any rope or lead had been attached to his head, let alone a bridle, he was wearing his first saddle. He was asking me lots of questions, his ears flicking back and forth and his nostrils blowing, but he trusted me.

At this point I stepped away from him and squared up to him, driving him away, not aggressively, but with the confidence I had developed over the last 200 or so horses. He went into flight and began to canter around the perimeter of the round pen. I wanted to familiarize him with the saddle before a rider was on. He bucked hard for several minutes, which I was glad to see because I did not want Ray Hackworth to think this was a fluke. Within a few minutes the colt was cantering steadily around, the bucking over. I saw the same signals—the licking and chewing, the inside ear settling on me, his coming off the wall to get closer to me. For a minute or two I worked him around the outer limits of the pen, and let him find comfort in carrying the saddle, first one way, then the other. After three or four revolutions in each direction, the colt was telling me he was ready to come back in. I let him join up with me, adjusted his girth, and generally soothed him with my voice. He was doing fine. There was nothing to be frightened about, if he stuck with me. I would look after him and have fun with him, love him like I loved all his brothers and sisters. I took the bridle and lifted it over his ears. The colt accepted the snaffle with no more than a brief lift of his head. I secured the reins under the rear portion of the saddle and took the stirrups down to prepare for long-lining. Then I sent the colt back to work, cantering him around the perimeter, first one way, then the other. He was fully tacked-up, wearing a saddle and a bridle and the long-lines.

I called out, "I want to gain his confidence and make him happy to follow the bit and bridle—as he'll be doing just that for the rest of his working life. I want to make it a happy experience for him."

I turned the colt six or seven times before stopping him and reining back one step. I again adjusted his girth; I brushed the saddle with my hands, rubbed his neck and belly. Then I put my left toe in the stirrup and prepared to lift myself on to his back. I felt the strain in my thigh muscle as I asked the colt if I could put my full weight into the stirrup, testing for his reaction. He took a sideways step to help redistribute the extra weight, but he held firm.

I lifted myself up. Instead of swinging a leg over, I lay across his back for a while, waiting to see if he was comfortable with this. I hoped I was answering any questions he had with the things I was saying to him. I would find him a good name. We would find him a good home. Perhaps he would enjoy being a ranch horse, or maybe he would go into a Western show, in the pleasure-horse category. He might end up with a kid like me, learning to ride. I let the colt catch sight of me out of both eyes before calmly swinging a leg over and sitting up. I was riding him after only forty minutes.

I sat there jubilant on the back of that horse. An idealistic youth, I was convinced that it was only a matter of weeks before I would enjoy the respect and admiration of my elders and betters all over the county. And especially, my father.

"That was a fluke!" Ray barked out.

He was staring at me, a concerned look on his face. The sound of his voice coincided with the colt's first steps, and I did not try to stop him. As the colt and I walked around together, I heard Ray say, "You're wrong to go against your father. He's worried about you getting hurt—and you could be hurt. These horses are dangerous. I suggest you stop it now."

He walked from the viewing deck and disappeared from sight. I rode the colt, feeling crushed at the very moment I should have felt triumphant. The people whose respect and guidance I needed were refusing to give it. I vowed never to mention my ideas to anyone again.

CHAPTER 2

Growing Up
with Horses

My first and most vivid childhood memory has me on the back of a horse. The ears of a horse flicking back and forth, the neck bobbing in front of me, the mane bouncing as the horse's rhythmic stride carried us along—well before I could walk, horse geography was as familiar to me as the human kind.

I was not like other toddlers, lifted onto a saddle as a diversion or so that a photograph might be snapped. I sat on a horse in the crook of my mother's arm for many hours at a time, while she gave riding lessons at the horse facility where she and my father lived. The feel of leather reins and horsehair, the sound of a horse blowing, the smell of fresh hay and horse lather: my senses first stirred in the world of horses.

I was born in the midst of the Great Depression, on May 14, 1935, in the little town of Salinas, one hundred miles south of San Francisco. John Steinbeck grew up in Salinas and set many of his classic novels—*The Grapes of Wrath, East of Eden, The Red Pony*—in this region. Perhaps he drew inspiration for his characters from my ancestors, among the immigrants and natives who came to settle in edenic California.

The first thing I would have seen when I was carried outside our little gray house would have been 2,300 acres of prime land situated in the so-called Salad Bowl of America. I remember the smells of the valley: the awful sweet, fermenting smells from Spreckels, the big sugar plant; the pungent hothouse smells of broccoli, onion, garlic, and the other cash crops growing in the alluvial topsoil that was twenty feet deep in places.

In *East of Eden*, Steinbeck talks about the Salinas River valley, how the river raged in spring, then went underground in summer—"a part-time river" he called it. The novel describes how a man bored a well in that lush valley and up came white sand full of shells and pieces of whalebone, along with bits of redwood—proof that the valley had once been a forest, and later an inland sea. Steinbeck sketches the flowers that grow there, the California poppies the color of gold—"if pure gold were liquid and could raise a cream," the blue lupines, the buttercups, the stands of Indian paintbrush, the yellow violets with black centers. He describes the valley's yellow mustard, once so tall that, if a man were to ride a horse in a field of it, only his head would be visible.

The valley is prone to extremes: occasionally too much water in winter, too little in summer. Topsoil thick in the valley bottom, scant on the mountainsides. Spring grasses were luxurious, but in summer the hot wind—"a rasping nervous wind," Steinbeck called it—forced men working in the fields to wear goggles over their eyes and kerchiefs over their noses to keep out the dust.

And Steinbeck refers to the place names, like Wild Horse Canyon and Mustang Grade, a reminder for me of how horses figure prominently in the valley. And in my life.

We did not live in a rural setting. Our place was set on the edge of town in a built-up area, but every one of our buildings was horse-inspired—from box stalls to a showring with bleachers to enclosures and breeding barns.

By the time I was two, I spent most of the day on a horse, having graduated to a mount of my own. My childhood was unique: few people can say they were born and raised on a rodeo competition grounds. The grounds came to exist when Eugene Sherwood died and willed to the city of Salinas 2,300 acres to be used solely for horse-related activities.

When the estate and the city called on my father to manage the land, he agreed, and shortly thereafter construction began on more than 800 box stalls and a competition arena with a 20,000-seat grandstand. At the time, it was the largest equestrian facility in North America. It still exists but was recently rebuilt: I plucked as a souvenir a slab of concrete from the old grandstand.

In addition to managing the facility, my father, Marvin, also operated his own riding school on the grounds. Physical education classes in Salinas grammar and high schools offered horseback riding. And so every day my mother, Marguerite, would make her rounds in our big station wagon, picking up students and bringing them to the grounds for their lessons, then returning them to class. Marvin Earl Roberts also trained and boarded horses for private clients, and leased the facilities to various horse trainers, as stipulated by Eugene Sherwood in his will.

My first horse was called Ginger. No one asked about his breeding: he was that kind of horse. Ginger was a red roan, with a bit of Thoroughbred in him, some Spanish pony blood, and maybe some Belgian four generations back, judging by the bit of feather on his legs.

He was thirteen years old when I first met him, a reined cow horse from the Uhl Ranch who in his time had been a fair entry in Western competition. Now, in his retirement, he was required to be both my baby-sitter and my teacher. Ginger had the perfect temperament: well-disciplined and steady, and marvelously calm, collected, and amiable. "Bomb-proof," as horse people say.

He had done all the cowboy stuff for years, and he knew it intimately. Even with a three-year-old kid bouncing on his withers and flapping his arms and legs in every direction, Ginger was patient. He knew me and nickered for me. His was not a noble or a peaceful retirement, but I think he too had fun. In my eyes he could do no wrong.

I can remember people saying, "That boy's just three years old"—but I could walk, trot, and canter a horse, do flying lead changes, and perform figure-of-eight maneuvers without a great deal of trouble.

My father soon noticed my riding abilities and made plans to exploit them. Before I had even started kindergarten, my father told me I had to practice harder and spend more time riding than I already did. He seized on me rather than on my brother because Larry was younger and born with a condition that, during his early years, made him somewhat frail. Larry was a gifted rider, more gifted than I was. But where he needed looking after, I could be pushed to the limit. I entered horse shows regularly and competed almost every weekend. I still have some shaky old footage of Larry and me entering the junior stock-horse class when I was four years old. The grainy, flickering film shows us running our horses around, spinning and stopping them, and racing them back and forth like miniature versions of the cowboys who had taught us—all in eerie silence.

When I see how I hauled Ginger around by his mouth and mistreated him, it makes me sad. I hope he understood that I was only a small child who knew no better.

In the Salinas junior stock-horse competition most of the children were older, but I had Ginger on my side and he knew how to score high marks in these events; he had been doing it for years against stiffer competition than this. The publicity that accrued from this unlikely win on Ginger had an intoxicating effect on my parents. Their business suddenly expanded—Mr. and Mrs. Roberts were plainly the best teachers because they had a boy of only four who won a trophy. It confirmed my father's belief: I was the child who would make the Roberts name famous in the world of show horses.

My father was an important figure, both in my personal life and in my working life with horses. Everything I achieved came to me because of the early and concentrated exposure to horses that he gave me. But if my professional life can be described as having a direction, it is one that runs absolutely counter to my father and his thinking.

Eventually my stance against him and his methods amounted to outright rebellion, for which I paid dearly. My father died in 1986, but calling him up even now, all these years later, is a bitterly hard thing to do. To understand *who* I am and *how* I am with horses, you must understand who my father was and how he was with horses.

My father was a tall man of a slim, muscular build, with chiseled features and light brown hair. He was as neat and orderly as circumstances allowed. If he met a friend in Salinas, he could be friendly, even inviting. Later in life he showed great tenderness to members of my family, but I never saw that side of him. I never shook hands with him, never got hugged by him. He would pass me on the street and not say hello. From the outset, he turned a cold and critical eye on me. Generous with others, he demanded perfection of me. He was unforgiving and scrutinized everything I did, more often than not holding it up to ridicule. As a boy I was serious and polite, and when I look back on those times I see that I never was a child. Child prodigy, perhaps. My father's protégé, yes, for a time. But a child? Never.

My father's methods of dealing with horses were what I would describe as conventional—but that is to say, cruel.

The standard way of breaking horses in those days remains popular even today. A television program from 1989 celebrated twenty years of space travel and made the point that while outer space is the great frontier of our era, the "Wild West" was its previous counterpart. As the program noted, some things have not changed since those times. Among their featured examples was how we break horses.

My father had a special corral built, with six solid posts fixed at equal distances around its perimeter. This way he could break half a dozen horses simultaneously. First he put halters on them. This might involve running horses through a squeeze chute to gain close enough access. Next, he attached strong ropes to their halters and tied each horse to a post, wrapping the rope around the post about six feet off the ground and tying off the end on the rails. Imagine, then, six animals tied thirty feet apart around the edge of the corral. The horses were already terrified and the process had only just begun.

Next, my father stood in the middle of the corral with a heavy tarpaulin or weighted sack attached to the end of a rope. He threw the sack over the horses' backs and around their legs, moving from one horse to the next. When the sack dropped on their hips and around their rear legs, the horses panicked. They rolled their eyes and kicked, reared, and pulled back against the ropes as though their lives depended on it.

Who could tell them that this was not some awful precursor to death? What primordial fears of attacks by predators were provoked?

Fear is in the horse's nature, and they were driven wild with it. They plunged back and forth and sideways on the ends of the ropes. Their necks and heads swelled up and frequently they injured themselves. It was, and remains, a desperately cruel sight.

This process is called "sacking out." It continued for perhaps four days, its purpose to break the horses' willpower and thwart their capacity for resistance. In the next stage, a leg—usually the near hind— was tied up. (Originally to accommodate swords, riders mount and dismount on the horse's left; so the "near" side of a horse is the left side, the "off" side is the horse's right.) A rope would be caught under their rear pastern and pulled tight to a collar placed around their necks. With the horses now disabled, a second period of sacking out further reduced their ability to resist. They struggled valiantly, heaving their weight pitifully on three legs and groaning in pain at the pressure on their halters. Each leg in turn was tied up; sacking out now took less and less time to sap their spirit. Then, with the hind leg again tied off, a saddle was fixed on. The horses renewed their resistance, fighting the girth. More sacking out wore them down. Some fought for many hours; others gave up more quickly and descended into confusion, waiting for more pain.

By now, eight to ten days had passed. The horses had blood tracks on their pasterns where the ropes had worn through the skin; in places, friction burned off the hair. Bruising and more serious leg injuries were common. The horses' relationship with their human masters was now defined: they would work out of fear, not willingness.

To destroy the willingness in a horse is a crazy, unforgivable act. Inherent generosity is among the dominant characteristics of the horse, and if nurtured can grow into the most rewarding aspect of their working lives. Of the horses I have been close to in my life, I have marveled most at their willingness to try for me, over and over again.

At this stage in the sacking out process, the six horses were untied one by one and fitted with a hackamore—a rawhide noseband without a bit. For a further week, the horses were long-lined. Essentially, lines are attached through the stirrups to the horse to get him used to the bit. The aim is to introduce the horse to the notion of brakes and gas pedal, ideas that do not come naturally to him. The rider to come will need the horse to know about stop and go.

I have a dramatic black-and-white photograph of my father long-lining a horse in the corral. He is bent low, hinged forward at the waist, his whole body tensed and focused on the poor horse at the end of the two lines. One might think a charge of electricity runs along the lines between man and horse. The horse kicks up great clouds of dust and reels off the corral fence. The whites in his eyes showing, the horse desperately tries to escape my father, and one eye looks back at him in fear and dread.

When my father came to ride these horses for the first time, their rear legs would be tied up again to prevent bucking. He mounted and dismounted, kicked them in the belly, tried any way he could to provoke some fight in them. If they moved, they were whipped.

If convinced they were "broken," he would untie them and ride them in the round pen. Those not yet ready to ride spent part of the day with their legs tied up, groaning in pain and despair. The whole process took a minimum of three weeks.

Given those same six horses today, I would have them ready to ride without tethering and whips, and without inflicting a moment's discomfort. I would communicate almost entirely with my body language, using my voice in only a minor way, and the result would be a willing partner that would try hard throughout his working life. All this and all six horses in just three hours, not three weeks.

———

My father was standing next to a stranger, beckoning me over to him. "Monty, this is Mr. Don Page."

The man loomed above me, holding out his hand for me to shake. It was 1939, and I was four years old; I was in competition at the Pickwick Riding Stables in Burbank, California. This area was also home to many Hollywood movie studios such as MGM, Paramount, and Warner Brothers. My father continued, "Mr. Page works at Warner Brothers, Monty."

They were both looking at me expectantly, and I waited to hear what was coming. Mr. Page dropped to his haunches to bring his face level with mine. "You know, horse stories are real popular at the moment. You seen any? Everyone's hungry for stories with kids and horses and nice things like that, so they can forget all the trouble we're in, what with the Depression, and the war in Europe. And we haven't got enough kids who can ride for us."

I squinted across at him and began to think I knew what he was after. "Your dad tells me you can ride pretty well. How do you feel about coming along to show us what you can do?"

Mr. Page suggested we stay over for a day and visit a nearby location where the studio's stunt team kept their horses and perfected their routines. At the appointed time for my audition, we turned up at this studio facility and were greeted by a line of people—likely stunt directors and casting directors. They had a steady, predictable horse ready for me, one presumably accustomed to the peculiar demands of Hollywood film directors. He was a bay gelding and led the low life of a studio mount in those days when the film industry was not so concerned about the safety of animals.

Someone called out, "OK, Monty, just canter past from left to right." I did. "And now back the other way, if possible." I successfully completed this difficult maneuver; difficult, that is, for most four-year-olds. "Now, can you pull up to a dead stop, and jump off?" This time he sounded more questioning; he was no longer issuing instructions. But I had been jumping off horses for some time now.

There was some whispering between my father and the line of studio observers. The man issuing all the orders came over to where I was standing by my horse. He looked at me and asked in a serious tone, "You see the sandpit over there?" I looked to where he was pointing.

"If you're comfortable about it, could you just ride over the sandpit and sort of... fall off? While the horse is moving?" I cantered the gelding over the sandpit and took a dive off the right-hand side. The sporadic outbreak of applause was no doubt led by my father. I stood up and brushed the sand off my clothes; someone had caught the gelding and was bringing him back. Next they had me doing all sorts of tricks. "Can you fall off the rear end?" "Could you just canter him past us and be invisible, hanging off the other side?"

Like most kids, my brother and I watched motion pictures on Saturday mornings. We would then go home and try to copy the stunts using a trick riding saddle our father had found for us. I left that studio facility pretty sore, but I had literally tumbled into the movie business, and over subsequent years I would appear in a hundred or so films.

I doubled for Roddy McDowall many times. On one occasion the crew was setting up the massive film camera they used in those days, pointing the wide-angle lens into the corral. We all gathered round. "OK, Monty," said the director, "you rope the horse here in the paddock. The pretty little girl is watching you from over there, sitting on the fence. Got that?"

"OK."

"The horse yanks you off your feet, but you cling to the end of the rope as though your life depends on it." He frowned. "Now don't forget to let the horse drag you around the paddock for quite a while, because we have to get coverage of that."

"No, I'll hang on to the rope until you tell me to stop."

This cheered him. "Great! And we'll cut the sequence back-to-back with Roddy bringing the girl here and then taking off with her afterwards. Go along to wardrobe now, and they'll fit you out in the same clothes as Roddy's wearing."

It was a simple requirement, although my father was shaking his head and telling the producers how dangerous this was going to be for his son and suggesting that the fee should reflect the level of risk. I roped the horse and dug my heels in to make it seem like I was being pulled over by the horse. I bit the dust, literally, and was dragged along the ground as planned. Then came a shredding sound; the pants given me by the costume department were of a thin, crepelike material. With this rough treatment they had bottomed out, and my bottom was equally out for all to see.

I got to my feet mortified. No one could help me out of that predicament quickly enough.

There was some consternation among the crew and much running about. They needed more shots of me being dragged, so I was to carry on, but wearing my own jeans instead. No new clothes to match

Roddy's could be found—they would worry about the continuity problem later.

But it seems they did not worry much. In the finished movie, Roddy McDowall wears off-white pants one moment, and in the next a pair of jeans while he ropes a fairly wild-looking horse, and afterward he is back in his off-white pants again.

I doubled for many child artists. I was Elizabeth Taylor in *National Velvet*—though I never actually met her until much later in life; they simply gave me a wig and a horse, and I followed instructions. I was Mickey Rooney, Charlton Heston, and Tab Hunter, and you can spot me, if you look carefully, in *Thunderhead* and *My Friend Flicka* and scores of other films. It was a good career for a boy just starting grade school, although my father made all the decisions in dealing with the studios. He negotiated and signed the contracts. He was not legally obliged to consult me or to inform me how much I had earned, nor were there laws governing the use of minors in film production. Provision for schooling, minimum wage, and safety rules did not exist then. And today, the parents of such a child actor would have to follow certain ethical standards.

As my filming schedule increased, my father often congratulated me on how well I was doing financially. He told me he was investing the money on my behalf, that it would be waiting for me when I was old enough to use it wisely. If I asked for some of it to buy a new saddle, for example, he would shake his head. "Monty, I'm telling you, I'll keep the money for you."

He stuck to his word; I never saw a penny.

——

For a seven-year-old child, a horse auction is a heady atmosphere. The crush threatened to carry me away, and I had to keep my father in sight or lose him. There was much squealing and calling, the auctioneer hammering away in his high-octane sales patter, and horses of every description were hurried into the ring to be put through their paces.

We squeezed into a spot near ringside and watched the first few horses, my father impassive. Then a skittish chestnut filly listed in the auctioneer's program as eight years old entered the ring. She was playing up and pushing her nose in the air, bothered by the halter rope and walking into the back of the man leading her as though she were only a two-year-old. She was undoubtedly a horse with problems, and no one was interested. My father was. He raised his hand and bought her for peanuts.

He signed the bill of sale and then took hold of my shoulder. "Monty, time to go to work. Follow me," he said. I thought, Here we go again. I ran along behind as he scooted around to the stalls to find the chestnut filly he had just bought. Filly in hand, we hurried to a spot out of sight of the sales ring.

On the way, my father had picked up lunge ropes, a saddle, bridle, and whip. He put on the saddle and bridle and attached the lunge ropes, then ran the filly around in a circle, turning her in both directions for about ten minutes before reining her in and removing the lunge ropes.

"Overfed and underused," he said, making a snap diagnosis of the animal's unsociable behavior. "Ride her hard for about an hour, then bring her down to a walk and cool her off. Have her take backward steps every quarter of an hour. Clean her up, and we'll put her back in the ring in three hours' time. We'll do the usual show."

For the next three hours, it was just me and the chestnut filly. My affinity with problem horses—or, as I call them, remedial horses—dates from these early, rather dubious experiences with my father at the sales ring. Horses whose difficulties he thought stemmed from maltreatment by youthful riders—"child-spoiled horses," he called them—came my way. He felt that I was the best person to ease the horse's transition to a regular rider.

I took the chestnut filly and did as instructed. But every time I worked with such a horse, I also felt compelled to figure out for myself what was causing the behavioral problem.

When my father returned, he watched as I rode the chestnut filly steadily in circles at walk, trot, and canter. Then I slipped off, ducked my head, and walked repeatedly underneath her belly. "OK," said my father. "Let's go."

Back in the sales ring, buyers looked on as I rode what appeared to be a well-broken, gentle animal and put her through some impressive maneuvers. I dismounted and walked back and forth underneath the horse's belly. Buyers pressed closer; they were impressed.

The voice of the auctioneer quickened and rose a notch as the figure rose to twice, then three times what my father had paid earlier in the day. The auctioneer must have been aware of what my father was doing. There was nothing illegal about it, of course, but clearly the horse's problems had not been solved, only quickly masked over. However, the sheer range of horses I rode made it an experience hard to equal. In time I developed the ability to read and understand problem horses quickly and accurately.

By observing the horse's actions and reactions, I developed an inner ear. I believed the horses were telling me something and, most important, I learned, with rare exceptions, never to believe the people connected with the horse. The rider was not lying, simply not listening.

Over the years this came to be the cornerstone of my thinking, so much so that it became like a mantra, and one proven by experience to be true: *A good trainer can hear a horse speak to him. A great trainer can hear him whisper.*

———

Early in 1942 the California sun was baking the dry earth as my father and I moved across the corral where he broke horses. He leaned against one of the six upright posts used to tether young horses. The posts were even taller and thinner than he was.

He was coiling a rope neatly on the post, ready for the next poor animal who would dance on the end of it like a fish on a line.

"Maybe it's time," he said, "you learned how to break a horse." I offered no reply, for I wanted no part of sacking out. The posts in the corral were like grim sentries guarding the reputation of this terrible procedure.

"There's nothin' much you can't manage," my father told me, "despite you being only a kid." We walked over to a nearby corral where my father pointed at two young horses. "There. Those two."

They seemed of a gentle enough disposition. Then we climbed the rail and got closer. The two young horses stirred and moved away quietly, but they were receptive to our voices. They had been handled before.

"We'll have you do the pair of them together, OK?"

No, I wanted to reply, I was not ready to sack out and tie up a horse; I wanted to avoid it completely if I could. My father continued, "I'll let you know when I've got the time to take you through it and instruct you."

I asked, "Can I have a few days?"

He did not sense my reluctance. To him, it would have been incomprehensible to want to "break" a horse in any other way. "A few days for what?"

"You know, maybe get to know them a bit first."

"To get to *know* them?" he asked, mystified.

"Maybe."

"Well, OK, but don't go messing it up. And don't go trying any fancy business. A horse is a dangerous machine, and you'd be wise to remember that. You hurt them first—or they'll hurt you."

I took the horses to a distant round pen and simply familiarized myself with them. I was in no danger; adults were working on their horses nearby and keeping an eye on me. I merely walked around the pen following the horses and trying to cajole them into letting me closer. It was all trial and error, but on the third day I was surprised to find that one of the horses was following me around. Where I went, so did this gelding. To my astonishment, I could stand on my tiptoes and push a saddle on his back. There seemed to be no rhyme or reason to it, but it happened.

Wildly excited by what I had accomplished, I ran immediately to the house to tell my father. I asked him to come and watch. He reminded me what he had said about not messing around as he followed me to the pen. I could not judge his mood. Maybe he was reluctant to waste his time walking 200 yards for nothing. Perhaps he had sensed my disobedience already, and was angry about it.

When we arrived, he said nothing. He simply took up position on the viewing stand just above the fence and waited. I was confident as I brought the gelding into the round pen. The horse and I wandered here and there together. It was an odd sort of dance, with neither partner knowing what the moves were, but eventually I was standing next to him.

Then, moving quietly and calmly, I reached up as high as I could and slid a saddle on his back. It was, for me, a magical experience. At this point, I looked up at my father, who was staring at me with his mouth open. I was uncertain how to read that look, but I was hoping it was astonishment and maybe pride at my accomplishing this after only three days.

Slowly, he stood up, still fixing me with this look that could have meant any number of things. "What the hell am I raising?" were the first words he uttered. As he jumped off the viewing platform, I saw that he had in hand a four-foot stall chain; such chains were often slung over the fences, and he may have gathered one up as he was watching me. He burst into the pen and grabbed me by one arm.

"What am I raising?" he said again, as if I had done something evil. Perhaps he expected me to cleanse myself, to apologize for veering from his methods. Instead, I said, "You saw it work. I was right."

Then he raised the stall chain and brought it down hard, again and again, on my thighs and buttocks. I reeled with the shock of it and the blood drained from my skull until I felt faint. I can still remember the iron grip of his left hand on my upper arm as he used his right hand to wield the chain. The beating seemed to continue for several minutes while I writhed in his grasp, my eyes closed, my spirit shattered.

I was left in a pitiful, grieving state. He whipped horses into submission and now he was giving me the same treatment, and I felt the same anger and sense of failure that the horse must have felt. A lesson in how *not* to win respect and allegiance, it only enforced a reluctant obedience, instilled fear, and left me with a lifelong sense of resentment.

I was put in the hospital so my parents could call my injuries horse-related and to keep me from the glare of friends and relatives. The term "child abuse," and the will to deal with it in society, were still many decades away. Large areas of my body were swollen, and I could neither walk nor stand. The beatings continued weekly for three more years before finally starting to taper off when I was ten. Only when I was fifteen did they cease altogether. On three other occasions, injuries from beatings required medical attention. I am sure the doctor knew, but nothing was said. Amid this blur of pain and disappointment, I learned a second lesson. I promised myself I would never again show my father any part of my work in starting and developing young horses.

Forty-four years would pass before I once more took him into my confidence. In 1986, just before he died at the age of seventy-eight, I would invite him to take up a position on the viewing deck of a round pen. But by then, everything had changed. Even him.

———

Later that year, in September of 1942, a stranger appeared at the gates of the Salinas rodeo and competition grounds. A man in a jacket and tie and carrying a briefcase was not a usual sight in Salinas. My father and mother greeted him, and they stood in a knot, talking.

From a discreet distance, my brother and I watched as my father raised his hand and pointed in different directions. When they started to move off, we followed, poking our noses around the corners of barns to see where they were going next. We soon realized that this stocky stranger was visiting areas of the competition grounds not normally used. From time to time he would stride up and down the lengths of the barns, measuring off distances. He examined the perimeter fencing. More pointing, more note taking.

A month later a letter arrived. My father read it aloud as we all listened: "It has been confirmed that the competition grounds owned by the city of Salinas are to be requisitioned and used by the U.S. Government as a Japanese-American internment camp."

What was an internment camp? Pearl Harbor had brought America wholeheartedly into the war the previous year, but I had no idea what this meant. My father and mother explained it to us by turns. We were at war with Japan, so Japanese immigrants and their families were considered enemies of the state and were to be interned for the duration of the war.

But these people were our friends and neighbors; some had been living around here for as long as we could remember. We were confused and stunned. Uncomprehending, we asked, "Where will they all live?"

"The government plans to house them in the box stalls."

"In the box stalls? What about the horses?"

My father was silent, looking again at the letter. Then he read out, "Other buildings will be constructed to provide communal facilities." My father folded the letter and explained that we were being asked to choose the lesser of two evils. We could reduce our riding school and horse-training activities almost to zero if we wanted to stay living at the grounds. Or, we could leave.

This was a traumatic experience for us all. If we chose to stay in our house, we would be living under cramped conditions behind barbed-wire fences, as though we, too, were prisoners, and whether we stayed or left, we would have to sell most of our horses. I remember the arguments going back and forth; the atmosphere in the house blackened. There was no option: we would leave.

My life had come to an end. I could not sleep, and cried through most nights. Many of my concerns were selfish, as those of a small child tend to be. I already believed I was to be a champion rider, with a future in showing horses. Now, all our horses and equipment were to be sold. Larry and I watched resentfully as an endless line of vehicles came and went. Some brought materials to convert box stalls into the most basic of living quarters and to erect makeshift communal facilities. Other trucks carted off our equipment and our horses.

Many of the horses were sent to be slaughtered at the notorious Crow's Landing. I would later go there myself dozens of times, and I remember once seeing men with their lunch boxes open on the carcasses of horses. All my life I have believed that the time of a horse's death is a sacred one. You tip your hat, you think about it. Crow's Landing was a horrible place, but that was the final destination of these truckloads of horses as they rolled out of the competition grounds in clouds of dust.

Larry and I were beset with anguish. To help assuage our grief, our parents told us that horsemeat was required for the war effort. All over the world, American soldiers not much older than ourselves were living in desperate conditions. The outcome of the fight against tyranny depended on keeping these young soldiers fit and well fed. Horse-meat would go toward saving their lives and winning the war.

In truth, there was nowhere else for the horses to go. No one could afford to buy them or, with gas rationed, even transport them. On one of those trucks bound for Crow's Landing was my faithful red roan, Ginger.

———

We moved to a small house in the center of Salinas. It had concrete curbs out front, and was the only house I would ever live in with a number on the door: 347 Church Street. Dating from the 1920s, the clapboard house had three bedrooms and an elevated floor; you navigated a lot of porch before you finally arrived inside. In the backyard grew a large magnolia tree; its blooms, though exquisite, made me sneeze.

Living here, on this city lot, with neighbors in every direction, was unlike anything I had ever known. My mother tried to console me and always lavished affection on me. In one photograph, taken early in her marriage, she wears a suit with fur epaulets, and the ringlets in her hair spill in a coy sort of way from her elegant hat. She was the oldest of eight children, born of the union of a Portuguese farmer and an English/Irish schoolteacher. Her family called her "Flick," because of the way she darted about. My mother was also a subservient soul who walked in my father's shadow, but later on she stood up to him many times and literally threw herself around me to protect me.

We had not been in that clapboard house long when she picked up our large globe of the world, brought it to my room, and asked me to find Japan. I eventually did. Then she asked me to find America.

"Now, Monty, look at those two places. Japan is a collection of tiny islands. The United States is a massive country, isn't it? So you can understand why, in just a few months, the war will be over and we can return to the competition grounds." It helped, but there was plenty of evidence to the contrary, and I began to doubt my mother. If the war was winding down, why were people putting stickers in their car windows asking, "Is this trip really necessary?"

Meanwhile, my father was thirty-four years old and therefore not eligible for service in the armed forces. But when he was younger he had policed the mountains on horseback for the forest service, riding a horse and carrying a badge and a gun. The shortage of young men and the fact that he had once been a forest ranger made him an ideal recruit for the Salinas police department.

———

When the news came of his appointment, it seemed to me that we would never get back to the competition grounds. But one thing prevented my life from straying too far from the course that I had so firmly fixed for it: my father managed to rent a small holding on the edge of town. It was only a barn surrounded by a few acres, and nothing like what we were used to, but it would allow us to keep ten to fifteen horses in training.

We cleaned it out thoroughly with a hose. We hammered up partitions, mended gates, and scrubbed concrete floors until they glistened. We walked over the ground inch by inch to clear any nails and the remnants of fencing wire that might damage the horses' feet. We connected the water supply, set gates back on their hinges, contrived a bin for the feed. The smell of horses was in my nostrils again, and that meant happiness.

Although my father was a frightening man, he had given me back what I wanted most in the world: a future with horses. More specifically, my future lay with the brown gelding called Brownie, who was one of the first arrivals at the Villa Street facility.

Brownie was 15 hands, his mother a mustang mare and his sire a Thoroughbred—one of the government remount stallions. This was a project whereby the U.S. Cavalry took Thoroughbred stallions and set them loose to run with the mustangs on the open range. The ranchers got a payment if they shot a mustang stallion: the Thoroughbred stallions could thus take over the females and breed a class of horse suitable for the military. The cavalry had first call to come back and capture the young males for themselves, while the ranchers could keep the fillies as further payment for their cooperation.

As his name implied, Brownie was medium brown all over, except for about eight inches of a softer, doeskin color on his muzzle and a small white dot between his eyes, which gave him a concentrated, pointed look. He had well-shaped feet with flint-hard hooves—a legacy of his mustang heritage. Domestic horses raised on soft ground need regular visits from the farrier to keep their feet healthy. But owing to the minerals mustangs eat and the constant teasing of the feet from running over rocks, mustang hooves are so strong a nail could hardly penetrate them.

The minute Brownie arrived and I knew he was to be mine, I wanted to bond with him closely.

"OK," said my father, "let's break him."

My heart sank. How could I be this animal's best friend when his tentative trust in human beings was about to be abused? But I was too frightened of my father to stop it. As Brownie waited in his stall, my father rooted among some old slatted boxes used for the commercial transport of vegetables. He found what he was looking for—a cut of heavy, crepelike paper used to line the crate. He twisted one end and tied it to the end of a rope.

Brownie was tied to a single post that had been driven deep into the ground. He stood patiently while my father walked around behind him, coiling the rope with the paper tied to the end of it. My father lobbed the paper and Brownie jumped sideways as if his life depended on it, which to his way of thinking it did. His head snapped around, brought up short by the rope. This was just the beginning.

As I watched Brownie's eyes widen and roll in fear, I felt dread and sympathy in equal doses. I cursed inwardly and wanted more than anything to untie the rope. I tried in vain to think how I might make it up to him.

Years later, while Brownie and I were trekking over the high desert for days at a time, I felt compelled to offer him an apology for the vicious sacking out and the paper terror he would feel until the day he died. I talked to him, tried to put things right and hoped he understood.

Brownie never forgot the sacking out: all his life he was phobic about paper. Anything that sounded remotely like paper would send him into a panic, and he would be dangerous to himself and to others. He would bolt, and no one could tell him that it was only paper, nothing to fear. Never angry with Brownie for this blind spot in his nature, I accepted it as our fault, our crime against him.

———

When my father became a policeman, our car became a police car. The war had made vehicles of any description difficult to come by. When he joined up, my father was told he would earn a higher salary if he offered to equip his family car for police work.

Consequently, many policemen's private cars were fitted with red emergency lights, sirens, and radios. Special spotlights and lighting systems were installed to adapt the car for driving in blackout conditions. The West Coast was vulnerable to enemy attack and blackouts were common.

I recall my father coming home one day—we were then still living at the competition grounds—and saying we needed a larger vehicle to pick up riding students. The Mullers, who owned a mortuary in Salinas, had just the car for us: the limousine used by the immediate family in the funeral procession.

The huge 1932 Cadillac sedan, with enormous running boards, was like a car from a gangster movie. Fitted with every option under the sun, it had acres of space inside and would accommodate many more riding students than any new car we might have bought for the same price. As with many automobiles of its day, the trunk consisted of a large metal box, like a footlocker, which bolted onto the back of the car. Now the black Cadillac was a patrol car for my father.

I sometimes accompanied him to his training sessions. My father could handle every man there, and most instructors, with a smile on his face. He was fearless. There was never a cell of fear in that man. I can remember riding with my father when he got calls over the radio, or when he saw someone violating the traffic code. The red light would come on, the siren would sound, and we would race off to "apprehend the suspect." He carried his badge with him always, and kept a citation pad and handcuffs in the glove compartment. There was also usually a handgun.

Late in the evening of one spring day in 1943, we were driving home from caring for some pasture horses. It had been a long day of riding and attending to their keep. Now it was getting dark. Near the city limits, a call came over the radio concerning an armed robbery in progress at the Golden Dragon saloon on Soledad Street in Chinatown. My father picked up the hand microphone and responded, "I'm just a block and a half from the Golden Dragon and I'll answer that call." The radio dispatcher asked, "Are you armed?" My father replied, "Yes."

A bolt of fear ran through me. In all the times I had been with him when he answered police calls, he had never had to defend himself with a gun. He flipped the switches for the siren and the flashing light. The car veered wildly from side to side as it covered the distance. The headlights picked up people leaping out of our way.

He barked at me, "Get down on the floor!"

The tone of his voice conveyed the seriousness of the situation. I quickly slid from the seat and into the foot well underneath the dash, and waited. My heart was beating loud and fast, and I could almost smell my own fear.

What happened next changed me forever. I would push the incident I am about to describe into a dark corner of my mind, until one day, returning from a horse sale on a mostly empty airplane, I took out a tape recorder and the truth poured out of me. Fresh blood from an old wound. There are days when I regret disinterring these memories. The whole picture remains crystal-clear, as if it had happened yesterday.

Some members of my family advised me that this incident should have no place in the book, and I weighed their counsel carefully before making the decision to reveal it—probably the single most important influence in my life. But what I saw on that day had a profound impact on the way I deal with horses, though not a single horse featured in the events of that night.

Before then I was a different person. In a way, I was born that evening, at the age of eight.

My father, you should know, had been brought up in the tough, sometimes cruel, world of the American pioneer. So much changed during those early decades of the twentieth century that the single generation between my father and me felt like a great chasm. During his childhood, he would have faced almost daily the natural law of "kill or be killed." In later years he mellowed. When my wife, Pat, came to know him, he was no longer the cold, rigid man I had known as a child; the fight had drained from him. My children remember him as a fine grandfather.

I am also at pains to point out the difficulty my father had with the issue of race. Half Cherokee, he had suffered racial abuse in his youth, and he felt a deep shame about his Cherokee mother. (Ironically, a little Cherokee blood ran in his own wife's veins.) Yet he was angry that the Second World War had brought black people to our otherwise white community. Fort Ord was a twenty-minute drive away, and many black servicemen were stationed there. Given the chance, victims of racial prejudice are sometimes the first to inflict it on others.

This is not to excuse what happened, and neither am I trying to vilify my father. But for as long as I live I will go on trying to understand what he did that night and how it shaped me.

As the car sped toward the crime scene, my father issued a second order: "Get me the gun and the handcuffs."

I flipped the latch on the glove compartment and quickly removed the handcuffs, but I could not feel the gun. Frantically, my fingers swept through the maps, pens, and other detritus, but in vain. He was cursing at me to hurry. "Damn," he said, "I was sure I brought it with me." He had already grabbed the handcuffs and shoved them into his pocket.

The Cadillac slid to a halt a few doors down from the Golden Dragon. He leapt from the car almost before it stopped moving, shouting to me just before he slammed the door, "Stay in the car, *on the floor!*"

I lay there, curled under the dash, as the flashing neon lights of the saloon's facade filled the car with an eerie pulsating glow. It was cramped where I lay, with its smell of barn dirt, sweat, and damp wool from the carpet. I wrestled with the urge to sit up, partly to escape the smell but mainly to see what was happening. As I crept up to the seat, my eyes were now level with the bottom of the driver's window. I had a direct view of the bar entrance some twenty yards away. The street was lined with people, some talking to my father and pointing to the saloon. They were agitated, whispering among themselves as my father went inside. Though stiff with panic, I reached over to the door handle and eased it open. Everyone was focused on what was going on just inside the saloon doorway, so no one saw me crawling along. I crabbed sideways to gain a spot near the door. It seemed like everything had gone silent, because all I could hear was the thumping of my heart as I peered into the bar.

Inside, no more than five feet away, I saw my father with his back to me. The bar's patrons were scattered to the farthest corners of the room. A tall, heavy-set black man in army fatigues was the only person moving. I seldom encountered blacks in Salinas; he was not a man to me, but a *black* man. He swerved to point a knife that looked the size of a sword—maybe it was a bayonet—in the direction of the bartender and shouted, "Put the money on the bar!" The frightened bartender pulled bills from the register, scattering coins to the floor in his haste.

The robber, who may have been twenty years old, had spread his coat on the bar and collected a small heap of watches, rings, bracelets, and wallets. Evidently he had been cleaning out the patrons. The plan was to use the coat as a sack and then make his escape.

At this point my father lifted his badge high in the air so everyone could see his authority, and he shouted, "Police! Stand where you are. Put down the knife and place your hands on the bar." All time stopped now.

The black man turned to face my father, his knife pointing directly in front of him. My father was a big man, but the man at the bar was huge. I silently begged my father to give way. He did not. He stepped forward, walking toward the knife. Serious injury or even death awaited him. It was a brave act. Terror overtook me; in those few seconds I saw myself fatherless.

"Don't do this to yourself," my father said as he kept walking forward. "Put the knife on the bar, turn around and put your hands in the air, give it up."

When they were inches from each other, and just when I thought the man would give way after all, he struck. He made a quick thrust with his knife hand, aiming for my father's ribs. My father's hand snaked out and grabbed the man's fist exactly where it closed on the knife handle.

With a quick folding action he locked the robber's elbow backward and sent the knife spinning to the floor. The pressure on his twisted arm caused the man to fall back, and his head cracked on the edge of the bar. He continued his free fall to the floor and hit his head again, this time on the brass foot rail. He lay motionless, in a heap. It was over.

I experienced a rush of emotion. My father was alive and, though unarmed, had brought down a knife-wielding thief. He was a hero.

But it was not over. At this point, my father—a powerfully built man who weighed about 220 pounds—put the cuffs on the man and stood over him. He raised one foot and locked his heel behind his thigh, elevated his body, and then dropped, driving his knee into the chest of the unconscious black man. I was shocked, but my father's next move was even more appalling. He lifted one foot, took aim and, with all the force he could muster, slammed the heel of his cowboy boot into the mouth of the fallen man. He then picked up the knife and handed it to the bartender, asking him to carry it for him. Turning to his prisoner, he grabbed the chain connecting the handcuffs and hauled on it, dragging the black man who was limp as a sack of feed, his hands high over his head.

As my father turned toward the doorway, it struck me, almost too late, that I was not where I was supposed to be. I turned and ran. As I slid into the driver's seat and closed the door behind me, I saw my father emerge from the bar, surrounded by onlookers. He gave the torso an extra lift and then released the chain, dropping the back of the man's head onto the sidewalk.

When my father arrived at the car, dragging his prisoner behind him, he went round and opened the passenger side of the car, taking the knife from the barman and placing it carefully on the seat beside me.

Then he went to the rear of the Cadillac and opened that big, trunklike box. He took empty grain sacks and laid them over the rear floor space so the black man's blood would not stain the interior.

He opened the doors wide, heaved the man inside, then got in the car himself. The knife was an object of fear for me. But I was torn between sitting close to the knife or sitting close to my father. My father instructed me to pick it up by the blade and place it in the glove compartment. A measure of the size of a 1932 Cadillac's glove compartment is that this long knife fit inside.

As we drove off, I could hear sounds coming from the man's throat. But my father said he was faking his injuries: "He'll be just fine." By now, other patrol cars had joined us on our way to the police station. Their sirens joined ours in a wailing that precisely caught my own inner mood of anguish and despair.

My father used the car radio to tell his colleagues how the thief had attempted to cut him with the knife. The tale was told with bravado. Turning around, I looked down to see if the man was still breathing. I could only see bubbles of blood around his mouth. I pleaded with my father to take him to the hospital, not the police station. He simply repeated that the man was faking his injuries.

On arrival at the station my father opened the car door and dragged the man onto the sidewalk. For good measure, as if testing for resistance, he again drew the black man's shoulders up a few feet and dropped him with a crack onto the cement. Other officers, emerging from the station or their patrol cars, laughed and hooted at this display.

My father picked up the chain again and hauled, so the unconscious prisoner's hands were once more over his head, as if in surrender. Lifting the man's head and torso off the sidewalk, he used the handcuff chain to drag the man backward up the concrete steps fronting the police station. "Get the knife out of the glove box," he barked to one of the officers. "Don't touch the handle." He would take a few steps, hoist his prisoner, take a few more steps, and repeat the process. The man was being conveyed into jail like an awkward piece of furniture.

No one made any attempt to find a stretcher, or to help my father. This was his trophy. He had bagged it, and now he was bringing it home to display before his brother officers. They hollered and laughed behind him, sidestepping the trail of blood.

Inside the station, at the top of the stairs, was the sergeant's desk. Dragging the black man the last few feet to a point opposite the desk, my father dropped him on the concrete floor. "I've pulled an I.D. from his pocket," he said. "Here's his name; book him, and send someone to get his prints." By this time in his police career, my father was a sergeant talking to a fellow sergeant. His imperious manner was that of a hunter after a kill.

The sergeant fed a sheet of paper into the typewriter and the keys began their staccato beat. Officers lit cigarettes and gathered to hear my father's tale. There was a second telling, this time with more violence and drama.

The man lay unconscious on the floor and I feared he was dying. I pulled at my father's coat to beg him to do something. My father looked down and shouted, "You get back in the car and shut up. The man is just faking it! There's nothing at all wrong with him." At this point the man seemed to regain consciousness and struggled to stand. Still handcuffed, he staggered forward toward the shaft of light coming through the door. No one made a move to stop him.

"Get in the car, Monty," said my father, who almost casually turned to follow his prisoner. The man did not go very far; he stumbled at the top of the steps and dove headlong, striking his head against a tree. Again he lay motionless. By now I was crying uncontrollably. My father again yelled, "Get in the car!" as he approached the prisoner. Through the window I saw my father kick him repeatedly in the ribs with the toe of his cowboy boot. This last display seemed for the benefit of four or five officers standing at the entrance. Finally, he dragged the prisoner up the steps and deposited him through the door.

Back in the Cadillac I buried my face in the upholstery, sobbing. Soon I heard the sound of the car door opening and slamming shut, then the scrape of the key in the ignition. We were going home.

Four days later I summoned enough courage to ask my father what had happened to the man he had arrested in the saloon. He replied, "Oh, he died." He must have felt my shock, because he quickly said, "He didn't die of his injuries. He died of pneumonia. That boy refused to pull the blankets over him at night, and he caught pneumonia and died."

I believed the story and I believed him. From then on, throughout my boyhood, I was careful at night to pull the covers up to my chin. Years later, I was told that the black man had lain for two days with his ribs broken, his lungs pierced and his skull cracked. He died without ever seeing a doctor.

Later, in psychology courses, I would learn how kidnappers and child molesters kill small animals in front of their victims to instill in them such fear that they are unable to fight back. My father's brutalizing of the young soldier was not aimed at me at all; he tried, in fact, to hide it from me. But the effect on me was the same as if he had forced me to watch.

I understand now that I became a victim of my father's aggression—then I only knew how much I feared him. But from that point forward, I knew I had to direct my life away from him.

There is a postscript to this incident.

Two months later, my father asked me to come with him one evening. "We're going to the fights," he said, "and you're going to meet a very special man there." We drove to the National Guard Armory, passing crowds of people as we pulled up outside. We entered a room at the back of the exhibition hall where a large black man was seated on a table.

My pulse shot up. He was the first of his race I had seen since the robbery. My father drew me closer and said, "Come on, Monty. Meet Joe Louis, he's the heavyweight champion of the world."

Joe Louis greeted my father by name. My father had been hired as one of the bodyguards to protect the champion.

"Hi," said my father. "Meet my son, Monty."

I refused to go closer. "Come on," said the boxer. "I won't hurt you."

I shook the hand of Joe Louis, but I could not look him in the eye. Hoping to get past my shyness, he pointed at his shoulder and said, "Hey, little man, hit me, I dare you."

It was a game I could not play. In the end he took my hand, folded it into a fist and tapped it against his shoulder, feigning injury. "Now," he said, "you can say you knocked out the world champ."

A photographer setting up nearby signaled his readiness. My father lined up beside Joe Louis and the flash popped. I still have the photo of Louis—an imposing man—flanked by four uniformed, hatted men at least his size or bigger. It is hard to read Louis's look, but the others, all white, seem more pleased to be in his company than he is in theirs.

On the way home, my father was remembering how Joe Louis, a celebrity bystander that night, had signed autographs while sitting in one corner of the ring. He would sign hurriedly, then drop the paper onto the floor of the ring so the autograph seekers had to pick them up. "The nigger in him had to come out, didn't it?" railed my father.

A woman named Nola Hightower worked for us in our house, and though my father treated her well, behind her back she, too, was a "nigger." Later, when I played high school football, his advice to me was to hit the black players hard early in the game and they would not bother me again, because "niggers lack courage." My father was a racist, and the black-and-white photograph of him smiling, with his arm around Joe Louis is, for me, a powerful memento.

———

When I was eight, I started riding quarter horses in sprint races, and my education in horsemanship moved up another notch.

Quarter horses were, and are, stout, easy keepers with well-developed feet and calm dispositions. Typically small, the quarter horse possessed a conformation one might call the muscular "bull-dog" type, with exceptionally well-rounded hindquarters and a deep chest. "A deep heart," as horsemen say.

The breed was originally known in the 1930s as Copper Bottom and, later, as Steel Dust—after the two principal sires who launched this specialist breed. Easily trained, they were bred for ranch work because their terrific acceleration made them ideal for roping cattle and cutting a cow out of a herd. During the week they would work on the ranch, and during weekend rodeos they would be entered in the roping events and steer wrestling competition. After a few minutes' rest, the quarter horses would swap their heavy Western rigs for the jockey's "postage stamp" saddle, and they would be raced on the bush tracks that surrounded the rodeo arenas. In shorter races, no horse could beat them: they were the equine equivalent of drag racers. In fact, many of these horses never drew a breath until after they crossed the finish line; only as they slowed did they realize the need for a change of air in their lungs.

Because of the distance involved, a quarter of a mile, the breed became known as the quarter horse. This new type of competitive event was called sprint-horse racing. I loved the excitement of it. To minimize weight on the back of the animal, the smallest boys were picked as riders. My fee, which the owner paid, was five dollars to ride and ten dollars to win. Little towns up and down California—Salinas, King City, Fresno, Victorville, Stockton—held these "short horse" or "quarter horse" meets. The gambling was unregulated and unsanctioned. Like any backroom gambling, it made for a charged atmosphere. Riders were also unlicensed, nor was much concern shown for their safety. I had no serious accidents, despite riding in some 200 sprint races, mostly quarter horse races, until I was thirteen years old, although I did fall off a time or two, and I often rode in races without a protective helmet.

In 1949, no longer able to keep my weight down below the 130-pound mark, I rode my last race in King City. It was just a ranching town, but for quarter horse racing two owners there had become important: Gyle Norris and the McKensie brothers. The latter owned a top-class mare named Lady Lee, whom I was lucky enough to ride a few times. They also owned Dee Dee, who was 1946 champion older male of the quarter horse breed.

One of my fellow racers in those days was the aptly named Tucker Slender, a tall, thin fellow three or four years my senior and a much better jockey than me. He went on to become the head starter at many of the major tracks in southern California, and at Santa Anita and Del Mar he is still the head starter. Slender knew, and I would learn, that horses and starting gates do not always mix.

One day, I was at Frank Vessels's track—then still quite rustic—as his trainer, a man named Farrell Jones, coped with a young quarter horse. The horse wheeled about behind the starting gate, eyeing its doors as he might the jaws of a crocodile. The track spooked him, the blocks of hay where we sat spooked him, the sky itself rattled him.

Accompanying this young horse was an older stablemate who knew the ropes.

"Right, then," said Farrell calmly, "let's load him into the gates." Farrell was a ruddy fireplug who lost his hair early.

In training quarter horses to bolt from the starting gate, it was then common practice to shut the novice horse inside and put the whip on him. The thinking was to drive the horse into a frenzy so he would be anxious to escape once the gate flipped open. And, every subsequent time in a starting gate, he would remember the fear, and the instinct to run would guarantee a better performance. Occasionally, electric shocks were applied to achieve the same effect.

I watched as Farrell Jones now took the nervous horse and walked him *through* the starting gate. Then he went around again. And again. This continued until the few of us watching began to get dizzy; the horse himself must have been on the edge of being bored with these endless circles. Finally he led him in and shut the front gate, offering a mouthful of feed in a bucket to make him feel at home. His stablemate was nearby, easily visible through the slatted sides. And there they stood.

I was confused. Was the training session designed to make the novice horse learn effective starts in a race? Or was this, in fact, his new stable?

However, once the horse had grown comfortable behind closed gates, they were opened. But he was not led out. No, he was allowed to take his time and to decide for himself whether he wanted to leave, if ever. When he did so, it seemed to me like an exciting moment.

Farrell Jones was eliminating every ounce of pressure from the training procedure. I also began to see another reason for having the stablemate on hand. With the gates closed and the novice horse inside, the stablemate was walked down the track a ways. The gate was opened and, without any encouragement, the novice stepped daintily out of the stall and strolled up the track to join his friend. A while later, the older pace horse was set going at a faster walk and allowed to get farther down the track. Now the novice had to shrug into a gentle trot to catch up with her.

Not many hours later, Farrell Jones had his novice horse entering the stalls without the slightest fuss, waiting with his nose pressed against the front gate in a state of great anticipation. The horse's only thought was to go forward, to fly out the gate of his own free will, and to canter down to the pace horse—who was always held back a touch to allow the novice to overtake him and "win" the race.

The once nervous horse was having fun. I was deeply impressed by what I had witnessed, and I wanted to know all about it.

"You know," said Farrell as he sucked on the wad of tobacco parked down the side of his back teeth, "I've watched a whole lot of these races, and I've watched them pretty carefully—as you do when there's maybe a sum of money riding into your pocket if you make the right choices. And I saw an interesting thing. It ain't the horses who're all jazzed up who're starting the quickest. Those ones are so busy bang-ing about from side to side and running on the spot and thinking about what evil-doer is behind them, that they have less time to no-tice whether the gate's flying open. No, it's the animals who are the most relaxed—they're the ones making the flying starts."

Farrell proved to me that the cruelty of whipping horses in the stall to make them afraid and want to escape was not only unnecessary, it was counterproductive. It made the horses *slower* off the mark.

I learned a great deal that day. My way of thinking about horses was enriched by this critical idea: a rider or trainer should never say to a horse, "You *must.*" Instead, the horse should be invited to perform because, "I would like you to." Taking that a step further—to ask a horse to perform is not as clever as causing him to *want* to perform.

Horses naturally want to run, and if they are trained correctly we can harness their willingness to do just that, to race to their poten-tial. As it turned out, I would work for most of my life in the Thor-oughbred racing industry, and to this day I am fervent in my belief that whips should be banned; there is no need for them if training procedures take advantage of a well-bred horse's overpowering desire to run.

At Flag Is Up Farms, exercise riders sometimes carry a crop: we are, after all, training horses for the track, and a horse that has *never* seen a whip may throw the first jockey to use one. A rider at our farm, then, may tap a horse; but if that rider raises a welt, that rider is gone.

Trevor Denman, the track announcer at the Santa Anita and Del Mar racetracks in California, has actually timed horses under the whip; he has determined that most horses slow down when they are whipped. The whip is simply a bad tool. We have no need for it.

Farrell Jones would become the leading Thoroughbred trainer in the United States several times over; his son, Gary, one of the top trainers in North America. Farrell's methods and original thinking have stood me in good stead since I learned that first lesson from him.

Frank Vessels, one of the major quarter horse owners in the United States, would launch the Quarter Racing Association in 1945—and soon he would elevate sprint racing into the same class of event as Thoroughbred racing. By 1946, the American Quarter Horse Association had formed, with a team of inspectors touring the United States adding to their register those horses with the right conformation.

From hanging on to the neck of a quarter horse as it blasted down those rough tracks, we all started the quarter horse racing industry. And I learned something about horses and starting gates.

———

When I was nine years old, my uncle Ray told me a story from our Cherokee ancestry—an old way that would have a place in my new way of thinking about horses.

My grandfather, Earl Roberts, was born in Wales in 1870. My love of horses may have come from him, because he farmed with them and also used them for foxhunting and pleasure riding. But at seventeen he was lured to the West by the promise of steady work, building roads over the Sierra Nevadas. In Spanish, Sierra Nevada means "snow-covered mountains," an unassuming phrase for the massive natural barrier that forms the border between California and Nevada. In North America only the Rocky Mountains are bigger.

In the Sierras, crews could work only six months of the year. Passes were otherwise closed. In 1846, the ill-fated Donner Party wagon train tried to cross the Sierras in the fall and were swallowed by one of its fierce, early winters. I can barely imagine the work involved in cutting through those mountains using only man and beast. Young Earl was hired to supply the horses that pulled the equipment on these road projects, as well as to provide saddle horses for the foremen directing the crews. The laborers were typically immigrants like my grandfather, but also among them were Indians of the Cherokee nation, who were brought to Nevada from their reservations in the Midwest by the federal government.

In that number was the woman who would become my grandmother, a young Cherokee girl in her late teens. I wish I knew her Indian name; they called her Sweeney, after the agent who had transported her family to Nevada. Among her few possessions were papers qualifying her as a full-blooded Cherokee entitled to specific native-born rights. Earl petitioned her family for her hand in marriage and in quick succession she bore him nine children—five of whom survived, including my father and my uncle Ray.

When Ray, her youngest child, was eleven years old, Sweeney decided that her marriage contract with Earl had been fulfilled. One day when the family got up in the morning, they found her gone.

Months passed while they searched for her. In the end, they discovered that she had walked from Tulare back to the Cherokee Indian Reservation, a distance of 600 miles. When I knew her, she had gone salt-and-pepper gray. She was about five feet six inches tall—fairly tall for a Cherokee woman of the late 1800s.

My father told disparaging stories about her and was not pleased that I sought her company. She was forbidden fruit. My grandmother spoke little English, words, not sentences, and she never said anything in front of my mother, but she seemed to come alive when we were alone together and she would rattle on in Cherokee, holding me close.

But in her life she was not content.

Shortly after she walked away, Ray developed pneumonia. Earl decided to take the boy back to Sweeney on the reservation, where Ray was adopted into the Cherokee tribe and raised to adulthood. He thus had the benefit of learning the Indian way as well as the white man's way.

Uncle Ray told me that when the Cherokee wanted to capture wild horses on the great plains, their problem was how to get close enough to rope them. They overcame this obstacle in remarkable fashion. Instead of driving them into the neck of a valley or building other traps of that sort, difficult given the landscape, they used a much quicker method. First of all, they followed the herd of horses. They did not drive them hard, but simply walked after them, pressing them away. This would continue for a day or two. Then, when the time was right, the Cherokee would turn and walk in the opposite direction. Invariably, in a kind of yo-yo effect, the horses would turn around and follow them. The Cherokee would then simply lead the wild herd into corrals between two and five acres in size.

Apparently the Cherokee used similar tactics to get close to the beasts they hunted—deer, antelope, and buffalo. To be effective with the bow and arrow, the hunter needed to be within forty or fifty feet of his target. He would press the animals away from him for a while, then turn around and head back the other way. The animals would turn and follow. After this pattern between hunter and prey had been repeated several times, the hunters found themselves near enough to make an easy kill.

When my uncle Ray told me the story of hunted animals circling back to check out the hunter, it was a mystery to me. Later on, when I had the opportunity to observe horses in the wild for myself, I would come to understand the reasons for their curious tendency to turn back and seek intimacy with their pursuers. I would give the phenomenon a name, "Advance and Retreat," and it would form the basis of my technique in working with horses.

————

The years of the Second World War had been filled with death. In one way or another, whether actual or metaphorical, war brings darkness. I was ten when the war finally ended in 1945, and in my small world the death of my dreams seemed as certain as it had when we first moved away from the competition grounds. I had seen my Japanese-American classmates rounded up and interned at a prison camp located at my former home. I had witnessed the death of the black man at the hands of my father, which caused me to lose respect for him and to seek my own path in life. Ironically, while I was trying hard to dissociate my life from his, he was giving me what I wanted more than anything else—a life with horses.

With the war over, it was a mad scramble to return to normalcy. For my father, this meant gearing up to return to our business at the competition grounds and entering me in as many equestrian competitions as he could find around the country—which was exactly what I wanted to do. But it was frantic. The grounds were in a horrible state. We dragged magnets around for weeks because the workmen who had dismantled the living quarters had left nails and roofing tacks on the ground, where they posed a threat to the horses' feet. We put the stables back in order, restored the feed stalls, repaired floors, and mended roofs. My mother's entire family turned up to volunteer their help. We sawed the back off the Cadillac to turn it into a pickup, and it went back and forth to the dump, carting away rubbish.

I recall the day when the new saddles arrived—twenty or thirty of them, all dumped in the yard at the same time. I tore at the packages to get them out and ready for the start of lessons the following day. We were back in our old house, back in business. But with the cost of all this equipment, not to mention the horses themselves, came heavy overhead. We held grave family conferences around the kitchen table. It was decided that my father would remain in the police force because he had risen to the rank of lieutenant and his salary could help to fund our debts. If we were to succeed, my father told us, we would have to do it on our own and without much hired help. We could afford only one man, the same Wendell Gillott who had worked for us beforehand.

Wendell was jockey-sized and claimed a jockey past, but no one could find a trace of it. He was full of stories whose details shifted with his moods. Wendell also claimed he had boxed, and he certainly had the face of someone who had been on the receiving end of many punches. His ears were elephantine and cauliflower, his nose flat and pushed off to one side. People said he had the look of a monkey: he would use his knuckles to rise up from a table.

His were the hands of a worker, and few worked as hard and fast as he did. Wendell was not vulgar, did not drink like so many ranch hands. He was a good man, not the brightest, but always with a joke or a laugh, and we could not have gotten along without him.

To fit in the necessary work of helping Wendell, schooling for Larry and me was cut back to bare bones. Wendell would arrive at the stables at four-thirty A.M. and immediately start feeding the sixty horses we were now stabling. I rolled out of bed some time before five o'clock and struggled into the same working clothes that had lain in a heap on the floor where I had dropped them the night before. I scooted, for I had twenty-two stalls to muck out before breakfast. Because he was younger and not as strong, Larry had ten stalls to clean.

I barely paused to call out a greeting to Wendell before cleaning and raking each stall, rolling back the bedding, adding straw—and on to the next one. As I went, I counted the seconds: the aim was to take no more than three and a half minutes, or 210 seconds, for each stall; ideally, all twenty-two stalls were done in just under an hour and a half. It was like a race; when I finally threw the pitchfork back against the wall I would raise both hands in the air like rodeo calf ropers do to stop the clock.

Breakfast was at six-thirty. As Larry and I ate, our father issued instructions on which horses to ride and what exercises each required. After breakfast, Wendell cleaned out the remaining thirty-odd stalls while Larry and I were out riding. From seven to nine, I rode perhaps six horses with a variety of training programs and tasks to be accomplished. After that, we trotted back to the house and showered and changed, ready for the start of school at nine-thirty.

At one-thirty we returned to the competition grounds and were straight back in the saddle training five to six horses apiece, so by mid-afternoon I had four hours of riding behind me. Then all of us—my father, mother, my brother, and I—gave riding lessons to classes ranging from six to twelve people. Some were scared stiff of horses, others were above it all, some were attentive. We pressed on, doing the best we could. At five-thirty P.M. my mother took the Cadillac and delivered the children back home.

Larry, Wendell, and I would finish up by stabling and feeding the horses, and cleaning the tack. By six-thirty my mother was preparing dinner and I was her helper, which got me interested in cooking. Then, after dinner, there was schoolwork. Even though I was only in school for between ten and forty percent of the normal time, my father insisted I keep up the best possible grades. By anyone's standards, he was a hard taskmaster.

A child's capabilities are elastic at that age, and he stretched mine to the limit, but perhaps as much credit should go to the tutor hired for me—a Miss Marguerite Parsons. That I wanted to take the school tests at all is a credit to her kindness and understanding. Despite my prolonged absences from the classroom, I would achieve near straight-A grades at school.

Like a cartoon character, I had the carrot in front of me, the whip behind.

—

The end of the war created a surplus of cheap military hardware, and among local ranchers it became fashionable to zip around in nearly new military jeeps or armored cars. My father joined in this craze, but in his own remarkable way: he leased a railroad car once used by the U.S. Cavalry. Framed in metal, its wood painted dark green, the car bore military numbers on the outside and, barely discernible beneath the paint, the American eagle.

A minimal payment secured it for several years. Designed to take officers' horses around the country on the rail network, it came equipped with shipping stalls for fifteen horses. My father reasoned that though competitions were few and far between, and even less publicized, the railroad car would get us there. He was also confident that the competitions would inevitably increase in number when normal life returned and he wanted to be prepared to take full advantage.

Builders removed six stalls in the car and constructed in their place a bunk room and a feed room with a bin for the grain and a large container for water. A minimal kitchen area offered a hot plate and a spot for making coffee. For the next few years, this railroad car would crisscross the United States. It was my home away from home during long spells in summer.

My father and I would consult the advertised schedules for horse shows, select the best ones, and then take our itinerary to Southern Pacific. Railroad officials would give us a series of pickup times and siding numbers; we might be car twenty-one in siding number fifty-six, for example, and at the appointed time—the railway did run on time in those days—a switch engine would pull us from the siding onto the main track. The train would back up to us, our car would be hitched up, and off we would go.

My father stayed behind to attend to his duties as a policeman, and as a trainer/manager of the horses. Traveling in the car with me were my favorite horse, Brownie; anywhere up to eight other horses; a groom (sometimes Wendell); and Miss Marguerite Parsons.

She was a central figure in my life. I still own a striking portrait photograph of her: she has her hair up in the 1940s style—we called it the "Rosie the Riveter look" after a cartoon character of the day— and what a luxuriant mane of hair it is. The chin is slightly pointed, the nose prominent. She has deep brown eyes, kindly eyes. You would look at that photograph and say, Here is a woman of character.

In the bunk room of the railroad car, the tiny-waisted Miss Parsons slept on the other side of a curtain strung along a pole. When we had all retired for the night, I would hear a strange whispering sound from her side of the curtain. It was not a human sound, and no horse ever made one like it. It had to be emanating from Miss Parsons. I did not know what it was, and I never asked. It was only some years later that the whispering was made plain to me: it was the pleasing sound of a woman's underclothing, silk on silk or the rustle of nylons. But in my bunk I could make no sense of the whispers, which only added to the quality of mystery that enveloped Miss Marguerite Parsons.

She had been our baby-sitter since I was two or three years old, and now she became my teacher as well. Neat, clean, and steady as a rock, she read me stories and made learning fun. Always in long skirts and dresses, she was strict and serious, but very caring and warm. Above all, she was instructive. If Miss Parsons had a fault she kept it hidden from me, and I loved her as pupils always love their favorite teacher.

She was only in her mid-twenties, but mature beyond her years, even wise. It seemed to me that she was always right in what she said and did. She would not leave us until 1949 when I was fourteen years old. She understood me better than my parents did and sympathized with my problems. She gave me lessons I value now: she taught me how to communicate with people; she encouraged me to relax; and she made me understand that if I was to pursue a career as a horseman with such single-minded dedication and from such a young age, I would have to pace myself—or burn out.

I remember heading for a show in Pomona, in southern California; it was one of the first times we used the railroad car, and simply preparing for it put me in a state of high excitement. We cleaned and sorted the saddles and bridles and arranged them in boxes fitted to one wall of the railroad car. In this way, we could simply lift out the boxes and stack them in the van so the equipment would not be damaged or soiled en route to the show ground.

"Ramp up, ramp up!" exclaimed Miss Parsons as soon as the horses and equipment were loaded and we were all inside. There was some urgency in her voice; a ramp was a welcome mat for mice. She worried obsessively about rodents, which were plentiful at all the railway sidings. Grain spilled during transport offered them a healthy food supply. Miss Parsons maintained a keen mouse vigil as well as a comprehensive extermination program inside the railroad car. And when not chasing mice she continued a brave but futile crusade against dust as we rolled from one siding to another.

A perfectionist, she posted lists of rules and regulations around the car, which we were asked to read every day. Many signs had mice in mind:

- Keep Doors Closed.
- Spill Grain, Clean Up Every Kernel.
- Horse Droppings Are to Be Cleaned Immediately.
- Keep Lids Tightly in Place on Manure Cans.

Before heading off, Miss Parsons would sort out the homework she would take with us to let me keep pace with my schooling.

She prepared my homework and wrote out tests for me at the little desk she set up in the car. She performed her task and I mine during long stopovers, and at night when the train was stopped, lest both of us become too ill with motion sickness from trying to read and write while underway.

The switch engine would pull us onto the main track, and a gentle bump and the clink of the hitch told us we were now one of many wagons hitched to the engine that we could hear steaming away at the head of the train. Southern Pacific took us down through San Luis Obispo, Santa Barbara, Ventura, and on toward the Los Angeles basin. Peering out through the heavy wire mesh guarding the windows, we could look ahead as the train snaked around a mountain or into the dozen or so tunnels that went right through the mountains. Rolling along the then pristine, unpopulated coast, we could look out to the tranquil beauty of the ocean. This was train travel, but wind-in-your-hair train travel, which most people never experience. The slow rhythm of the wheels rolling over the tracks settled all of us—horses, Wendell, Miss Parsons and me—into a routine as we made our way south.

After the tunnels and the slow route beside the sea, Los Angeles was an eye-opener: so many cars and buildings and people squeezed together constituted an alien land. But finally, we arrived at Pomona. This was an upscale, fiercely competitive show, and I faced it with trepidation. I could be reasonably confident of winning in some of the shows I went to, but Pomona was different, and, in one way, unique.

The owner of the facility—Dr. John Harvey Kellogg of Kellogg's cereals—had built a spur line connecting his grounds to the main Southern Pacific network. No need to park in a siding and transport horses and equipment to the show ground. We simply chugged down the spur line, dropped the ramp, and the main arena lay right before us. The other contestants, who had to stable their horses a mile away, looked on in amazement at this kid who just parked next to the arena in his own train. It was a good psychological tactic. I had already won pole position.

But I would need any advantage. This was a serious event, with a 2,000-seat stadium and a parade of superbly equipped competitors mounted on expensive horses. I would have to give Brownie all the help I could muster to cut a path anywhere near the top. A current of excitement coursed through Brownie, too; he was as charged up as I was. Because of his breeding—part aristocrat, part mustang—his nerves were always highly tuned, and he knew this was something special.

As I led him out and then returned to help Wendell with the other horses, a line of children began to form a small audience. They continued to observe impassively as I—only eleven myself—warmed up Brownie, putting him through his paces as any athlete would—to warm up the ligaments and tendons and to push his blood around his body a bit faster after the long journey with inadequate exercise.

As the children watched, I had the sense that Brownie and I were the "other team," tagged as the opposition. During the warm-up, something caught my eye in a ring some distance away—a horse coming to a dead stop from a gallop, a cloud of dust under his belly, the hind feet tucked neatly underneath and taking the strain of the sliding halt. I was impressed, even elated at the sight, but depressed, too. Surely, I thought to myself, there is the winner of my junior class.

As I rode over I saw, with no small measure of relief, that the rider was an adult; he would compete in a different division. Drawing closer, I recognized Clyde Kennedy riding Rango, the southern California champion reined cow horse. I had been impressed, even from afar, with good reason.

Still somewhat daunted by the professional atmosphere, I felt uncertain and unsure of our prospects. When it was time for my class, Wendell brought Brownie across to me. Watching my horse stride over, the single white dot like a third eye as he carried himself along in his usual, steady fashion, I suddenly knew I had the best horse. In the saddle with my hand on his neck, I sensed his low pulse rate and his capable attitude and adopted it myself to calm my nerves. I had doubted him, but no longer. We felt like professionals.

Figure eights were Brownie's Achilles' heel, but he hit the flying changes on this occasion unusually well. I knew Clyde Kennedy was watching me. I had found a new hero, and I wanted to impress him. When it came to do the stops, Brownie accomplished the first two reasonably quickly, but without any reaction from the crowd. The third stop I can remember to this day because I asked Brownie 'Whoa!' when we were galloping in the center of the ring, and he slid to a quivering, perfect halt in thirty feet. We stood in that cloud of dust while the crowd roared; it was the kind of applause that goes up at a football game after a touchdown, and I knew then, before the backing up and the offsets, that we had done fine.

At the out gate, Clyde Kennedy was there to congratulate Brownie on his performance and to ask me if I had a trainer. I told him no, but that I had seen him on Rango earlier and I would take any lessons I could from him. Clyde came over to the railroad car and looked around inside, intrigued by the arrangement. That night, he joined Miss Parsons and me in the railroad workers' cafeteria a short way up the track. As we sat down to our meal, I learned about the rivalry between Clyde and Jimmy Williams, the local favorite in Pomona.

Clyde continued to ask questions about the railroad car. Miss Parsons was proud to tell him how we were strictly tied to a low budget. There was no candy or soft drinks for young Monty Roberts; if he was lucky, he might get to open the box of scrap leather and mend some of his equipment—if he ever had a spare moment after collecting used Coca-Cola bottles so he could get the deposits back. Clyde shook his head in amusement.

That night as I lay in the railroad car I could hear children whispering and running around outside; they were looking for Brownie, who had become something of a hero. On the outside of the railroad car was pinned a line of rosettes, as well as spurs and belt buckles and other prizes. Brownie took this celebrity in stride, as though he thought it was his due. He was not an arrogant horse, simply one unfazed by almost any experience that did not involve paper.

On the last day of the show, the rivalry between Jimmy Williams and Clyde Kennedy was played out in the open division. Jimmy's horse Red Hawk could spin like a top. His sliding stops could be seen for miles around, the dust like Cherokee smoke signals. The crowd was rooting for him.

Clyde Kennedy, though, was superb on Rango. With only Miss Parsons, Wendell, and me to cheer him on, Rango executed the figure eights with style, effortlessly flying from one lead to the other as if he were ambidextrous. His pirouettes were a blur—all the while holding his head and neck straight, and never allowing his front feet to tangle while spinning in both directions. I had already seen his marvelous stops, and was not surprised when he won, but it was thrilling to witness nonetheless.

Wendell, Miss Parsons, and I loaded ourselves and our horses back into the railroad car, ready to be hauled back to the main line. Next stop: Tucson, Arizona, more than eight hours away. My whole life, invariably a life with horses, seemed to stretch out before me, as straight and as uncomplicated as the railway track itself.

Recently, I had occasion to revisit Pomona to give a lecture at a breeders' symposium. As I drove the car past a wild grassy area and a broken-down fence line, I had a flashback. I said to Pat, "Hang on, I've been here before. Follow me and I'll show you." I cut a path through the tall grass and we went about one hundred yards up the valley.

"I bet you," I said, "there's a disused single-track railway line up here." Pat followed me but gave me a doubting look. A little way off, I found the old length of iron and some wasted railway ties. We walked down the track to the spot where the show ground had been. The spectators' grandstand had been dismantled but the main ring itself was still discernible as an oval shape, the railings grassed over and choked with weeds. Suddenly, that day half a century ago, its clear sense of triumph and excitement, came back to me. The reality of the place, the show ground itself, was eroding; the event lived on only in the minds of those who had taken part. In a few years all trace of it would be gone.

It was a powerfully nostalgic feeling to stand where I had stood as a boy. It stirred my soul and took me totally by surprise.

I had once thought that life would be a straight progression, like an iron line through the wilderness. I knew better now, but looking out to that faded oval, with my arms around Pat, I felt a certain joy in our maturity. After forty years of marriage and raising a family, we had made it. To stand in Pomona, amid the ruins, was to make a neat and tidy circle.

———

Small wonder that entrepreneurial instincts were strong in me even as a boy: I had been riding for prize money at horse shows and working as a stunt rider in movies since the age of four, and even school was shaped around work in the stables. By the time I was twelve, money-making schemes—some quite epic—began to hatch in my brain. One involved Coca-Cola bottles.

My brother and I had been picking up bottles at horse competitions and bringing them home in the railroad car to earn the two-cent deposits. In 1947, it was announced that the first big postwar rodeo was to be held at the competition grounds in Salinas, and visions of all those empty Coke bottles were too tempting to pass up.

The outdoor grandstand was five stories high with a concrete wall behind and bench seating from top to bottom. The 20,000 spectators each day would stuff wrappers and spent bottles into the cavity below their seats—and down into the off-limits area below.

I went to Doc Leach in the competition grounds office with a proposal. Larry and I would clean up under the seats when the rodeo ended—"just for the coins and stuff we might find." Doc Leach wondered vaguely why we might volunteer to do so much work just for the odd coin, but he agreed. He would not have known about either the deposit system or Coke itself: inventions too new for old Doc Leach.

After the rodeo, however, our profits appeared to be in jeopardy. Before taking the measure of our haul, I had asked my father to call a representative of the Coca-Cola Bottling Company. I had in mind a very busy scene: wooden crates stacked by the doors, a line of trucks to take them away, with Larry and me in charge. But a Mr. Carlson of Coca-Cola warned us that people were catching on to the deposit idea and taking bottles home. We might do a great deal of work for almost nothing.

When, after the rodeo, my brother and I first entered that cavernous space below the seats, we were greeted by an amazing spectacle. Sunlight filtered through the slatted seats, like light through a Venetian blind, throwing wide stripes across ground that was ankle-deep in rubbish.

Anxious to find that first bottle, we held it up to a shaft of light. It was not broken, and few were. We were safe. We were also knee-deep in work: it took us two and a half months, working mostly at night, to complete the task! But at the end was a glass bonanza—80,000 bottles, one for every ticket sold over the four days. A convoy of trucks did indeed cart the bottles away. Larry and I earned $800 each, then a small fortune.

A tribute to the glass then used, only a thousand bottles had broken: some, remember, were dropped from a great height.

In the local newspaper, Doc Leach cheerfully conceded: the rodeo association had missed out on quite a profit and two young entrepreneurs had taken an old guy for a ride. He would not make the same mistake again.

The next year, when I went up to the high deserts of Nevada to bring back wild mustangs for Doc Leach and the rodeo, our partnership would be more equitable. But the heady Coca-Cola success certainly led to my life-changing encounters with the wild horses through the summer that followed.

CHAPTER 3

East of Eden

By 1949, when I was fourteen years old, I had essentially been a professional rider for a decade. I never really had a childhood; my youth had been an apprenticeship dedicated almost exclusively to horses, and my amateur competitors in the showring could not have known that the fuzzy-cheeked kid opposing them—on Ginger or Brownie—was a pro in every sense. Small wonder the trophies often went my way.

I had grown up on rodeo grounds, and it was inevitable that one day rodeo competition would beckon and that one day I would heed the call. My father's credo was simple: if there was prize money, I was to try for it. And so I entered skeet-shooting contests, chuck-wagon races, I rode bulls and even bucking horses—though I loathed riding broncs and had no talent for it. At fourteen, I began to practice the rodeo event called "bulldogging," which would prove to be the one at which I was most capable. Bulldogging started on ranches in Texas. Cowboys would have to hold herds of cattle together for hours at a time while various animals were singled out and roped—for veterinary treatment, perhaps, or for branding. Occasionally, a grown animal would run out of the herd, and the cowboys would chase after him and turn him back. For their own amusement during the long hours on the range, they started to compete among themselves in this chase-and-turn work. Some tried jumping from their horses onto the animal's neck, turning him back using their bare hands.

One day a black cowboy named Bill Pickett rode after a steer, jumped on its head, leaned over and grabbed its upper lip in his mouth, and bit down hard. The animal was so surprised by the pain that it fell. This was the very method that the English bulldog used to drop deer. Pickett would then turn the animal around and drive it back into the herd. The ranch put him on a tour to demonstrate his remarkable methods, which evolved into the event that we know today as bulldogging.

In the modern version, two men on horseback dart after an adult horned steer. One stays on the right and hazes the animal to keep it going in a straight line. The other runs alongside it on the left-hand side and leaps off his horse. The aim is to land on the steer's neck. His goal is to "throw" the steer. The bulldogger will want to stick to the animal like glue to prevent falling underneath his hooves. He wraps an arm around the animal's horns and takes its nose in the crook of his elbow, then gives an almighty twist to the steer's neck. The forward impetus of the animal causes it to flip on its side. It's like performing a judo throw with a 700-pound steer at breakneck speed. When the steer's flanks hit the dust, the clock stops. Injuries to the animals are virtually nil; the cowboys are often not as lucky.

I won the National Intercollegiate Rodeo Association (NIRA) bull-dogging championship in 1957, and I did well to win it—generally, rodeo championships go to cowboys from inland states such as Texas, Idaho, and Montana. My first steer was a bad draw. He was a big, slow-handling animal, and by the time I had thrown him I was placed seventh in the event, with a time of 6.2 seconds. But I could still win the championship if I placed well in the second round (the two rounds are averaged to produce a final score). I drew for my second steer, and got myself perhaps the best on offer. However, I drew in the "slack," which meant my second round would fall late at night, long after the public had left the arena.

Worse, by ten P.M. a sleet storm blew up. Particles of ice dripped off our hats. There was no cover, and I piled whatever clothing I could find on my horse and myself. Every now and again, I would run around in circles for ten minutes to keep my muscles warm. I would trot my horse, called Miss Twist, in circles for the same reason. Just past midnight, with only two more bulldoggers to go, I got the call for my second round. My college crew (my teammates) were all drinking hot coffee, and they swore it was the best thing for me in these crazy conditions, so I took half a cup and drained it, though coffee and I did not agree.

The bulldogger before me was in the chutes and ready to go. With the steer set on its way, the hazer's horse slipped on the muddy ground and failed to keep up. The young bulldogger found himself galloping alongside the steer with no one on the other side to keep it in a straight line. The steer peeled off to the right and the boy got his horse over and alongside the steer as best he could. But by now the steer was running alongside the fence and just as the boy leaned out to pitch from his horse, the steer carved a line to the left, toward the horse, and the rider was upended, bounced over the top of the steer, and into the metal pipe-and-rail fencing. He hit his head on an upright post and lay still where he fell.

The ambulance was called, and there was a sorrowful delay. The realization sank in that the boy had died instantly; the sound of his head hitting the upright had been ominously final.

The weather further blackened our spirits. And to add to these increasingly desperate circumstances, I began to feel nauseous; the coffee was working away in my gut and producing the allergic reaction that I subsequently learned to avoid at all costs. While my stomach churned, I backed Miss Twist into the box and threw off the sheets keeping her more or less out of the sleet and rain. I signaled to my hazer, Jack Roddy, that I was ready.

The steer was let out and I blew after him as fast as I could, Jack Roddy's horse maintaining his grip in the mud and keeping the steer in a straight line for me. I leapt from my saddle onto the steer's neck and with a giant twist of his head I brought him down in 4.3 seconds. I knew as soon as I felt him hit the turf that this great score meant I had earned myself a national championship in bulldogging.

When my college crew ran over to applaud me they found me staring at the ground, almost embracing it. The allergy had taken effect and I was more sick than I believed possible. I threw up everything, even my heels. The crew put it down to overexcitement, and I could not draw a breath to tell them otherwise and to plead: could they please stop pounding on the back of such a sick and sorry man.

———

Of all the events performed in the rodeo, perhaps the most dangerous is bull riding. In bull riding, your life depends on the draw. After your ride, the bull receives a score between one and fifty for his efforts, and the rider receives a score in that same range for his. You might even call it a team event. Each contestant has eight seconds to stay right side up on a professional rodeo bull. Bulls are more ferocious in their tactics than bucking horses. Horses arch their backs, curl their heads between their front legs and jump, stiff-legged, in a pogo-stick type of action, all of which is difficult enough. Bulls, on the other hand, have extraordinary strength and traction in their cloven feet that allows them to dive, then twist up to the left, come down again, crack into a right spin, and so on. A bull is like a hairy, snorting roller coaster. You hold on to the braided rope around his middle, and eight seconds on a bull's back can seem like a lifetime.

Of course, once you jump off or are thrown the bull straightaway turns and heads for you. His intentions are clear; he wants to see you as dust under his feet. So-called clowns run into the ring and distract his attention, which they do with any number of humorous antics. The clowns are amazing athletes and bullfighters who risk everything to entertain the crowd and save cowboys from injury.

When I got married, Pat asked me to give up bull riding since competitors are particularly prone to serious injury. She argued that my other rodeo events would improve without the stress and strain of bull riding. I agreed, and it took no more than one rodeo event to prove her right. Still, long afterward I would have strange flashes about bull riding. At a rodeo I would find myself worrying about which bull I had drawn, then remember. Without knowing it, I had been suffering from enormous tension, and I was glad of Pat's advice.

Most rodeo events evolved from common working practices on the ranch. In team roping, a pair of day hands would rope the steer's head and hind feet and stretch him out on the ground. Using a medicinal kit carried in their saddlebags, the two might have to deal with a hunk of barbed wire around his leg or a foxtail in his eye. Ranch horses were trained to maintain the tension on the rope until the job was done. Rodeo took that task and turned it into a competition—team roping. I was to win the NIRA national championship in team roping in 1956. To win that title requires a year of preparation.

Once, in Scottsdale, Arizona, Jack Roddy and I had drawn a perfect steer; he was steady and moved in a straight line. In my mind, this steer was important if we were going to get things going for the year. The steer was in the chute; Jack, the header, was behind the barrier to the left; I, the heeler, was in position on the right.

A piece of string is attached to the steer. When he takes off, he goes a prescribed distance before the string trips the latch holding a cord across the front of the header's horse. A ten-second fine is imposed if the header breaks through the cord. The trick (an art, really) is to have the horse moving forward just as the cord is released.

On this occasion, Jack Roddy timed it perfectly. In the arena he threw a great loop: a time below ten seconds and the championship trophy appeared before me like a vision. I was on a horse called Berney, and we shot off after the steer that Jack was drawing across our path. I leaned out, my loop built and whirling above my head, well within range and, suddenly, I had no horse. Berney took a dive and somersaulted, throwing me onto my chin.

In my hands was a rope, one end of it tied to the steer's hind feet. With a neat bucking action, the steer pulled it through, and the palms of my hands were like hamburger, practically smoking. Logically, I should have let the rope go but my subconscious had taken over. I had to apologize to Jack Roddy. No trophy.

Albuquerque, New Mexico, was a different story. We drew a steer that rodeo competitors call "a blue screamer." He was more like a racehorse than a bovine. "Don't worry," said Jack, "we'll beat these pot lickers." *Pot licker* was a derogatory term for the competition; when everyone else had finished lunch, a pot licker got to lick the pot.

The steer was in his chute wringing his tail, anxious to run, and Jack and I were lined up. Jack had his horse, Chongo, backed all the way up in the chute, aiming to time it so he pushed through the cord at a full gallop.

The steer lit out of the chute like it was on fire, and Jack rolled Chongo forward just as the string was tightening. He had Chongo flat out after only a few strides, and he roped the steer's head with a superb long throw. However, the long rope meant it was more difficult for me because the steer was swinging back and forth in a long arc. I had Berney on his tail and I could see his hind feet going quicker than I thought possible. I faced a twelve- to fourteen-foot throw instead of the usual four or five. Berney was practically scratching his inside ear on the ground, leaning that hard into the corner to get me close enough to rope the critter's heels. But this was the only chance I would get, and I had no time to widen my loop. I made the throw of a lifetime, and the steer's hind legs ran into the coil. We had him laid out flat on the ground and the field judge dropped the flag in less than eight seconds. The world championship was mine.

As a young man in the rodeo arena, I did more calf roping than I care to admit. In the calf-roping event, a small, 200-pound bovine scatters from the gate, moving more nimbly than the bigger animals. Dexterity is the name of the game. A cowboy races after him. As he builds his loop and closes in, the calf knows he is there. He ducks his head and flattens his ears, expecting his pursuer—as a predator—to catch him on the back of the neck. The cowboy throws the loop around the calf's head, keeping the other end of the rope tied around the horn of his saddle. All in one motion, the horse stops hard, the roper dismounts, and the calf is jerked off its feet and lands with a thud on its side.

The cowboy runs at him with a small length of rope in his teeth, waiting for the calf to rise to his feet. The roper's task is to throw the calf to the ground again and then wind the rope around any three of his legs—usually one front leg and both rear legs. The instant the cowboy completes the tie and throws his hands in the air, the field judge drops the flag and the clock stops.

Calf roping is not a pleasant event, and bears no comparison with what actually happens on a ranch. Roping calves is a necessary practice—for branding, castration, and medical purposes—but the calf is allowed to run with the rope and is brought to a halt slowly. Usually calves are roped by a team, to minimize stress on the calf.

I recently did a day's roping on a neighboring ranch and my horse, Dually, a champion reined and cutting horse, never broke out of a walk during the whole day's work. Ranchers prefer it this way: these babies, after all, are their livelihood. Protests against calf roping on the rodeo circuit have increased to such an extent that now the event is seldom seen by the paying public. It still takes place, but in the slack when the seats are empty.

As for bronc riding, another competition that has stirred an outcry, the distress that some people feel for broncs is misplaced. The bronc is not just any wild animal; he is a highly prized specialist. Not many horses are suited for the work. Far from being a cruel sport, this is a competition event in which the horse truly enjoys himself.

The champion bronc is a valuable animal who gets the best care and nutrition. He is not bored by repetitive exercises, like many horses working in other rodeo events or in the Western show-horse categories. He is respected as a bronc. He is a wild thing, and nobody spends hours trying to bend his will. He quickly learns that he has nothing to fear.

He is taken into the chute, a man gets on him, and the gate opens. The bronc then does as he pleases, and what pleases him is to put that rider on the ground. It's a good life.

———

In 1949, a group of American amateur equestrian associations banded together and established rules for a new amateur contest called "horsemastership," open to anyone under the age of eighteen. They laid a grid on the map, and each state was divided into districts. The winner would climb a ladder, from district to state to regional competition. At the end of this long trail of hard work, the reward was to be invited to the international final of the horsemastership contest, held in New York.

Parents across the country entered their children in this enormous and comprehensive competition. Surely the nation's gross national product dropped during the few years the all-consuming contest was held. My brother and I entered the first year. It was a hot day in Santa Rosa, California, and we were roasted in more ways than one. We were unprepared and came home losers.

Within days, we began to prepare for the 1950 horsemastership title. Next time I did better. Victorious in the district, I went to the state competition at Palm Springs. Judges had numbered different bits and bridles and ancillary equipment, and we were asked to name them. For every buckle and strip of leather, I gave a crisp answer. The judges might have taken my confidence as patronizing, but they liked the philosophy behind the phrase I repeated over and over, and they gave me full marks. "The most important part of any bit or horse headgear," I told them, "are the hands that hold it."

I won, but it was no surprise—I had been training horses for this event obsessively for two years in the manner of an adult professional yet I was pitched against young people who undertook their horsemanship more as a hobby. When I traveled to New York to win the final event with points to spare, I was still only fifteen. Nearly all the other twenty finalists were at the maximum age of eighteen. Fifteen of them came from various states in the United States; the rest were from Canada, Mexico, Panama, Puerto Rico, South Africa, and Argentina.

Between the rodeos and the show grounds and the horsemastership contests, and all the traveling on the railroad car, I did manage to fit in a little time at school, but my attendance record was slim. It consisted mostly of turning up on examination days to prove that I was up to standard. I was, though, registered with the local Catholic school administered by Notre Dame nuns. One nun, Sister Agnes Patricia, was the most influential teacher I ever knew. What I will always remember about her is her statement that there is no such thing as teaching— only learning. She believed that no teacher could ever teach anyone anything. Her task as a teacher was to create an environment in which the student can learn.

Knowledge, she told us, standing very straight in her long black habit, her face framed by her white wimple, pointed at the top like the spire of a cathedral, needs to be pulled into the brain by the student, not pushed into it by the teacher. Knowledge is not to be forced on anyone. The brain has to be receptive, malleable, and most important, hungry for that knowledge.

I apply the same philosophy to training horses. To use the word "teach" implies an injection of knowledge. Like Sister Agnes Patricia, I came to agree that there is no such thing as teaching, only learning.

———

When I was sixteen, Larry and I were part of a mad enterprise: a roundup of wild steers that had the look and feel of a wild goose chase—in the dark.

A woman named Dorothy Tavernetti owned the Laguna Seca Ranch, fifteen miles south of Salinas and some 6,000 acres in size. In 1950 she became the financial backer of an enthusiastic rodeo cowboy, Trevor Haggeman, who specialized in team roping, and they may have been connected romantically as well. She bought batches of young "Mexican Corianti" steers with long horns on which Trevor could practice his roping. My brother and I would go over three times a week to practice as well.

Within three or four months the steers got too heavy and stopped running; they grew weary of being roped all the time. Instead of selling them, Trevor would turn them out on the range and Dorothy would buy another batch of steers for him. The cattle lived on the range and grew bigger and bigger. When, a year later, Dorothy grew disenchanted with Trevor and asked him to leave, she decided to sell all the steers that had been put out on her ranch. The first group of 400 steers were easy to round up, and were shipped off to market. But the remaining one hundred head were now quite wild. You were lucky to glimpse them in the daylight hours and only rarely at night. Dorothy's hired hands concluded it was impossible to catch them.

She did not accept this defeatist attitude, however, and contracted Ralph Carter to catch her renegade cattle. Ralph and Vivian had been our partners in the mustang roundups, and since roping was a part of our lives, Ralph asked Larry and me, then fifteen and sixteen, to help. We felt like rustlers, for the roundup would take place under cover of darkness. The first few nights we were able to gather about forty head without too much difficulty. The remaining sixty head, however, were elusive. Ralph devised a plan: he would drive out with a load of hay in the pickup and feed them on open, flat areas five miles from the ranch house.

It was high summer, and food was in short supply. The cattle quickly found the new hay and would listen for the pickup as it came at nine or ten at night. They grew to like the sound of the truck's engine. Once this routine was established, Ralph hid Larry and me, on horseback, in the trees nearby. While the steers were eating the dropped hay, we were to break from the trees and gallop through the darkness, heading them off before they could reach the safety of the brush. The task was to rope a steer in near darkness.

It was hair-raising to be riding hellishly fast over broken ground, trying to see enough by the scant moonlight to rope some of the wildest steers known to humankind. You only knew you had caught one when you felt the sudden yank on the line. It was like fishing in the dark.

We would hold the captured steer with a dally—the rope wrapped around the horn of the saddle—until Ralph arrived with the truck and trailer. We then passed the ropes through the front of the trailer, so that by pulling from in front and pushing from behind, the steers were drawn up and into the trailer. Over six nights, we captured twelve steers in this fashion. The remaining forty-eight grew wise and would not be tempted from the brush. Ralph had to devise another plan. This time, Larry and I left headquarters on horseback, heading north of the cattle. We then pressed south, driving any cattle ahead of us through the brush into the open areas where we ran the horses flat out to catch the steers before they thought to circle back to cover.

I was chasing a steer I could barely see when it ran into a small clump of oak trees. I was concentrating hard on not riding into a low-hanging limb. The steer obviously knew that in the center of this clump of trees lay a deep pit. He also knew (though Brownie and I did not) about a trail that skirted round the edge of the pit. When the steer suddenly veered off, we continued on—airborne—down into the pit.

I was thrown over Brownie's head and, as I passed over his ears, accidentally caught my hand on the crown of the bridle. I found myself at the bottom of a sixteen-foot pit, standing in sand up to my knees. In my left hand was the whole bridle and part of a rope; in my right hand was my loop, still built. Brownie stood beside me in sand up to his knees and hocks.

Outwitted by a steer! I felt sore about this, but I was less pleased to discover that this fifty-foot-wide pit was truly a sand trap. I would scramble up the side, hang on by the tips of my fingers, then slide back down again. Once or twice I reached the top, but could not persuade Brownie to join me. I was spitting dust, and my boots were full of stones. It took me half an hour to fight my way out of there, horse included. Back at the pickup, they were wondering what had happened to me.

Larry and I began to make inquiries about our salaries, and whether danger pay ought to be included. Our fee was a meager ten dollars per steer. But we carried on anyway because we were having fun. Finally, there remained about twenty steers to capture, and Ralph had yet another new plan.

We had learned that the steers were frightened only of the horses, whom they could smell from afar. Horses were their nemeses. But they still liked the sound of the pickup and the hay that came with it. We would use subterfuge.

Ralph stowed me in the back of the pickup, well hidden but with a loop already built. The other end of the rope was attached to the trailer hitch. Ralph drove slowly through the herd, while I tossed flakes of hay over the side from my position lying supine in the bed of the pickup. Ralph was muttering out the side window in a low voice, "Three coming up now on the left side . . ." At an opportune moment, I leapt from my hiding place and roped a steer. Ralph gunned the accelerator and jerked the steer to the ground. Larry and I jumped on the steer and held him down while Ralph got a rope around his horns. We then tied him to a tree, to be picked up later in the trailer. We were doing very well with this method until the accident.

I reckoned the steers were going to be on the right side of the truck, but they turned and approached us from the left. As usual, I jumped up, but then had to face in the other direction to throw the loop. I did not stop to think about where the rest of the rope was lying. As Ralph accelerated, the rope—caught around me—whipped up, crossed over my left cheekbone, and slammed my head into the tail-gate.

He dragged the steer for thirty yards, while the rope massaged my head. I was unconscious for several hours; I awoke in the hospital with bandages covering my head and wondering what had happened. We eventually caught all the steers and made a fair amount of money for those nights' work. We were lucky to live through it, but it was fun and taught us to see in the dark.

———

During my trips to Nevada, I had become acutely aware that Brownie was due an apology from us. In the high desert, I had seen how he must have been brought up. Predators aside, it had looked to me to be idyllically happy. Brownie would have been been raised in a close family group, with affection tempered by discipline, and with all the security of a large extended family communicating effectively with one another.

He had then been wrenched into an alien environment, and right away beaten and frightened into submission. I had taken it upon myself to try to make up for the sacking-out procedure. I talked to him all the time, listened to him, gave him the best possible care; I wanted to do everything right for him. His health was always good; I thought carefully about his diet, I read his every mood. And he had responded. He had become as close as a brother to me. Save for his paper phobia, he was a steady and well-adjusted horse. He had recovered, I think, as well as could be expected.

However, not long after our steer-roping adventure together, when he was fourteen and I was seventeen, I began to notice a sorrowful air come over him in the stable, a certain reluctance when I swung into the saddle. He was not crisp and ready for the day as he usually was. Concerned, I began to experiment with his diet and exercise.

One of Brownie's favorite exercises was one I had devised to prac-tice for the heeling event in rodeo competition. I did not always have a header to work with me, so I trained one steer to cooperate with us in these training sessions. The steer's job was to hold in one corner of a large rectangular pen; we would gallop toward him, and the steer would run toward the center. Brownie's task—and he excelled at it— was to execute a U-turn placing his right shoulder near the left hip of the steer, giving me a perfect opportunity to rope the hind legs. Both Brownie and the steer seemed to enjoy the game.

But when I included a touch more of this favorite activity in Brownie's training schedule, his apathy seemed worse rather than better. Suddenly, it hit me. He was bored with me; he needed a holiday. A young person as driven as I was will almost always overwork his horse, and despite all the attention I gave Brownie, it had proven too much. I had crowded his life with my own.

I realized this only weeks before the biggest horse show of the year in Salinas. Were we to duck out of it, and give up all we had worked for? More than ever, I wished that we shared the same language.

One day I leaned into Brownie's stall and had a conversation with him. I put an arrangement to him: "Brownie, I will love you from Monday to Friday, feed and exercise you from Monday to Friday, but I won't badger you or bother you. You can do what you want during the week. In return, can you give me everything you've got on Saturday and Sunday?"

Knowing he could not understand, but fresh with the knowledge I had gained in Nevada, I made a promise to him that I would dedicate my life to understanding his language. This was a vow made to a horse, but solemn nonetheless. I meant to keep it. On that day, which was a focal point in my life, I set out my goal. My ambitions became focused from that point.

Brownie won everything at the Salinas show. It was as though he did understand.

———

These were the last summers spent on the railroad car traveling to horse shows.

The shows themselves were a flurry of activity and hard work. My father employed an advance man to sort out transportation from rail yard to show ground, to identify where we could restock with provisions and, more important, to sell as many tickets as possible to a "clinic" I would put on after the weekend shows, often on a Monday evening. Miss Parsons took the gate money and banked our share; she kept accounts in a steel box that would then be pored over by her and by my father, though I was not privy to that. The advance man also secured the venue for the clinic. Often the tickets were sold to clubs and schools. The advertised appeal was: "Monty can show you how to win." My father no doubt hit on this initiative to help cover the considerable costs involved in hauling the railroad car around the country with all those horses and two full-time employees. He must have needed more than my prize money to keep that show on the road.

At the shows, I generally won everything. And why not? I had Brownie, plus up to eight highly trained horses to mop up any prizes left over. I was a professional with years of experience behind me. The American Horse Shows Association recognized me as a professional but did not exclude me from entering amateur competitions as long as I was within the qualifying age. I competed against boys and girls who might enter two or three horse shows a summer and only ride on weekends. Horsemanship was their fun, not their life's work. In a way, I was a freak occurrence on the show circuit in those years. At the clinics I was supposed to reveal the secret of my success before what we hoped was an enthusiastic audience. Brownie was on hand so young riders could see the famous champion horse. I listened hard to every question and gave as much advice as I could.

I spoke about equipment, work ethic, training. I watched my pupils' horses and counseled what should be done with them next. I learned to project my voice and speak clearly. I felt a great weight of responsibility, because all these riders had paid and deserved the best attention. But, for all that, the clinics could never deliver what they promised. The "secret" of my success was a life obsession with horses. I would look at the eager young faces lined up before me: no youngsters were going to dedicate six to seven hours a day to riding, and no parents would let them. Sometimes I felt sorry for those kids, but just as often I felt sorry for myself. My life during those summers was like that of young evangelists who travel the country preaching; in many ways, it was a trying existence.

Not having had the opportunity to behave as a child, I was separate, isolated, with a different set of values from most young people. I had never visited a toy shop, for instance, never possessed a toy as a child; only much later did that fact strike me as odd. I would see a child go into a shop, point at a train set or a doll, and say, "Can I have that one, please?" It struck me that I had never done that, and I felt an overwhelming sense of regret. On the other hand, because my world was focused so tightly on horses, I was prone to think I was better than anyone else and that I possessed unique qualities. After all, I was *the* high-profile junior horseman on the North American showring circuit. Behind my father's back I had started to investigate the silent language of Equus. I could not wait to be free of him and to start using my own methods.

Luckily, Miss Parsons kept my feet on the ground, reminding me that the whole circus of our operation offered tremendous opportunities for both adventure and education. She kept me humble, pointing out that my success owed a great deal to the many hours of work I put in, which my competitors could not. There were no magic wands in my possession, no mystical qualities unique to Monty Roberts.

But I was already more man than boy. In terms of my life experience, my travel, and my education, I was a man in his twenties. Even my body carried the message that I was older than my years. I had turned to weight lifting, and my 190 pounds was spread over a powerful frame with a forty-eight-inch chest. Silently, I was conveying a message to my father: "I will be bigger than you." When I won the "Mr. Salinas Junior" bodybuilding contest, my father ridiculed me. We were like two bulls, and though the younger one still feared the older, time, as it always is, was on the side of the young.

The already strained relationship between us grew increasingly difficult. As a boy reaching manhood, I had good reason to believe I should be testing my wings. We had many aborted conversations about starting to train horses using my own methods. What was wrong with his methods? he would ask. He had done pretty well with them—what was there to change? He wanted his ways to be my ways; he could not conceive that I might do anything other than what he had taught me. The mere thought of it stirred anger in him.

At fifteen, I had wanted to play football and try out for the wrestling team, but he would have none of it. I might as well have asked his permission to fly to the moon. Anything that took me away from the life he had made for me was beyond contemplation. He had given me first breath, and he owned the ones that came after.

I would try again. "Maybe you could release some of the income I earned from the motion pictures I did, so I could buy some equipment?"

"What money? You used that up long ago."

"OK, what about the clinics we just held?"

He would counter with a question of his own. "Who paid for your education, who paid for your room and board, who paid for your upbringing?"

Then he made the point crystal clear. "I, as your father, am responsible for everything you've done, and you owe me, not vice versa."

Sometime later, I was in the house talking with my mother, explaining to her how working with the mustangs over the last few years had taught me a great deal.

"Like what?" she asked.

"Something very important. For instance, I just know that no one needs to sack out a young horse anymore. I'm doing it a different way. I don't even hit a horse once, not ever—not the way I do it. I don't even tie a rope to their heads before I ride them."

"Well," she said, "that sounds like a lot happier way of doing things." Just then, a movement caught my eye and I turned and saw my father. He was staring at me from the doorway, and I knew he had caught the drift of my conversation. He stepped forward wearing a hard, unforgiving look. I knew what that meant. He stepped in front of us, his color heightened by his terrible fury. The veins stood out in his neck as he shouted, "I don't want to hear any more of this sort of talk."

"Dad—"

He shouted louder, one of his hands curling into a fist, the other jabbing at my chest. "You are ungrateful to me."

"I'm not."

"You are too stupid to do anything without my help." I swallowed hard, knowing what was coming, as my mother pleaded, "Marvin, please..."

"You owe everything to me!" With that, he raised his fist to his opposite ear and brought it back across my face, knocking my jaw hard. On this day, finally, I was not going to take it. I advanced on him, my hands on his arms, and backed him against a wall. I looked him in the eye, and he seemed to grow a little smaller. I had anger now to match his, and I came within a hair of unleashing it.

I felt then what I have occasionally felt since but always resisted: an urge to strike. But at that moment the chain of violence was broken. I would not be like him—either with other humans, or with animals.

I registered that my mother had screamed, briefly. I heard my mother say to him, "Marvin, stop at once." She had his arm and was staring at him hard, like she wanted to turn him to stone.

"Listen to him for once," she said. "Let's just see what he has to say. He's not a child."

We moved slightly apart, and he dropped his shoulders. He was not afraid of me, but he wore a look of shock and resignation. "Listen, uh?" he said, as though anything I said would not be worth much. Nevertheless, he went quiet. We moved to the living room and he sat on a couch by himself while my mother stood close by me.

Something clicked; I recognized my opportunity. This was no conversation now. I was telling him what was going to happen. "I want to start up on my own. I figure there are people who will give me work training their horses, and I want to be left to do as I think fit. I want a chance to prove I can do it. It's not much to ask, it's only what anyone in Salinas could do—lease some facilities from you so they can work with horses here at the grounds. Same as Ray Hackworth or anybody else."

There was a moment's pause while my father digested what he had just heard. A look of disbelief stole over his face, then he said, "Good! You can do just that! I'll rent you barn number eight, course I will. And we'll see how you get on." Then he stood up and pointed a finger at me. "And while you're about it, since you're so damned grown-up all of a sudden, you can pay us money for your board, you can buy your own vehicle and your own clothes." His parting shot was: "The rent for your room here is thirty-five dollars a month!"

The rent for the entire house on Church Street had been thirty-five dollars a month. He wanted to show me the kind of payments he faced, and by setting such a high rent he thought he was sowing the seeds of my failure. Nevertheless, I eagerly accepted the arrangement. He named my mother as administrator for all the various charges, and the days she was to expect them.

I took him at his word and opened for business as a trainer of show horses and cutting horses.

In other ways too I made it clear that I was now in charge of my own destiny. Rodeos would no longer dominate my time: I joined the football and wrestling teams at school. As far as making a living, I was a world champion horseman, was I not? Surely there would be more than enough work training other people's horses.

Reality struck home quickly: had it not been for my mother helping me out surreptitiously most of the time, forgetting a month's rent here and there and slipping me some cash when she saw I needed it, I certainly would have crashed quickly and would have had to find myself a job digging ditches. But my mother cheated on my behalf in ingenious ways. She bought pants, supposedly for my father but in my size, so she could give them to me instead. Without her adjusting the accounts in this way, my father would have been right and I would not have survived.

Thanks to her, I was out from under him for the first time in my life. It was a start.

———

I was mounted on Brownie, standing in one corner of the corral. In the other corner stood one steer. While Brownie jigged on the spot, wanting to be set loose and run at the steer, I counted the seconds and judged when to give the command. I gave a cluck and he jumped forward in the usual gleeful way. Brownie ran in, rolling the steer out of the corner and bouncing it out from along the rails—his particular skill.

Suddenly, he felt all wrong beneath me. As if his nervous system was plugged into mine, I felt the sharp, fearful breakdown within him just as he did. When he stumbled and made a crashing fall, this was no horse tripping over a piece of rough ground; this was the rug pulled out from under his feet.

By the time I stood up, I knew he was dead. He was lying on the ground, not moving a muscle. A terrible grief overtook me. I could not imagine life without this horse as my friend and companion. I suffered true bereavement, as bad as any I have known. I stood there for a long while in dumb silence, not doing a thing.

As I stood there, I remembered. I remembered first seeing that single white dot between his eyes, remembered hearing his name. Brownie. Standing nose to tail with Oriel in the pale moonlight up on the high desert in Nevada. Rocking back and forth in the railroad car, keeping his balance. Walking forward to collect many, many championship trophies as a working horse. Spinning calves out of the corner of the corral...

I set about to bury him where he died, at the south end of the competition grounds. The ground was rock hard, and I went at it with a pick and shovel. To my surprise, my father understood my sorrow. He rented an air chisel for me so I could break through; it was the kindest thing he ever did for me.

The old grounds at Salinas were recently rebuilt and one of the mementos I plucked from it was a board from Brownie's stall. Not that I needed anything to remember him by.

It is a bitter pill to watch a horse die, but to lose one you love is to lose a part of yourself. The tears do not stop coming for a long time.

"Rest in peace," I said to Brownie as I laid him in his grave. I meant it.

———

Mr. Fowler paced back and forth at the head of the class, while we waited with our pencils sharpened and our paper at the ready. A tall man with an erect bearing and an olive complexion, he always dressed immaculately.

"I want you all to think about this very carefully," the teacher said, waving his long, elegant hands. "It should be like painting a picture of your lives in the future, as if all your ambitions had been realized."

A voice piped up. "How much detail do you want, sir?"

"As much as possible. It should be a complete portrayal of what you envision for yourself in the future." He turned to gaze at us calmly.

"And my last instruction to you is perhaps the most important: This vision should be realistic. I don't want to hear about some crazy, off-the-wall plan. I don't want to know about any Hollywood dreams, either."

There was a smattering of laughter at this. We were in California, after all. Mr. Fowler ended, "It should be a fair and accurate assessment of where I might expect to find you if I were to visit you in your mid-thirties. It's to be called "My Goals in Life" and should be returned within three weeks."

In my last year of high school, I knew precisely what I wanted to do in life; from the time I was nine I had been sketching plans for stables and training facilities. Mine was no Hollywood dream. I turned in what I thought was a good paper that captured my life's ambition: a ground plan and associated paperwork for the operation of a Thoroughbred racehorse facility. Five days later, the paper was returned to me with a big red F printed across the top of the page, along with the traditional words: "See me."

This was a shock, because I normally got good grades. Essay in hand, I went immediately to see Mr. Fowler after class and asked him what I had done wrong. He leafed through the pages. "You know that my last instruction to you was to be realistic in this projection of your future?"

"Yes, I did realize that."

"Do you realize that the average annual income of a person in the United States is sixty-three hundred dollars?" I had a clear idea of what was coming. "So how many years would you have to work and save up to earn the amount of money you'd need for your plan?" he asked me.

"I don't know."

He snapped his finger against the red F and advised me, "It's a wild, unattainable dream. I gave it a failing grade based on the instructions I issued at the outset." He handed me back the paper. "I know your family and background; it would just not be possible. Take it home, think about it, change your vision to an appropriate level, and hand it in again. The last thing I want is to fail you based on a misunderstanding."

It felt like he had driven a knife into me, so unexpected was his re-action. I was suddenly awakened to the reality of finance, and I faced the prospect that my dream was of the impossible kind. The next few days were depressing. I agonized over what to do. My mother saw I was troubled and inquired, so I confided in her.

She read my paper and suggested, "Well, if that's truly your life's dream, then in my opinion you can achieve it. I think you ought to consider turning the paper back in just the way it is, without any changes." She added, "If you think it's unattainable, then you can change it yourself. But I don't think it's for a high school instructor to set a level on your hopes and dreams."

My mother was a meek woman, but this is one of the few times I saw her angry. I felt renewed. I returned to school and handed the paper back, this time with a note attached to Mr. Fowler. I told him that while he had every right as my instructor to call my life plan un-attainable, I did not see it that way. I further suggested that he did not have the right to put a cap on my aspirations, but that he should grade the paper as he saw fit.

When the grades were mailed to us at the end of the year, I got an A for that particular course. I never did find out to what extent my teacher changed the mark, but clearly an F on the project would have scuttled any chance for a top grade. I would encounter Lyman Fowler much later in my life: he would have more to say on the subject of hopes and dreams.

———

One night in the summer of 1953, I was in the railroad car, winding through the Imperial Valley in California. It was still strange not hav-ing Brownie with me—we had spent so long together in this rattling wooden structure as it rolled around the vast countryside. His was a ghostly presence, especially at night.

I had gone back over the roof of the train to the caboose where the railroad crew rode. Nothing much was happening. The cards were put away and no one was drinking or eating. I was looking out the window into the moonlit desert of southern California. Quite sud-denly the image of a young lady named Patricia Burden came into my mind as clearly as if I had invited her to sit by me. It struck me that she was going to be a major factor in my life. Pat Burden had been one year behind me through primary and secondary school. Her father owned a major company that drilled and installed water wells, but she had relatives who were involved in the horse business and in rodeo as well.

What to do next preyed on me. This was not a decision I had made; it was as if someone else were pulling the strings. Once home, I went up to her in the corridor of Salinas Union High School and simply informed her that she was my "chosen woman," or words to that effect. She had a different reading and shooed me away.

Pat was then involved with someone in an on-again, off-again relationship. Curiously, I discovered later that in grade school she *did* have a crush on me and even named her black cocker spaniel Monty Blue. But that was then; Monty Blue the dog had since been run over. This was now.

Soon after my announcement in the corridor, Pat was with friends, Sally and Jim Martins, who happened to be related to my family and she told them I was pestering her every day for a meeting of some sort, suggesting no end of things we might do together. They dared Pat to go out with me just once. Not being the type to turn down a dare, she said she would. The next day, I made my usual overture. This time she said yes to a date—dinner and a movie. Since then we have been together for more than forty years.

———

A major Hollywood picture was scheduled to be shot in and around Salinas in the summer of 1954. It was to be called *East of Eden,* from the book by John Steinbeck, who had been a Salinas resident in the early years of the century. I had gone to school with members of his family.

The director was to be the noted filmmaker Elia Kazan. He had cast a kid from a New York stage school in the main role, and naturally the producers were worried about asking a city boy to play the part of a small-town Californian. Our old friend Don Page was the first assistant director on the film, and he suggested that I take this young, unknown actor under my wing and show him around, let him live with me for a while, to help him soak up the local atmosphere. I thought it was a terrible idea, imagining some drama school graduate slowing me down. But when Don pointed out that there was a $2,500 payment for the three months, plus food allowances, I saw what a sensible plan it was after all. "What's the actor's name?"

"James Dean."

He turned up at the competition grounds with a little suitcase, wearing jeans, a T-shirt, and a leather jacket. He was disheveled and careless, goofy and irreverent, unstructured and confident. He was twenty-three years to my twenty, but it seemed the other way around; he was young for his age. I took his bag and showed him to my room, where I gave him the top bunk. Then I noticed his boots. They were a city-slicker's idea of cowboy boots, with the jeans an inch too short to show more of the leather. I said nothing at first, but then could bear it no longer. We had a clothing allowance for him, and I suggested we go to the Garcia saddlery store to buy him some real boots.

Jimmy was stoic about it, though he wanted to hang on to his original pair. "If you don't burn them by the time we're through," I told him, "I won't have done my job properly." A little later, when he was comfortable with his new footwear, he gave the original boots away. The boots episode tipped us into a firm friendship. He would sit on the fence and watch Pat and me riding, either at shows or in the practice corrals. We went to Mac's Cafe and had dinner; we introduced him to everyone we could. He would melt into corners and sit balled up, running his fingers through his hair. I advised him to straighten up, to come out of his shell, not to slink back all the time if he wanted to appear like a Salinas-born Steinbeck character. "Yeah, yeah. I'll do that," he replied, unconcerned. Then with genuine interest he would ask, "Can you show me how to spin that rope?"

We sat up till three in the morning teaching him to do the "butterfly." Jimmy thought that mastering that spin would be his ticket to local social acceptance. He was right. He did it everywhere, showing off his new trick while the assembled company nodded their heads in approval. He also wanted a pair of chaps. He would borrow mine and wear them to horse shows, but for a spectator to wear the uniform of a competitor was considered poor form, and he soon stopped. He was pleased when I gave him an old pair of my father's chaps.

Jimmy fell in love with Pat and followed her around like a puppy. He was never a threat because he never advanced his case—he simply looked at her all the time, and wherever she went he would go too. After the three months were up, Don Page and Elia Kazan called me in for a meeting. They were close to shooting now, and they wanted to know how their young prospect had fared.

I told them I really liked him, that he was like a brother to me, and that I was impressed with his character, with everything about him. I had to add one caveat, though. I knew plenty of actors from my film work, and James Dean was not like John Wayne or Roddy McDowall. He was not gregarious, did not engage people in conversation, did not evoke enthusiasm. He just did not seem to me like an actor.

The two men thanked me for my report, and I went away to begin my various tasks on the shoot. I was the wrangler looking after the horses my father had provided for the movie, as well as a stuntman and an extra. Soon the film crews turned up. Jimmy moved out of my bedroom and into the hotel with them, although we still formed a threesome, still went out every night.

Filming started and after two days Elia Kazan and Don Page asked me if I would attend what are called the "dailies"—a session to view footage shot the day before. They wanted me to comment on the authenticity of all aspects of the film. I felt a certain dread because I was sure that Jimmy's acting ability, or lack of it, was about to be cruelly exposed. I pictured the scene: when they asked, "What are we going to do to save this movie?" I would have to stop myself from saying, "I told you so."

I could not have been more wrong. I went back to being an environmental consultant and never breathed a word about his acting again. It was immediately obvious that James Dean brought a new and magical presence to the screen. He was absolutely electric.

When we were out together at night, Jimmy would act out scenarios for our amusement. First he would pretend to be on the telephone to someone, describing his spectacular success. He was the Hollywood star who did not know what to do with all his money—there were girls beating down the door to see him; he was going to buy a huge ranch in the area; Pat and I were going to manage it for him; he would fly in from whichever part of the world he was shooting in. Then he would act out a darker scenario. *East of Eden* was a terrible failure. No one watched it; the studios wanted their $150,000 fee back; they wanted the clothing allowance back; they came and took the boots off his feet.

None of us knew then which it was going to be.

History recorded the answer. Over the next year I was with James Dean when he shot *Rebel Without a Cause*, as well as *Giant* with Elizabeth Taylor and Rock Hudson. As it turned out, Jimmy's Hollywood star scenario was the right one, and he gained the fortune to go with it. And he really did want to buy a ranch that Pat and I would manage for him. There was a property for sale near Salinas, and we had even driven out together to look at it.

Late one summer, Jimmy called to say he was due to take part in a road race in Salinas. He would drive up from Hollywood with his mechanic in his Porsche Spyder, and stay with us at Pat's parents' place. We would begin looking at property in earnest. Pat and I felt our future was decided—through our friendship, we were following a promising new track in our lives.

On September 30, 1955, we were waiting for his telephone call. We had told him to call us when he was near to let us know his estimated time of arrival. His mechanic, Wolf Weutherich, had our names and telephone numbers in the pocket of his overalls and was getting ready to stop when the Porsche collided with another car. The other driver walked away with a bruised nose. Weutherich broke his leg and jaw. James Dean died of a broken neck.

In the aftermath, Wolf was so dazed and traumatized that the first call he made was to us. Through his fractured jaw, he mumbled that James Dean was dead.

It was a numbing experience. What made it even harder was that Pat and I were alone with our grief. We had known him for only a year. We knew none of his family, and they were unaware that we existed. His body was taken back to the Midwest and we never attended the funeral. The life that we had been expecting to lead with our friend closed down in front of us. We simply went back to school.

In 1955 I won a football scholarship to the California Polytechnic State University, San Luis Obispo (better known as Cal Poly), where I would major in three areas: biological sciences (specializing in psychology), animal science, and agri-economics. The "full-ride" scholarship meant that both tuition and living expenses were paid for. However, because of a football injury, I declined the scholarship and joined the rodeo team instead. They welcomed me, a four-event man, with open arms.

I had registered for the military draft but had not yet been called up. Their medical examination confirmed that I was completely color-blind. I was glad to have it proven that I saw in a way that most others did not—that I perceived movement more clearly and from a far greater distance, and that I could see better at night.

Many years later, when I was sixty-one, I went to a specialist in Britain who gave me contact lenses that offered a taste of what it is like to see color. The vibration of energy that resulted caused me enormous agitation. If this is what normally sighted people have to put up with, I thought to myself, small wonder they are so distracted and nervous. It was a revelation that left me certain: I could not have done what I have in my life had I seen color. (And when I describe colors in this book, say the coppery color of a horse I may be using what others have told me. But the most delicate shadings and depths of shadows and light I do see. I see density of pigment, which allows me to see the sheen and sparkle of a healthy horse's coat.)

Woody Proud, who owned the Proud Ranch near the university, allowed me to live there while I was a student. Convinced my reputation would bring him significant business, he let me occupy a house rent-free if I agreed to share it with two other rent-paying students. It was not so much a house as a hut—Woody had bought several old motel cabins and parked them on his land.

Nevertheless, this arrangement let me keep my three horses—Miss Twist, Finito, and Poco Hyena—and still afford to go to college. From the outset, I practiced hard with the college rodeo team. As we drove to competitions far afield, I became interested in how horses transported in trailers countered the stress and strain of road travel. A year or two later, I would team up with Sheila Varian and conduct an in-depth study of horse transportation, hauling horses over twisting roads for long periods of time. We used an open truck with no partitions, reasoning that loose horses would be free to find the most comfortable position. Almost all the time they chose to arrange themselves at forty-five degrees to the roadway, with about half facing forward and half facing backward. The common element, though, was the clear preference for forty-five degrees. At that angle, they were better able to brace themselves against the stopping and starting and against the pull of the corners.

Subsequently, in 1960, I took my old trailer to a welding shop and had them change the partitions so all were hinged to one wall and would swing open. I could then haul my horses at forty-five degrees. To my knowledge, mine was the first trailer adapted in this way. I made inquiries about taking out a patent on the design, but never pressed the matter. Years later, forty-five-degree-angle trailers were being factory-built, and now half of all horse trailers built in the United States follow that design.

———

On June 16, 1956, Pat and I got married and together moved into something on the Proud Ranch that was a little closer to a real house. Our first child, Deborah, arrived less than a year later. That day was the greatest in our lives, to be matched only by the births of our other two children, Laurel and Marty.

Suddenly, money disappeared more quickly. The dollars left my pocket and I waved good-bye to them, then wondered where the next ones would come from. I simply could not win enough at competitions to pay for our own needs and the upkeep of the horses. I was a twenty-two-year-old rodeo competitor who brought back prize money maybe four days a month during summer, but only one day a month in winter.

While Pat was pursuing a diploma in business, we opened a shop to which we were able to give the famous "Garcia" name; the arrangement amounted to an early franchise operation. Garcia made the best Western equipment in North America, and our store was conveniently located between Cal Poly and the Proud Ranch.

Toward the end of our college years, the economic climate for us appeared to brighten with the arrival of one Homer Mitchell. He had put a horse or two my way for training and had been impressed. Now he wanted to find a property near the ocean and San Luis Obispo. The plan was that I help him build a training facility there, which I would then manage for him. When he was older, he would retire there.

I found him an eighty-acre property near Edna, California, five miles inland from Pismo Beach. In those days the whole area was as beautiful and unspoiled as any along that coastline. Homer agreed that the property, called Laurellinda, was perfect.

Pat and I watched Homer as he reached into his coat pocket and took out a checkbook and pen. It was a simple thing to write a check for $160,000, but to us he was walking on water; we did not think that kind of money existed, even in a bank. We agreed in writing to lease the property. Homer would put three horses into training for a fixed amount per month, meaning that we started out already halfway to covering our costs. We counted ourselves lucky. By now our second daughter, Laurel, had been born. We were about to leave college and make a living doing what we loved. We were young and rightly optimistic. All was well.

———

The 1960s marked a period of great upheaval: men burned their draft cards, women burned their bras, and students—especially in California—started leaning far to the left on the political spectrum. We seemed not to be touched by any of this. Our concerns were elsewhere, and we had too much else on our plates. We had two infant daughters, Debbie and Laurel, with our son, Marty, on the way. We had to finish constructing a 2,000-square-foot ranch house and the outbuildings. And we had our horses. What we did not have was money.

Laurellinda was just eighty beautiful acres with a couple of broken-down shacks on it. Homer pointed at one shack and said, "A nickel box of matches will do the job here." It was his way of instructing us to torch the buildings.

"Where will we live?" we asked him.

"You'll have to rent a place in town and drive out here to work. Money dictates that we build the horse facility before we build the house." Pat and I had no money for rent, and running back and forth was out of the question. Horses are not nine-to-five; horses are all hours.

Since the pair of little shacks stood where the training barn was to be built, we moved them away a short distance. One was a very old, very small railway car, and the other was a garage-shaped box. We nudged them together and plastered over the holes. I saw this as a temporary arrangement—surely, with my reputation, horses in need of expert training would arrive any minute. We could then rent a big house trailer until a proper house could be built. But the horses did not arrive. And we had given up our saddle-shop franchise now that our third baby was on the way. I had a few mares to breed and I gave a few lessons, but with only four paid horses in training I was desperate. I was trying hard for prize money in rodeos, but the figures just did not add up. I had to find more work.

It was then that someone said to me: "Go live with Don Dodge for a while." Don Dodge was possibly the most successful trainer of Western horses in the United States, and he did have a line of vans waiting to turn into his place. "Study hard with Don," the advice went. "Give him one hundred percent. If he believes in you, you'll have it made. He'll recommend people to you." Then came the warning: "He's impossible to impress!"

With nothing to lose, I called him up and asked to work for him for a while.

"Yup. Come up if you want. Prepare to go to work, though. You can bring a couple of your own horses, and when it's time for you to leave I'll figure out what you owe me. 'Cause I'm going to teach you something. God knows you need it. Oh, and Monty, you have to promise to do exactly as I tell you. OK?"

"I promise."

I took two of my horses in training, Selah Reed and Finito, and drove north to 3400 North Del Paso Boulevard, North Sacramento, California, an address forever engraved in my memory.

Don Dodge was about forty-four, a six-footer with dark hair. He had a slim build, a beaky nose, and close-set eyes that gave him an intense look that women seemed to adore. He cut a good figure on a horse, and he had about forty horses in training for some of the best owners in the world. Bad owners do not pay their bills; they dictate to the trainer and make sore losers. Good owners, on the other hand, pay bills on time, get involved enough to take good or bad news in stride, and they let the trainer train. Don Dodge was blessed with a fleet of such owners.

I had no sooner pulled up in his yard than he had me working. "Glad you're here. Billy Patrick here could use some help." He waved at a red-haired kid scurrying back and forth with water buckets. I backed out my two horses, and they were allocated open booths of distinctly inferior quality to the box stalls occupied by Don's horses.

I helped Billy feed all forty horses and topped off their stalls (removed the top layer of manure). More bucket carrying ensued because Don did not believe in automatic watering systems. After that, we had to clean all the tack used that day.

At about seven P.M. Billy and I were through, and I went indoors. I was looking forward to a wash and brushup, changing into some clean clothes, then maybe having dinner with Don. I imagined we would share a drink and a chat, and during the meal I could begin to cultivate his friendship.

"Where you going to stay?" Don asked me.

My jaw dropped. "I thought you might have a bunk room for me somewhere."

"Nope. You can go down the road a way, and there's a sort of rooming house. Old Mother Harris." Don telephoned to tell her I was coming. He added, "She'll fix your meals for you." Cursing in disbelief, I drove to Mother Harris's place. A room with board included would be ... a figure I could not dream of paying. A room without board was two dollars a night; I had no other option.

I telephoned Pat. The children were crying in the background; the shack was falling down around her ears; and there was, she assured me, no more money. The only thing I could afford to eat was a product called MetreCal, a liquid meal designed for people trying to lose weight. It cost ninety cents a can, and I lived off it for ten weeks.

On the bright side, there were different flavors. I had a choice of chocolate MetreCal, vanilla MetreCal or strawberry MetreCal. I would make my decision, punch holes in the top, and suck out the contents.

I had to be at Don Dodge's at four-thirty in the morning to feed the horses and attend to their stalls. Don would appear at seven-thirty and start barking orders. I would ride a minimum of ten horses for him during the morning, then crack another can of MetreCal and keep going. At some point in the afternoon, he would always spend time with me as I worked on my two horses. A hard taskmaster, Don Dodge would shout at the top of his lungs. I did what I was told. I learned a lot.

During these afternoon sessions, he would pepper me with questions about the other two horses left at home. Surrounded by his sleek horses, it sounded pitiful to talk about the four I had in training. I told him about one of them, a stallion owned by Lawson Williams called Panama Buck, who tried to mate with his reflection if he caught sight of himself in glass. I told him many other details, including who their owners were and how much I was charging for their keep and training. I could not fathom his interest. Did he like hearing how badly I was doing?

For the rest of the afternoon, Billy and I would finish the chores and top off the stalls and clean the tack. Work ended at nine P.M. I would swallow some more MetreCal and head back to Mother Harris's place. Occasionally, Don asked me in for a meal and I fell on the food like the starving person I was. Once or twice we went to a rodeo and I won enough for a few meals, but basically I was on a MetreCal diet. I turned into a skeleton; my ribs popped out and I had a deathly pallor. My hands were calloused from carrying water buckets, and I was worn down by Don's constant shouting.

As the time for my departure drew near, Don invited me into his office for a formal meeting to settle up—and he warned me that he would tell me how much I owed him. After his stern treatment of me and my unflagging slave labor for him, I looked forward to the payoff—he would say he was going to recommend me to everyone he knew and my labor would all have been well spent.

He sat down on the opposite side of the desk, stared at me, and said, "Well, Monty, I have you figured. You have a little talent, which maybe you could build on. But it's a lot different now. No college bullshit rodeo team."

"No, I realize that, but I hope I'm ready to do it on my own."

"You're going to have to work a lot harder than I've put you through if you want to make any progress at all."

I could not believe what he had just said. Suddenly I was so tired and dispirited I could have chewed nails.

"Now then," he went on, "there is this matter of your promise to do exactly what I instructed."

I nodded in agreement. "Sure." A promise was a promise.

He leaned forward and spoke slowly and precisely. "Go home, call Lawson Williams, and tell him his horse is no good and you're wasting his money. Tell him he's to come and pick him up immediately. Then do the same with that other horse you got back there."

I went into a tailspin. "How can I do that? I've only got four horses, and you're asking me to cut my income in half? Why? Why on earth should I do such a thing?"

"I don't owe you an explanation, but seeing as you ask—you're going to do it for a very good reason. You're going to do it because he'll be impressed with you. That horse of his isn't going anywhere. You know it; I know it. You'll tell him the truth, and he'll respect you for it and send you five horses right back again."

I let this sink in. I could see his psychology, but it seemed too risky for someone with only four paid horses-in-training to send two of them away.

"Now," he added, "the reckoning."

I waited for him to congratulate me on my hard work. He might even weigh the poor straits I was in and press a few dollars into my hand. Instead he said, "You owe me fifty dollars per day; that's a total of thirty-two hundred dollars." And he wrote out a bill. "Pay me just as soon as you can. You'll realize some day it's the best bargain you ever had."

Driving home with my tail between my legs I was devastated, but not totally surprised. When I showed the bill to Pat she was *absolutely* devastated. But perhaps because I had paid so dearly for Don's advice, it began to sound good. I started to like the feel of it. I delayed for a while, trying to work out the best way of saying it, but there was no other way but head on. I rang Lawson Williams.

"Mr. Williams, I don't want to waste your money, and it's my judgment that Panama Buck isn't worth spending any more on. I'd like you to come up and collect—"

Lawson Williams cut in. "You useless son of a gun, you wouldn't know a good horse if it leapt up between your legs. That's the last horse you'll ever get from me!" He slammed down his receiver, and the next day a man arrived to take away Panama Buck. I had a vision of all of us—Pat, the children, and me—on MetreCal.

Shortly afterward, Selah Reed, the one paid horse-in-training I had with any promise, fractured her hind leg and had to be taken out of training. I was now running on empty. I walked about the place thinking about suicide the whole time. Life was all wrong, and I was letting my family down. Then I got a telephone call.

"Hello. Joe Gray here. I'm a pipeline contractor."

"Hello, Mr. Gray." Who *was* this?

"I was having lunch with Lawson Williams yesterday. He was complaining about you, but from what I understand you must be about the only honest horse trainer I ever heard of."

A wave of emotion overtook me. I remembered Don Dodge's intense stare, and his advice. It had seemed harsh at the time.

"What can I do for you, Mr. Gray?"

"Well, I know that Panama Buck wasn't any good, and I just want to take a flyer on you. I have this horse I want to send you; she's called My Blue Heaven."

In my heart I felt I could glimpse daylight.

"I'm a little worried for the safety of my daughters," he said. "My Blue Heaven is a six-year-old quarter horse mare. I thought she would be a good show horse for them, and she has been trained extensively. But she went wrong, and no one can stop her now."

"Is she dangerous?"

"Extremely. They can't pull her up."

At shows with one of his daughters in the saddle, she would apparently take the bit between her teeth, run away, and crash into fences or try to avoid fences by turning sharply and falling down at high speed.

Joe Gray sent the little gray mare to me with the instruction that she be sold. The family was going on a three-week vacation, and no matter how low the sum offered, I was to find a buyer before they returned.

When she came out of the van I saw she was a pretty mare with a good action and a lively eye—highly sensitive to the bit and bridle. Joe had used increasingly fierce bits to try and get her to stop. I put on a hackamore, a bitless bridle, and rode her into the arena.

To my surprise, My Blue Heaven was a well-trained mare. When she was frightened, she would indeed run out of control—I discovered that soon enough—but she also performed better than any horse I had ridden in the showring up to that time. I removed the hackamore and saddle and turned her loose in the round pen. I wanted to earn her trust, then perhaps I could encourage her to enjoy stopping and thus end the vicious circle of crime and punishment.

I squared up to her and sent her away, cast the light sash line in her direction and pressed her away harder, until she was traveling at a smart canter. I fixed my eye on hers; she began to drop the odd signal that she was prepared to talk—I saw her tongue briefly, and her large mandibles rippled, showing the chewing action. She was keeping one ear fixed on my position, then she dropped her head. After one more turn of the round pen, I turned my shoulders through forty-five degrees to the front of her action. She stopped immediately, and my eyes left hers. Although I was not looking at her, I could sense her waiting. I could hear nothing but my own heartbeat.

She was wondering whether to trust me or not. She was asking herself, Where would this lead? Moments later, she took her first step toward me. Then another. She was tentative, and all I could do was wait. Eventually she was there, standing by me. I soothed her and told her I would not abuse her trust. Together we would work it out; we were going to help each other. She would help me make a reputation as a trainer; I would help her avoid harsh bits in her mouth.

Her early training for stopping had been conventional: if enough pressure is put on a horse's mouth, the horse can be forced to stop. As her riders had become increasingly frightened of her, increasingly severe bits were deployed. It was an unhappy progression. The worse the bit, the worse she got.

My aim was to get her to like stopping, schooling her with signals from my body and voice that would cause her to ease into stops. I tried to put as little pressure on her mouth as I could. I created a situation whereby she herself wanted to stop, by pushing her on until it seemed like stopping was her idea. My Blue Heaven began to welcome the stop signal—the word "Whoa" and my weight pressing down into the back of the saddle—once she learned that she could avoid the pressure if she made the stop comfortably and without resistance. Though her problem was deep-seated and fairly long-standing, she was smart enough to sort it out, and she became extremely effective at stopping.

About two weeks after the Grays left for their vacation, I decided to enter My Blue Heaven in a popular, high-quality show at the Alisal Guest Ranch in the Santa Ynez Valley. If I put in a good performance there, the mare would bring a better price for Mr. Gray and his family. Unable to reach the Grays, I made the entry myself and continued to school her.

The winner of the event would get a fair bit of money, and, more important, a Jedlicka saddle, a Western saddle made of hand-tooled leather. Letters depicting the trophy embellished the fenders—the part of the saddle above the stirrup and below the seat. Today the saddle would be worth $5,000.

There were close to twenty good horses in the competition. My Blue Heaven performed like a professional and won. Don Dodge's advice was working well. I was getting what I wanted, so was My Blue Heaven, and the Gray daughters might get what they wanted, too: a top-flight show horse. I called friends of the Gray family and was able to get into their house. I put the saddle in their dining room, with a note on it to the effect that I needed to discuss My Blue Heaven with the family before selling her.

When they returned, Joe and his family were elated with My Blue Heaven's win. The daughters particularly were excited, and the family agreed that she should stay in training. The following year, she ranked second in the world for the reined cow horse division. Twice she finished second in the world, and only because she happened to come up against Mona Lisa, one of the greatest reined cow horses of all time. Mona Lisa was owned and shown by none other than Don Dodge.

My Blue Heaven was the first horse I campaigned in open professional competition, and she was a significant part of my learning process. After I showed her for two seasons, she went on to compete under the two daughters successfully throughout the western United States.

I did eventually pay Don Dodge's bill—and I wrote and thanked him for the best advice I ever had. Within six months I had fifteen horses in training.

———

In 1961 we moved out of the shack and into the now finished ranch house at Laurellinda. On February 1, our son Marty was born, and it seemed a good time for my mother and father to drive the 125 miles south from Salinas to visit us and their three grandchildren.

I took my father to view the horses I had in training, but as we walked around the property he sang the same old song: "You wait, I'm telling you, that bastard horse is going to go the other way with you. He's going to come loose and get you. You've got to keep them tuned up."

I looked at the lines now carved more deeply into his face. I was twenty-six; he was nearly fifty-four. He could not hurt me anymore. I had escaped him, and his opinions were almost irrelevant. Even so, I felt anger as new as the day he created it. I never wanted any horse of mine to suffer that same anger, fear, and resentment.

During the visit, he played with his grandchildren—Debbie was then four, Laurel two, and Marty a newborn. The two older children had their little responsibilities around the house, such as keeping their rooms tidy. Each had a horse whose stalls they helped muck out daily. At one point, my father said, "You know, Monty, you're too tough on these kids."

Incredulous, my mother left the room. The world briefly stopped turning.

"Me, tough?" I replied. "Do you by any chance remember how tough you were on me?"

"I know, but these are good kids."

I was startled. "And I wasn't?"

He added, "And they're little girls."

What deflated my father more than anything was the undeniable fact that my method of training horses worked. It was especially effective in dealing with remedial horses.

Hey Sam was a Thoroughbred who came to me that same year. He was raised on the Parker Ranch in Hawaii and purchased by Robert Anderson. I started him and gave him his pretrack training before he went to Hollywood Park for racing. Hey Sam started well and went to the track in exceptional form, but he was then sent to a trainer who was not Anderson's first choice.

Something was going wrong. I was called to come and see the horse at Hollywood Park about three months after his arrival, and I quickly identified the root of the problem: The rider had been pulling up Hey Sam on the racetrack at exactly the same place—the half-mile pole—every day, so the horse had begun to anticipate this. Insisting on going back to the barn, Hey Sam would pull off the track in dramatic fashion, whether his rider wanted him to or not. He would run up against the outside part of the track and almost bury himself in the hedge, a quivering wreck. The rider thought to correct this habit by severely whipping Hey Sam before he got to the half-mile pole so as to beat him past the troublesome area. Then, when the horse started veering to the outside of the track to pull himself up, the exercise rider would whip him on the right side to drive him back to the inside rail.

These methods appeared to work for a while, but by the time I arrived to see him all that had been accomplished was that Hey Sam would quicken his pace when approaching the half-mile pole. When he saw his chance he would veer violently outside and stop at the hedge, bracing for the whip but refusing to go anywhere. It was a dramatic display, and the stewards ruled him off the track.

This was distressing for me since I had sent him from my establish-

ment in good order and ready to begin his training for his racing career. My reputation as well as the trainer's was at stake. I had no
choice but to take him home and reestablish communication.

Once again I harked back to the lessons I had learned from other
horses, like Brownie. Horses do not move away from pressure, they
move into it—particularly if the pressure is applied to their flanks.
Horses are into pressure animals. I knew that the whip inflicted by Hey
Sam's riders on his outside flanks was causing him to go the opposite
way to the one that might be expected, and we had to change that. I
worked for about six months, taking all pressure off the outside. Instead, I started to use my leg well back on the inside, schooling him to
bring his head more toward the rail and to be happy doing it.

He was not a bad horse and had no evil in him. He learned, and he
changed significantly. When he went back to the track, I sent him to
Farrell Jones. I had known Farrell for so many years and we communicated well with each other. It was the best thing that could have
happened to the horse. Farrell watched me ride Hey Sam on the racecourse at Golden Gate Fields in northern California, and then he put
a rider on him who employed the same techniques. Soon enough he
was entered in his first race, and he won at odds of fifty to one. My
heart lifted; he was on his way. I also felt a personal triumph. Hey Sam
went on to win twelve races, and earned his owner more than
$100,000.

It was a success story, and the start of my love affair with the American Thoroughbred racing industry.

———

The horse I loved perhaps more than any other had the all-boy name
of Johnny Tivio. He was a registered quarter horse stallion, fourteen
hands, three inches high, and weighing 1,200 pounds. He was a light
bay, but his coat had a brilliant coppery sheen that made it almost
glitter.

I had seen him at the show grounds and had been eyeing him for a
long time. Though he was not kept in top condition, his coat seemed
to outshine any other horse's, as though the polish came through from
the very heart and soul of him rather than from constant grooming.

His trainer, Harry Rose, had enjoyed a lot of success with Johnny Tivio. Harry was a rough, tough kind of man who lived hard and played hard. One day Pat and I were on the horse-show circuit, driving to a competition in Watsonville, California, when we saw a horse trailer parked outside a scuzzy, honky-tonk bar. Inside the trailer I could see Johnny Tivio and another horse.

I said to Pat, "There's Harry, drinking the town dry again."

We were in Watsonville to compete in a show for working horses. We unloaded Fiddle D'Or and My Blue Heaven and put them away for the night at the grounds, then drove back the same way. Harry Rose's trailer was still parked outside the bar, the horses still inside.

The next morning we turned up early to prepare our two horses for the competition that day. Two blocks from the bar, the trailer was now parked outside a house, with Johnny Tivio and the other horse still inside. They had been standing there all night.

After the usual preparation with our horses, which included an exercise or two to warm them up, we were ready for the eight A.M. start. Minutes before the hour, Harry Rose came tearing down the hill, his trailer swerving behind. He jerked to a halt, dragged out a girlfriend, then backed out the two horses.

He threw a saddle on Johnny Tivio and sprang onto his back; then he hauled the girl up behind him and the pair of them started prancing around.

Johnny Tivio won everything that day. Locked up in a trailer all night and without a moment's preparation, he beat my horse for fun. He walked into the arena as if he owned the place and we were lucky just to rub up alongside him. I was amazed and angry that Harry Rose would treat such a wonderful horse so badly.

"That horse is solid gold," I said to Pat. "Some day he'll be mine."

Only months later the local humane society got a telephone call about a horse left in a trailer outside a house for two days. Horse and trailer were impounded and the registration number led the police to the home of the owner, Carl Williams. They attempted to arrest Carl for cruelty to a horse called Johnny Tivio but he put them right and set them on the trail of his trainer, Harry Rose. Then he rang me because he knew I had been angling to buy his horse. He asked me for

$6,000. I leapt at the chance, though I had to call George Smith, a customer and an old friend, to put up half the money.

Johnny Tivio had foundered, his feet were sore and inflamed, and his shoes were grown in, but he was mine. We looked after him and cared for his feet. He was always a willing animal, but he grew stronger and better with every kind word and every kind deed.

But from the minute he joined us at Laurellinda, he was in charge: we were working for him and not vice versa. He had several complaints about his stall, and we had to shift the bedding around so he could drop his manure in one particular corner. With his fastidious stable manners and superior attitude, he was quite the best horse he himself had ever seen. Other horses were allowed to exist but only with his approval. Palominos were out of the question: early in life he had had a palomino stablemate, and now he could barely tolerate the sight of one.

Johnny Tivio became a monumental success; year after year I could enter him in any category of the Western division, and he would win. He was one of the few horses on the show circuit who everyone would agree was the best on the face of the earth.

———

Sometimes a horse comes along who is too troubled, too mean, to engage in conversation. Barlet was a horse made mean by humans.

A movie studio had hired an actor, Slim Pickens, to feature in a film for Disney called *The Horse with the Flying Tail*, about a palomino jumping horse. They would use a foal, called Barlet, to depict the early years of the equine star. I was on the set as a stunt rider at a ranch in the Salinas valley where much of the footage was shot. I had known Slim since I was a child; he was like an uncle to me.

"Hey, Monty, look at this!" Slim called to me. "Isn't this the cutest foal you've ever seen?" Slim was toying with a stick, and the little palomino foal was trying to nibble at it.

"Watch this," he said. He tossed the stick and the foal turned and ambled over to where it lay, picked it up in his teeth and brought it back like a retriever. Then the foal wandered back to where Slim was standing.

"Incredible," I agreed.

"He's like a little puppy," said Slim. "Watch this as well." He turned to the foal and slapped his own chest, calling, "Hup! Hup!" The foal jumped up and put his front legs on Slim's shoulders. "See?" said Slim. "Ain't this going to be the brightest Walt Disney horse?" While it did seem fetching at the time, Barlet also thought it was fun to perform the same tricks as a two-year-old, whether he was asked to or not.

By then his owner, Marten Clark, had been showing Barlet throughout the western United States, and he was virtually undefeated as a halter horse, an in-hand competition judged only on the horse's conformation. He was in line to be the national champion that year; it was almost a certainty. But when I next saw Barlet at the championship show in 1962 at the Cow Palace in San Francisco, I found that Marten Clark had him in a box stall with an electrical circuit. Two wires had been set up: one all around the stall and halfway up the wall, and a second wire around the top. Astonishingly, if the electric current were switched off, Barlet would climb right over the wall.

The palomino was smart. When he heard a pulsating sound, a signal that the charger was on, he posed no problem at all. When Marten wanted to take him out of the stall, however, he had to turn off the charger to open the door. Once the switch was thrown, Barlet became more like a tiger than a horse, and he literally attacked Marten.

During the days before the competition, Marten could not get Barlet out of the stall; handling the horse was impossible. Marten made me an offer: "If you can catch Barlet in the stall and get him through the show ring and win with him, I'll give you a half interest in him; then you can take him back to San Luis Obispo and put him in training." Since Barlet's value stood in the $35,000 range, this was no mean offer. I was excited by the challenge and convinced there was no horse I could not handle. Still, I was disconcerted when I arrived at the stall and saw the security arrangements. After shutting off the power, I opened the door and Barlet bolted toward me from the rear of the stall with his ears back and his teeth bared. He wanted to hurt me.

I jumped back and closed the door before he got hold of me. Unable even to look him over, I had to reassess the situation. This horse was too far gone to even ask for his trust. From a very young age he had been spoiled, not through cruelty in his case, but through unintended psychological abuse. He had been trained as a lapdog, and something had gone terribly wrong.

Using a lariat rope, I was able to swing the rope around in such a fashion that it kept Barlet at sufficient distance. I got him roped in the stall and was able to put on his head a piece of equipment Don Dodge had taught me to use; we call it the "come-along." The come-along is a cute phrase to describe a useful but dangerous tool. The rope is put over the horse's head and arranged in halterlike fashion: the rope applies pressure to nerves above the horse's cheekbones and behind the ears. Too much pressure at the wrong time can be exceedingly dangerous for horse and person. But with some remedial horses, the come-along is the only option if they are to be introduced to a better life, or any life at all.

I led Barlet out of his stall and started schooling him, using the join-up method. I was trying to restore his trust. It took a good deal longer than it did with My Blue Heaven, and the results were not as consistent, but he did eventually come to trust me a little. I was then able to show him in hand at that show and when he was named national champion, I became half owner. I took him home, and he went on to win a great deal. But he was never a mentally balanced horse after being spoiled as a foal. As is so often the case with horses made mean, even by well-intentioned people like Slim Pickens, they can seldom be trusted. This type of chronically distrustful horse should be handled only by professional horse trainers fully aware of what they are dealing with. The consequences can be too grave otherwise.

Barlet was a truly mean and severely troubled horse who attacked me on several occasions. One can only guess at what had triggered his disappointment with human beings. He and I had an understanding built around a well-developed discipline-and-reward system, so I was able to control his neurosis for three or four years. Unhappily, his problems eventually got the better of him, and he died in a fight with a gelding on my farm at Laurellinda. He smashed a fence to get to the other horse and broke his front leg during the ensuing skirmish.

CHAPTER 4

The Sand-Castle Syndrome

Imagine a beach on a blistering day in August. Down at the water's edge is a child with shovel and pail building an elaborate sand castle. The child has taken great delight in this creation, fussed all day over its turrets, fashioned moats and stairs and dwelt on every intricate detail. But at the end of the day, when the tide comes in, the greater joy is in watching as the waves level it all.

Now imagine an adult who acts like that child on the beach, an adult with the power and the wealth to construct on an epic scale— and a dark urge to crush the very thing he has so lovingly created. Such people bear no distinguishing marks, no telltale warning signs. No one told the crewmen of *The Bounty* before they set sail that her captain was a madman; no one told me that the bold dreamer I cast my lot with would be so keen years later to destroy.

In 1964, when I was thirty-one years old, I fell in with just such a man. He would take my family and me to dizzying heights and bring us lower than I ever imagined possible. I would find my fiber tested as never before; I would find what friends are made of; and I would find the courage to continue.

That year, at a quarter horse sale in the Santa Ynez Valley near

Solvang, I watched one man buy several horses. His name was Hastings Harcourt, son of the founder of a giant textbook publisher, Harcourt Brace & World. Married, with a grown son, Hastings Harcourt was in his sixties and had gained a reputation as an eccentric and difficult millionaire. He owned property at Juniper Farms in the Santa Ynez Valley, and in Montecito—among the most exclusive residential areas in all of California.

A few days later, after hearing about me through a veterinarian, Mr. Harcourt called and asked if I would be interested in training his recent acquisitions. Within a day I was transporting three young quarter horses the sixty miles from Santa Ynez north to my place at Laurellinda.

After a week, I reported back to him that one three-year-old gelding, in particular, a horse called Travel's Echo, possessed talent. Mr. Harcourt seemed pleased and invited me to meet him at Juniper Farms.

Juniper Farms stood at the end of a long, treed driveway. The place was a tangle of architectural styles tacked onto a 1920s early-California house, but the property was immaculately maintained. On first impression, Hastings Harcourt struck me as an unfortunate-looking man. A skin condition had marked and pitted his face. He wore thick, black-rimmed glasses; he carried too much weight on his six-foot-two-inch frame; and I was acutely aware that his smile touched only his mouth, it never reached his eyes.

If he seemed possessed by a boyish enthusiasm, bouncing up from his lawn chair to greet Pat and me like old friends, his wife, Fran, was impassive. Uninterested in our arrival and disinclined even to get up from her chair, she bore the look of someone who had seen many like us come and go.

Hastings Harcourt admitted that he knew nothing about horses, but his desire to learn seemed genuine, even refreshing. He struck me as a nice man enjoying the first flush of excitement at becoming involved in the horse business. I mentioned that I would show Johnny Tivio at a show in Santa Barbara three months away. Why not, he pleaded, show Travel's Echo, too? Putting a green horse in a high-caliber show with little time for training was not my style, and I warned him to keep his expectations low. But I was also grateful for the work, and it seemed there was the promise of more.

Both Pat and I had some solid horses to show in that event, so at the very least the Harcourts could see his trainers competing on three world-class horses. I had Johnny Tivio, who would no doubt organize all the major trophies for himself, and Night Mist, who could be almost as good. Pat had Julia's Doll, a well-established mare competing in the pleasure-horse division. Travel's Echo was progressing so rapidly that I thought maybe there was a chance that I could show him, and I covered my bets by entering him just in case.

On the appointed day, the Harcourts had rented an exclusive box seats at the center of the ring. They brought along a party of eight to ten friends, all prominent in the Montecito society circuit. The entourage was as much on display as the horses.

Johnny Tivio performed as expected; Night Mist was her sterling self, winning both her events; and Julia's Doll was in top form, winning with Pat in the saddle. I was due to show Travel's Echo in the Western pleasure-horse division, open to horses four and under. Entering the arena, I was stunned when I saw that we were up against more than fifty competitors. But Travel's Echo surprised everyone, including me and those of Harcourts' guests who were savvy about horses and who could appreciate the achievement. Travel's Echo made the ten-horse finals. In the runoff, he finished third to two of the nation's top competitors, defeating other horses who had already won many championships. As I rode forward to collect the trophy and the rosette for third place, I was looking straight at the Harcourts. They were beaming, their friends all standing and applauding.

Afterward, they all came to the out gate to stand with Travel's Echo and pat him. It was embarrassing because this was the exit for competitors in the arena, and the Harcourt party seemed oblivious to the traffic jam they were creating. Because of his standing in the community and his reputation as a philanthropist, photographers and journalists crowded around to chronicle both his enthusiasm and the spectacular success of his young horse.

Sparks were flying now. Three days later the Harcourts flew in their private plane to San Luis Obispo to see our modest operation and discuss a greater involvement.

"Have you got any experience with the Thoroughbred racing industry?" he asked me. He owned a few Thoroughbreds, but he had the feeling they were not of the highest quality. I told him that we always had a few Thoroughbreds in training, but never the class of horse needed to win top races in California. Two days later he had me flown in his plane to three different locations to see his Thoroughbred stable: some brood mares, three foals, two yearlings, and two horses-in-training. He was right to doubt their quality. Now Harcourt upped the ante yet again. He proposed sending me to the Del Mar Thoroughbred yearling sale with a budget of $20,000 to buy two horses of my choosing.

Harcourt was offering me a chance of a lifetime. I had bought Thoroughbred yearlings for other clients who imposed limits of $2,000 per horse—low-class, fair-track horses, but they had done fairly well considering their breeding, and it seemed I had the ability to choose horses who could run and stay sound. Harcourt's offer meant a chance to leap into top-flight racing on California tracks: it was like a professional baseball player moving overnight from single "A" ball to the big leagues.

At Del Mar, where the restaurant menus included champagne, I decided that my cowboy hat should stay at home, and I wore instead a soft tweed cap. During the auction I saw a chestnut colt walk by at a distance of fifty yards. I will never forget that moment. He caught my eye as no young Thoroughbred had. Stock still, he had perfect symmetry and balance, but the extraordinary thing was how those qualities did not diminish when he moved. I went immediately to the stable where the chestnut was kept. On closer inspection, he proved even more impressive. No one else much fancied him. The nameless horse was brought into the auction ring and I won the bidding at just $5,000. When the hammer came down, Sharivari—as we later called him—was mine. I was now in business with Hastings Harcourt.

Sharivari would later be ranked the best three-year-old in California prior to the Kentucky Derby where he was the early book favorite. He would later become a champion sire many times over. At Del Mar,

I also purchased a bay colt, whom we called Bahroona. As it turned out, the bay was the more precocious of the two horses and was ready to run by June of the following year. Gifted with blinding speed, he won his first start at Hollywood Park by ten open lengths. Harcourt was euphoric about Bahroona's success and insisted that I come in his plane to Montecito: he was holding a victory party at his home.

The pilot and I took off, settling into the journey. Flying over the gleaming black waters of Lake Cachuma in the Santa Ynez Valley, the engine died and we immediately started plummeting toward the water. I was certain we would die. The pilot switched over to the second fuel tank and started the engine again, and we pulled out of the dive. This incident did nothing for my nerves, but later it struck me as a symbolic moment in the roller-coaster ride I was now embarked on.

A driver took me from the Santa Barbara airport to their house where a party was in full swing. Over the noise and laughter, Mr. Harcourt shouted out to me, "We must have a major operation!" With those words, the noise of the party seemed to recede as I latched on to what he was saying so loudly. "I have property in the Santa Ynez Valley. What do you think of that area for creating a full-scale Thoroughbred facility?"

It had been my life's dream to be a part of a horse operation in that valley. While the party continued on its high-spirited course, I offered my opinion that the climate and the soil there were superior to any in the United States, and that it would be a wonderful choice of location for a Thoroughbred breeding and training farm.

Harcourt was bursting with plans. "Start studying the area," he advised, "and I will purchase enough property to encompass a world-class facility."

My education had prepared me well for my scouting mission. I knew about soils, forage grasses, fertilization, facility design, conformation, pedigrees, and most of all, training techniques. None of the various properties that Harcourt already owned in the Santa Ynez Valley was right. One was too heavily treed, another too stony, a third lacked water. We needed land along the river; just outside the town of Solvang I pinpointed a microvalley three miles long by one and a quarter miles wide. The valley bottom was almost level, and the top-

Wedding photo
of Monty's parents.

On Ginger in 1939, age four,
winning the junior stock horse
competition for age sixteen
and under.

Monty in football uniform.

Monty's father with Joe Louis.

Monty's father long-lining a young horse.

Pat and Monty in costume
on the set of *East of Eden*.

James Dean with a pair
of Monty's chaps.

Monty and James Dean on the *East of Eden* set.

Future wife, Pat, presenting Monty with hackamore champion trophy in 1955.

Monty and Pat on their wedding day, June 16, 1956.

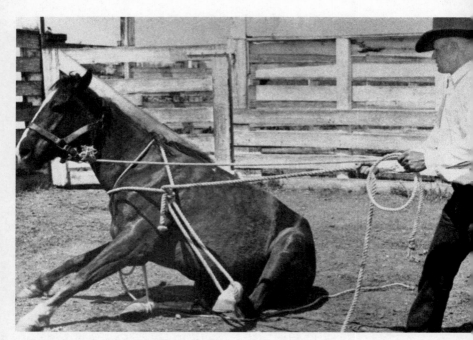

Monty's father's methods of breaking a horse: tying a horse to gain supremacy.

Monty achieving join-up.

Monty and Pat on Flag Is Up Farms, October 1966.

Johnny Tivio at home on
Flag Is Up Farms, 1967.

Monty cutting cattle on Johnny Tivio in Monterey, California.

Pat with a quarter horse
mare, 1996.

Flag Is Up Farms, late 1980s.

Monty and Pat releasing the first horses on the new pastures at Flag Is Up Farms, October 1966.

Alleged winning the Prix de l'Arc de Triomphe with Lester Piggott. As a team, they won in 1977 and 1978.

Lomitas refusing to enter the starting gate the day he was banned from racing
at the end of May 1991.

Lomitas, with Monty leading him to the starting gate June 23, 1991, ten days after Monty met him. He went in like a lamb, got the best start, won the race, and was reinstated.

Lomitas in winning form in the following months.

Her Majesty Queen Elizabeth II with Monty and Pat as they presented her with a copy of the British edition of *The Man Who Listens to Horses*.

Monty with one of Her Majesty the Queen's horses at Windsor Castle.

Grandma, early 1990s.

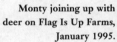

Monty joining up with deer on Flag Is Up Farms, January 1995.

Monty and Dually in competition, January 1996.

Monty on Dually with the mustang Shy Boy at side.

Monty works with a remedial horse who learns there is nothing to fear from a rider by carrying a dummy on his back.

The dummy rider with Monty at the stables of Gestut Fahrhof.

Monty and Pat attending Queen Elizabeth II's Golden Jubilee celebrations at the Royal Windsor Horse Show. Windsor Castle can be seen in the background.

Monty at a public demonstration of Join-Up in Australia. Monty travels 310 days a year to further his training concepts throughout the world.

Monty at The Horse Event held yearly in The Netherlands.

Photo: © Mariska de Hoogt

Monty with Shy Boy at the Konocti Unified School District in California, to promote the values of communication and nonviolence to students.

Her Royal Highness Princess Benedikte of Denmark, with Monty during a horse show.

Monty and Shy Boy on the viewing platform around Monty's round pen, after a demonstration for a group of young children at Flag Is Up Farms.

Monty with his granddaughter Loren, who is riding Shy Boy.

soil averaged seventeen feet in depth. Even better, below the topsoil lay a generous layer of diatomaceous material—microscopic sea-shells or crustaceans compressed into a chalky, calcium-rich earth, the legacy of a prehistoric ocean. In addition, ample underground aquifers near the surface meant wells with extraordinary flows, up to 600 gallons a minute. The climate was ideal: the influence of the nearby ocean kept the valley cool in summer and relatively warm in winter.

Harcourt began buying in one-hundred- and fifty-acre parcels, making offers no property owner could refuse. Within ninety days we sat down to discuss design concepts. As keen as I, he marshaled his considerable resources into a frenzy of activity. The train was rolling fast; then came a derailment, the first of many.

The day before a scheduled meeting in Santa Barbara, I got a call from his private secretary. In a roundabout way, she indicated that Mr. Harcourt had had second thoughts about building his sizable horse farm, and she advised me to consider him out of the picture.

Once it had sunk in, I was both devastated and dumbfounded. Only hours before, he had been plunging ahead as if his life depended on it. I spent that night pondering my next move. So much was at stake. It occurred to me that the secretary had implied, but not specified, that my meeting with Harcourt was canceled. I decided to go to his home at the designated time, as if the secretary had never called. At least I would hear him explain his decision to withdraw. Next day I drove the one hundred miles to Montecito, unsure of what to anticipate at the journey's end.

When I stopped at the gates and spoke into the security intercom, I half expected to be refused entry, but a voice buzzed me through. I drove down the driveway, the gravel crunching under my tires as I followed the circular drive around an imposing fountain. I parked by the guest house and walked to the front door of the main house where I rang the bell and waited. Clearly someone was in—I had been let through the gate. I reminded myself that it took a while to get from one end of such a large house to the other, so I waited longer than usual before ringing the bell a second time. No one came. It was deathly quiet. After some minutes, I gave up hope. I had one hand on my car door handle when a sudden movement caught my eye. I turned and saw Mr. Harcourt scuttle across an open area of ground on the far side of the fountain. He disappeared through a side door.

I was alarmed because he looked to be deliberately trying to avoid being seen. But perhaps he was hurrying into the house to be punctual for our meeting? I rang the bell again, but the house remained silent and uninviting. Clearly, I was persona non grata: it was all over. I tried calling him that evening, but the maid, not unkindly, said he was unavailable.

Pat took the philosophical attitude that we should get on with our lives as if Hastings and Fran Harcourt had never existed. Even if he did call to apologize, he was evidently unstable and we should ignore him. Four days later, while I was working horses at home, Harcourt called. I dismounted and went to the telephone, my stomach in knots.

Offering a cordial greeting and an apology, he said he had endured a psychological downturn and something untoward had befallen his family's publishing business. However, he had sought professional counseling and was once more ready to proceed with the farm. Full throttle.

Our whole family plunged into the effort to create the classiest Thoroughbred facility anywhere. The sudden emotional shift was enormous. Proof of his new seriousness was that he now had a name for the farm he envisioned. "I have always been intrigued," he said, "by that moment at the races when the announcer says, 'The flag is up.' " At one time, tracks employed someone literally to hold up a red flag—a signal that all the horses were in the starting gate. At that moment, no more bets were possible, and everyone paused to focus on the gate. "That's the moment," said Mr. Harcourt, "that this whole farm enterprise—the breeding, the selection, the training—is preparing for. At that moment, what will be will be."

But in his grand plan, I was no mere overseer. "I want you to be more than a manager, more than a horseman," he told me. "I want you to become the managing partner of Flag Is Up Farms, and for your input you should be entitled to five percent of the operation going in and have the right to buy deeper into it as we progress. I will create a contract with you, and I will pay for the legal work. You should go to the offices of my lawyer and outline for him all that you want in the contract. I will read it, but you can create it."

I did as instructed and outlined a contract that I believed to be fair and equitable to both sides.

Then he asked me if I would fly to Europe to tour the best horse operations there, and with that knowledge press ahead quickly with planning the facility. I had never been outside North America before and eagerly boarded a plane to England, where I hooked up with Tim Vigors. He was a bloodstock agent, a gentleman farmer, and a former fighter pilot in the Second World War. With Vigors at the controls, we flew to stud farms all around Britain and landed on most of the major racecourses. I made notes and took photographs. In France we toured more facilities, including the Guy de Rothschild breeding farm. The trip was better than a university course in the design and management of racehorse facilities. Then we flew to Germany and on to Ireland.

While I had been away, Harcourt had been reading about operations in other parts of the world, so I was not long back before I was sent off to Argentina, Australia, and New Zealand on the same mission. When I returned, I made a final report and recommendations to him. Both Pat and I prepared ourselves and our family for a twelve- to eighteen-month cyclone of activity to plan, construct, and open the operation of Flag Is Up Farms, Incorporated, Solvang, California.

The 1,250-acre property, then far and away the classiest Thoroughbred facility in California, had four main areas. First, there was a breeding and foaling operation with a stallion barn, breeding pens, laboratory, round pen, office complex, eight-stall foaling barn, and residential quarters for up to eight employees. The second area—a training and starting facility for adolescent horses—incorporated a covered riding arena, two covered round pens, box stalls for eighty horses, a five-eighth-mile training track, a two-and-a-half-mile cross-country gallop, three large hay- and straw-storage barns, a feed mill to make our own feed, a main office, and residential quarters for up to fifty employees. Third, a hospital and rehabilitation area included space for forty horses, a swimming pool for water therapy, an X-ray therapy facility, an office complex, turn-out paddocks, plus residential quarters for six employees.

Last, there was the main house. It sat on top of the "mesa" or 150-foot rise on the north end of the property. Designed in the early Californian tradition, though with much more glass than usual, the house looked south out over the valley.

We moved the first horses on to the farm in July 1966. Johnny Tivio strolled in and booked the best room in the place. In October of that year our family moved into our beautiful new home. We were all working hard, but we felt like we had stepped into paradise.

Not long afterward, my father and mother came to inspect our new digs. I gave them a guided tour.

My father criticized the fencing ("Should have got oak from Kentucky and made plank fencing.") and the many thousands of cedars and other trees I had planted ("Get in the way if you want to move anything around. You wait. They'll just knock your hat off every time you ride underneath."). The racetrack was too small. The training-barn loft badly built. The aisle floors ill-conceived. The round pens too costly. "Keep a foot in the show-horse business," he advised me before leaving. "This racehorse thing will eat you up."

Meanwhile, our horses were performing well and we won our share of good races, mostly from horses I had selected as yearlings: Cathy Honey, champion three-year-old filly of the United States; Gladwin, a beautiful First Landing colt purchased at Saratoga, was a Group I winner (that is, he won at the highest level in Thoroughbred racing); Aladancer, another Group I winner, was among the first crop of Northern Dancer foals; *Petrone, purchased as a three-year-old in France for $150,000, later won more than $400,000; Sharivari, eventual Champion Sprinter and Horse of the Year in New Zealand; and Bahroona, a major stakes winner, along with many other winners, were among the early residents of Flag Is Up Farms. The years 1967 to 1970 were successful ones for the farm.

One day early in 1971, Mr. Harcourt came to the house. He had had a drink and asked for another as we retired to the patio overlooking the farm. He took off his spectacles and I could see his eyes, now watering from all the emotion welling up. "It's no way for anyone to live, having this disease," he confided, striking his own chest. Then he described the effects of what he termed "bi-polar disease." From a very early age, he had suffered from manic depression.

It had driven him out of the family business and broken up count-less business partnerships. People were not willing to cope with him. I felt sympathy for his plight but had no idea how to help. I sensed, however, that he was asking me to look after him and understand his every whim, however illogical.

"Do you know," he said, "I've had thirty years of therapy? How does that sound?"

"Expensive," I suggested, trying for a little levity.

"Fran knows how to handle me. When I swing on the moon, she knows to draw me back down. When I'm stumbling through the cel-lar in the dark, she knows to bring me back up. Do you know, Monty," he said suddenly, "my relationship with your family and what we're doing at Flag Is Up Farms is the most important thing in my life, and I don't want to encounter these problems with you."

"I agree," I said, and meant it. We had already had a hint of it, and it had been devastating.

"I want you to know how to handle me. If we can do this, I see our relationship lasting all my days. I'll make an appointment for you to visit my psychiatrist. You can learn from him how to track me. I'm confident your intelligence will allow you to do that. You'll be just like Fran."

While I felt relieved that the situation was out in the open and that some kind of a plan to cope was taking shape, I also felt a great weight of responsibility for this sorry man.

His psychiatrist in Santa Barbara did not seem pleased to see me. A tall, lean man in his late forties with a sophisticated and soft-spoken manner, he queried me carefully—no doubt concerned about breach-ing patient confidentiality, even with Harcourt's consent. But on my second visit to the clinic, it became clear that he now knew everything about me and was more inclined to be candid. He described Har-court's condition as "sand-castle syndrome": he used the curious metaphor of the child on the beach taking as much joy in destruction as in creation.

Standing on the terrace later that evening, I looked down on the barns caught in the last rays of the sun slipping below the mountains, and I remembered Harcourt's wild enthusiasm as we planned and built. And I knew then we had built a sand castle for Hastings Harcourt.

In September 1971, I was at the racecourse in Del Mar, 250 miles from Flag Is Up Farms, when I received a call saying that the private plane would pick me up and fly me back to the farm. Mr. Harcourt wanted to see me that afternoon. He and another man were already waiting for me in a car outside the house. Pat was out with the children, so I was to face them alone on the back patio overlooking the farm.

They appeared to choose the seating arrangements carefully. I sat on one side of the table; they sat together on the opposite side. Harcourt was in a stern, somber mood. He introduced his companion as a business associate who was working with him on some new projects.

Harcourt produced from his jacket pocket a silver pillbox that he ceremoniously placed on the table between us. He opened it to reveal about twenty tablets of varying colors, shapes, and sizes. When he looked at me, the hairs stood up on the back of my neck. It was a cold, ominous look. What we had been dreading was about to unfold.

"I just want you to realize," said Harcourt, "that it takes me this many pills to get through a day. You know my doctor, and you know my problems. I won't bore you with a lot of the details, but I am sure that you realize I am in a grave condition."

He paused, then continued, "I must sell the farm and all the horses as soon as possible. It is devastating to me, but it must be done. I am saddened to give up my farm and my horses, but it is particularly painful to give up my relationship with you, Pat, and your family. You have been an important part of our lives for almost six years now, but where my health is concerned I can let no one get in the way."

I knew the signs. Hastings Harcourt was heading into free fall.

"My associate here will coordinate with you over the disposition of the assets. If you can find someone to buy the farm, obviously you could remain here under similar circumstances. And possibly that same person would be interested in buying some or all of the horses. Whatever I can do to assist in your quest to keep the farm together, I will do, so long as I can get out of everything very soon. I will leave you now and wait in the car for my associate, who will explain to you some of my ideas for disposition."

His speech over, he walked round the table toward me with his arms outstretched. I stood and waited while he threw his arms around me and squeezed. "I'm sorry," he said. "I have failed you and your family, but this must be done."

He turned and disappeared through the house. I felt sorry for this poor old man. I also felt an inexplicable wonder—awe, even—that such a destructive psychology could exist and continue to take such ruinous effect, even in a man who knew himself and who could afford the best possible treatment.

Harcourt's man ordered me to sit down. I felt like a student in the principal's office. He announced, "Mr. Harcourt is getting out of this thing in short order, so don't get in his way. We can work together on this, and I can help you make the transition."

"Mr. Harcourt," he went on, "feels the people in this industry would be more responsive to buying the property and horses if you remain involved in the sale. Your reputation and approval will bring significant value to the deal and increase the speed with which we can push it through."

"Fair enough."

"He would like you to explain to any potential purchaser that you have a five percent interest in the property, money they wouldn't have to come up with. You should also say that you will buy in on the horses to at least ten percent, which Mr. Harcourt would not require you to pay. So you would end up with ten percent in the horses as a commission. He might even consider fifteen or twenty percent, depending on price and conditions."

"That's fine, thank you." I prayed it was going to be as easy as this. It appeared we had our escape route and that Harcourt was acting sensibly. Harcourt's business associate wanted a list of horses I would not buy in to, since they would be consigned to the earliest sale possible. I said I would do that right away.

Then he dropped the first bombshell. "In addition to this, Mr. Harcourt has instructed me to tell you that he wants his riding horse, called Travel's Echo, shot dead... and disposed of."

His words stopped me cold.

"Why on earth—"

He cut in. "Mr. Harcourt doesn't want anyone else to have Travel's Echo. He wishes you personally to shoot him, rather than have him go to another home."

I said nothing. Wanting Travel's Echo not to go to anyone else was a sentimental notion—but to place such a cruel sting in the tail of it? I could not bear it. The image came to me of Travel's Echo doing so well for the Harcourts at that first show almost five years ago ... and their smiles as they accepted the applause of friends.

"He also wants you personally to shoot Mrs. Harcourt's driving ponies. She, also, doesn't wish them to go to anyone else." Fran had bought a pair of driving ponies, thinking she might like to come out from time to time and use them; she never did, though the ponies were kept in good condition by farm staff.

He paused and consulted some papers in front of him. "Mr. Harcourt has also been extremely disappointed with the performance of two horses, Veiled Wonder and Cherokee Arrow. He wants you to shoot them, preferably today. He does not want you to try to sell them to someone else; he feels they have disgraced him because he had high hopes for their performance and they let him down."

Gone was amazement, sorrow, or incomprehension. Now I felt anger and determination. No horse in my care was going to be sacrificed on the whim of an unstable man. Harcourt's henchman prepared to go. "I will be in touch with you on a daily basis to facilitate the disposal."

I heard the door shut with a click. I sat there, hollow with shock. I knew this much: There was no time to feel sorry for myself, because if I failed to move quickly, things would be taken out of my hands. Since I was empowered to sign papers, certain options were open to save the lives of these animals. The man's words squirreled around in my head: "... disappointed with their performance ... a disgrace ..." Cherokee Arrow and Veiled Wonder were young colts—well-bred stakes winners—who had only "disappointed" us because we had set our hopes extremely high for them. I went down to their stalls and looked them over. I stroked their muzzles and tried to think.

Just a month before, Veiled Wonder and Cherokee Arrow had been appraised along with all the other Harcourt horses. I double-checked at the farm office: Veiled Wonder was valued at $3,500 and Cherokee Arrow at $3,000. I had one option: sell them this instant and ensure that the money was logged as usual in the Flag Is Up Farms accounts. I could not leave myself open to any accusation of theft.

I called a friend and asked him to send me a check for $6,500, naming the two horses. I promised him I would get the money back to him. He agreed, and I quickly arranged to ship both horses to England for quarantine, then on to Alton Lodge in New Zealand, where Sharivari and Bahroona were standing at stud. As the trucks pulled out with the horses, I wondered how Harcourt would react when he found out I had refused to destroy them. No wrong was done to Harcourt since the farm received their full appraised value. I told myself that he was a sick man making irrational decisions, and I could not allow the animals to be the victims of this malady.

Next, the driving ponies. I telephoned a friend who would give them a good home, and she was at the farm within the hour to take them. Then I called a neighbor who lived close by.

"Can I park a horse with you, in secret?"

"What's going on?"

"I can't tell you, but if you can trust me that this horse's life is in danger, will you take him and not tell a soul?"

"Send him over, then. What's his name?"

"It's best if I don't tell you."

I led Travel's Echo out of his stall and loaded him into one of our vans. He would stay hidden until some sense could be made of these events.

This frenzy of activity occupied me through the afternoon and well into the night. I finished by visiting Johnny Tivio in his stall, just to check he was still there, alive and well. As usual, his stall was in immaculate condition, the dung piled neatly in one corner. He rarely urinated in his stall. I said to him, "You're almost house-trained, aren't you, boy? You want to come and live with us in the house, a room of your own, huh?" It felt good to break the tension a little. Johnny Tivio regarded me silently, impassively.

Early next morning, I got a call.

"Mr. Roberts?" It was a woman's voice, distant and cool. By her tone, she might have been calling about a malfunctioning dishwasher, not to cross horses off a death list. "I'm calling on behalf of Hastings Harcourt."

"Yes."

"Can you confirm for me that the horse named Travel's Echo has been destroyed?" I needed to lie but the nuns had taught me well. I hated lies, yet now it was imperative that I deceive, or at least stretch the truth.

"He's gone."

"And the two colts, Veiled Wonder and Cherokee Arrow, have they also been destroyed?"

"I can confirm they've gone, too."

"And can you confirm that Mrs. Harcourt's driving ponies have also been destroyed?"

"They're no longer here."

"And lastly, I need to confirm that you personally undertook the disposal of these animals."

"Yes."

"Thank you, Mr. Roberts." The phone clicked and the disembodied voice was gone. The next few months were chaos for us as we prepared brood mares, yearlings, foals, and racehorses for sales conducted over a radius of 3,000 miles. The children were now ten, twelve, and fourteen years old, and they had a difficult time making sense of events. They were not alone.

I desperately contacted potential buyers for Flag Is Up Farms. If one was not found quickly, the farm would be broken up and sold in lots. Although the family was tense and worried much of the time, I was reasonably confident that things would go well. I had avoided having to shoot the animals, Harcourt had obviously believed my story, and a Mr. Rudolf Greenbaum, from Los Angeles, had surfaced as a possible buyer for the farm.

Two months later, in the first week of December 1971, Rudolf Greenbaum finally agreed to buy Flag Is Up Farms, most of the horses, the rolling stock, and the equipment—in other words, the ongoing business. The price was negotiated, and by the third week in December, Greenbaum had deposited $200,000 in an escrow account opened at a title insurance company in Santa Barbara. The deal was done. We were safe, and on a better footing than before. We took comfort, knowing that the sand-castle man was behind us.

Then he came roaring back, and I learned that hell hath no fury like a Harcourt scorned. On January 3, 1972, his emissary called to say that everything was on hold and he needed to meet with me in my office at the farm. He arrived with a large briefcase and delivered what sounded like a well-rehearsed speech.

"Mr. Harcourt is very upset. He has discovered that you didn't shoot Veiled Wonder and Cherokee Arrow, and that you had a friend buy them only to transfer them to your name. It looks as though you stole them."

"I paid their fair market value," I said, "and since he wanted to shoot them, he got $6,500 more than he should have."

Harcourt's man paused and then said quietly, "By the time he gets through with it ... he'll make you look like Jesse James. If that's the route you want to go."

The Greenbaum deal was crushed, like a match underfoot. Moving with speed and power, as his wealth allowed him to, he used his web of contacts to "disappear" the records of the escrow account, and to send the $200,000 back into Rudolf Greenbaum's account as if it had never been sent. If Rudolf Greenbaum sued, as surely he would, I was the only third party who could testify in court that the deal had ever been struck.

"Mr. Harcourt," said his colleague, "has been very nice to you and to your family, and he can make it very easy on you or he can make it tough on you for the rest of your life. Mr. Harcourt needs you to come to court and testify that there was never an agreement to sell the farm."

I saw what was happening. The sale of the farm had gone too smoothly. Harcourt had not yet made enough waves. His castle still stood by the seashore. When I told this pacing hireling that I would not lie in court, and that I wanted nothing more to do with Hastings Harcourt, he sighed and bade me polite farewell.

There followed three weeks of calm before the inevitable storm. Whenever I saw Harcourt at the farm, he was saccharine, pleading for

138 · *Monty Roberts*

my cooperation. He even asked me to speak with Rudolf Greenbaum
and tell him I had changed my mind. I told Harcourt that during the
transition period I would cooperate in every way I could, but that my
days of doing business with him were over.

A few days later, on January 24, his secretary called. Sharivari and
Bahroona were to be sold in New Zealand and I was to go there immediately to consummate the deal. Pat would join me on the trip:
during these turbulent days we needed each other close. We were to
meet Harcourt at a certain barbershop in Santa Barbara, as a send-off.
It was indeed that.

While Pat went down the street to buy me a hamburger, for I was
famished, I entered the barbershop. Two hulking men who announced they were from the district attorney's office put me in handcuffs. "You're under arrest," said one. "We're acting on a complaint
that you've stolen two million dollars and that you're about to flee the
country." As we left I spotted Harcourt's black Lincoln across the
street; he was behind the wheel in almost comically oversized dark
sunglasses.

Pat, meanwhile, burger in hand, got the alarming news of my arrest
from the equally bewildered barber. She drove frantically to the sheriff's office in Santa Barbara where she would take up an agonizing
vigil from mid-afternoon to ten P.M.

That night, she and the children watched in horror and disbelief as
the charges led off the eleven o'clock news. So many friends called
Pat that finally she let the answering service take over while she tried
to calm the children. They had so many questions and their mother
had so few answers. They held each other like a family huddled in a
tent while a windstorm rages outside. What happened that day be-
longs in film or fiction. But it did happen, and it happened to me.

The two hulking men took me into an all-white booking room with
marble-top counters, first pulling rank on the attendants and shooing
them away like flies. The two had clearly never booked anyone before,
but the comic air soon evaporated. They wanted a guilty plea from
me, and quickly. I said I would never plead guilty when I was not. One
squeezed my bicep to the bone. "I must tell you," he said, "that we
have a murderer waiting in a cell for your company, and he is there to
convince you to plead guilty."

They took me down a long hallway, past cells full of men, some lying down, some pacing or playing cards, many shouting profanities. The noise was insane: the iron doors, the metal cups being banged on the bars, the screaming, the shouting—something you must experience to know. Bank robbers, town drunks, and druggies were all thrown together like sticks in a tornado. My jailers would stop along the way, ask me to reconsider. They seemed oddly sincere when they said they did not want me to go through with what lay in store.

I was taken to a solitary confinement cell, eight-foot-square, with a solid concrete front and a black iron door. The only light source was a bulb recessed into the ceiling and covered with a cage. Inside was an enormous chained man who looked like a cross between a grizzly and Bigfoot. I was introduced to Buffalo Babcock.

He was about six feet, four inches tall, and weighed at least 300 pounds. He stank in his jeans and undershirt. Red hair grew in tufts out of his neck; his arms were as big as my thighs and busy with dark tattoos. On the right arm was a snake's head, its body extending over to the man's pectorals. On the left arm was a woman, long and waistless in shorts and high heels. I was shackled to him, face-to-face through a floating ring, with heavy metal collars at our wrists and ankles. An X formed between us. The men showed Babcock a button near the door, which he was to press when I was ready to plead guilty. The noise of the door closing was deafening. My pulse was racing out of control, but I knew I had to think if I was to survive this. I wanted this man to talk.

"Why are you in here?" I asked him. Smiling at first, he said he "blew a jukebox," then explained what that meant: You enter a bar with a double-barreled shotgun and shoot out the jukebox, then announce that the next blast is for the first guy who moves—in this case, an unfortunate bartender who went for a hidden gun.

Babcock turned his attention to me. "I know you, Monty Roberts. I know all about you. You're my passport. I don't really want to hurt you, but my life is on the line and I couldn't give a damn about yours." The deal was this: He would convince me, nicely or not, to plead guilty and thus win for himself a dismissal of charges.

My mind turned somersaults. I had to get him talking again. As he spoke in rapid-fire fashion about his abusive father, drunken mother, his stint in Korea, this giant would stand up, then sit down on the iron bunk. Ranching and rodeo work had taught me to stay clear of ropes that might entangle you and kill you when a steer or mustang was on the other end.

Buffalo was too immersed in his tale to notice the chain sliding around his right knee, and as he bent to sit down again, I moved. I had been bulldogging in the arena, and I was quick and strong. With a power reserved for fathers lifting cars off children, I hoisted the chain around his ankles and he came crashing down, banging his head on the corner of the iron bunk. While he lay there, motionless, I went for the buzzer.

Help came in the form of a sheriff's uniform. "This has gone far enough," he yelled. They unchained me, took Babcock to the infirmary and me to a jail cell. Along the way, the several hundred prisoners were yelling and applauding, banging their metal cups against the bars in celebration. "Good man, you survived," praised one. It seemed I was a hero for vanquishing Babcock, whom they knew as a bully.

I mentioned to a cell mate that I was hungry—my last meal had been breakfast. All fifteen prisoners in my cell once more created pandemonium with their cups. A guard came, and soon after, a sympathetic young man who, oddly enough, had once worked for me in the broodmare barn at the farm. He brought me the most delicious roast-beef sandwiches I had ever tasted, along with a toothbrush, toothpaste, a washcloth, a bar of soap, and a towel. After the brutality of the day, this simple and humane act touched me deeply.

I paced the cell all night and had no appetite for breakfast in the morning. By then my hero's halo was fading: some of my cell mates, now deciding I was a millionaire, were showing signs of aggression. At nine o'clock came further evidence that even in dark times like this, my guardian angel—the one the nuns had told me about as a boy— was looking after me. I was taken to a small room with a telephone on the wall, the receiver off the hook.

On the other end was Glen Cornelius, a cattleman I had done business with. Harcourt's office had tried to sell him cattle that Glen knew belonged to me. Glen was on his way to a meeting at my home of concerned friends. But first, he had to know something.

"Did you take anything from this man?"

"I took nothing from him," I said. "It has to do with him wanting me to lie for him in court." He asked me again, and I made the same answer. "I knew you were honest," Glen would say later, "and I knew you worked for a man who wasn't." After Glen met with Pat and the others that morning, he came with a paper bag and $50,000 in bail money.

Within days, after hearings to plead for a reduced bail, and huddles with lawyers, I was out. When I finally got back to the farm, it was lit up with floodlights everywhere, and armed guards were patrolling the property.

Late that night, there was a knock at the front door; when I stepped outside a guard put a shotgun to the back of my head. He instructed me to lie on my stomach; his foot against my neck was meant to ensure I stay there. This fellow, too, wanted my guilty plea and perhaps a bonus for procuring it. But once again, my angel was on duty. At that moment, the guard's boss showed up and called off the uniformed thug.

In the days that followed, the friends who rallied around us saved our lives in every way. The help was emotional, logistical, financial, and if I name names here it is by way of thanks: to John and JoAnn Jones, Marge and Vince Evans, George and Kathy Smith, John and Glory Bacon, Dr. Jack and Cae Algeo, Peggy and Slick Gardner, Raymond and Rosalie Cornelius, as well as Glen and Ora Cornelius.

One loaned us a car, for we had none; the farm owned everything. Another took in our children for several months while the legal firestorm raged. Another housed Pat and me when our lawyers advised us to leave the property.

On that day, I ran down to the stables and immediately saddled Johnny Tivio, Jess, and Cadillac—the three horses I knew we had to get away from Flag Is Up Farms. While I was saddling Johnny Tivio, one of my office staff came to say that the horses should remain until everyone knew who they really belonged to. I smiled at her and continued tacking up. She knew who these three horses belonged to, and that an army could not separate me from Johnny Tivio, short of burying me a distance from him.

I put as much of my tack and equipment as I could on my horses. Then I mounted Johnny Tivio and led the other two down the long straight drive, past the buildings I had so carefully planned and the paddocks I had cultivated over the past six years. I wondered if I would ever return. It looked peaceful and orderly, and its beauty had the usual effect on me. I was proud of it.

In the paddocks grazed some of the horses I had trained or started. Horses know nothing of our troubles and we know too little of theirs. But I wanted to know more, and I felt renewed resolve to focus on my work with remedial animals and in starting young horses. The acres that spread out on either side of me would exist long after Harcourt was dead and gone, and long after I was too.

Johnny Tivio walked on, toward the safe haven of the Gardner Ranch, in charge as always, his ears flicking back and forth. At that moment, Johnny Tivio's belief in himself and his natural superiority to everyone around him seemed to me like gold dust—magical and priceless. I loved that horse.

During the following year, the case against me unraveled; the charge of theft languished in court. Harcourt panicked and started selling off pieces of Flag Is Up Farms for much less than their actual value. There followed a protracted legal battle: Rudolf Greenbaum sued Harcourt for $10 million; I filed a wrongful prosecution suit against Harcourt for $30 million.

A judge was hauled out of retirement to sort it all out. C. Douglas Smith was a slight, gray-haired, distinguished-looking man with a deliberate manner and a cool gaze. In his chambers, the judge said that he had read all the documents and he did not see a felony here—at least, not on the part of the accused. Pointing at me, he said, "I want to see that man smile." I liked this judge.

In the end, my attorneys came to me with a deal. They were not sure it was good enough, but the alternative was years more of legal wrangling and a full trial. I was to plead a *nolo contendere* to a misdemeanor for signing the two horses' ownership papers over to myself. Both horses would be given to me by Harcourt as final proof that I had committed no intrinsic wrong. And the California Horse Racing Board agreed that my licence—suspended early in these proceedings—would immediately be restored and a letter of apology sent to me.

Last, but not least, Flag Is Up Farms would be ours. The compensation paid to us by Harcourt allowed us to buy the farm. It was over.

A year later, Hastings Harcourt contacted me to say that he was terminally ill and wanted to meet. We sat in the den overlooking the farm. The first thing he did was congratulate me on being such a formidable opponent. He asked forgiveness for the injustice he had tried to perpetrate, and I said I appreciated the gesture, adding that two of my children, Deborah and Marty, had decided to take up law, hoping to bring some integrity to a legal system that sometimes seems to have none. Harcourt died not long afterward.

What a study in the variables of human psychology that tortured tale was. It drew me closer still to horses—the most wonderful and the most predictable creatures on earth.

CHAPTER 5

Flag Is Up Farms Regained

For Johnny Tivio, Jess, and Cadillac, the barn at the Gardner Ranch had been home for a year. Now I loaded them in the van and drove them back the short distance to Flag Is Up Farms. Johnny Tivio was pleased to see his real home again, with its gracious stabling and spacious paddocks laid out side by side in this stunning valley.

When Pat and I, with Debbie, Laurel, and Marty, walked back into our house, it looked to have lain empty for one hundred years, not twelve months. Our footsteps echoed as we walked over the wooden floors. Cobwebs hung from the rafters, and everywhere we felt the ghostly residue of all that had transpired before our hurried departure.

We switched on the electricity and the plumbing, opened the windows, and blew some life back into the place. We liberated our furniture from the storage company. A gifted artist, Pat started painting pictures and hung them all over the house. She wanted to bring light and color back into our lives. Later, she took up sculpture too, studied human and equine anatomy, and began to work in bronze.

We walked the farm, reintroducing ourselves to each paddock and building. Much of the original land and the site of the breeding barn had been sold off, but the core remained. We still had 154 acres. In time, it sunk in that Flag Is Up Farms was ours and we began to mend as a family. I was keen to get back to what I was good at: horses. Perhaps this renewed sense of energy led to overzealousness, and a critical error of judgment with a horse called Fancy Heels.

I had been talking to our friends Dave and Sue Abel of Elko, Nevada, about my coming to the Elko horse show to look over the large contingent of reined cow horses who compete there every year. These ranch horses work long hours each day, honing their skills without suffering the drudgery of exercises specifically geared for the showring, which tends to make horses resent their jobs. The Elko competition often showcases wonderful equine athletes, with sound work ethics and good attitudes.

I soon spotted a horse that impressed me. Tall, copper-red in color, with an unattractive head, Fancy Heels looked like a classic mustang/Thoroughbred cross, with a fair bit of feathering on his legs. He showed an enormous amount of cow sense and good athletic ability, with a light, responsive mouth. A little work, I thought, could turn him from a good working horse to a top show horse.

Fancy Heels won his class on the Saturday, which earned him a place in the championship on the Sunday. I was anxious to buy him before he started winning any championships outright, so that afternoon Dave Abel and I sought out the horse's owner, Randy Bunch.

"Well, he's for sale all right," said Randy. "That's why I brought him to town in the first place."

"How much do you want for him?"

Randy paused before saying $3,500. I was surprised at this low figure and agreed immediately. We shook hands and I wrote him a check.

"You looking forward to the championship tomorrow, just the same?" I queried.

"Uh-uh. Hang on. You own the horse; you show him tomorrow."

Startled, I said, "Now wait a minute, I've never even sat on him yet, and I don't even have any clothes or equipment." Randy crooked a finger at me and said, "I want to show you something." Fancy Heels shifted to one side as we walked to the back of his stall.

Randy raked back the bedding from one corner to reveal a half-empty bottle of Jim Beam whiskey. He picked up the bottle and held it between us. "That's how much whiskey it took to get me through the elimination classes. I don't intend to have to drink the rest of it to get through the championship. I came to town to sell him; I've sold him, and now I'm going back to the ranch. Good luck with him—you're showing him."

I looked across at Dave Abel. My expression was a plea for his help. Dave shrugged, "That's the way people are up here, Monty. If you want a shot at that prize money, I guess you show the horse. We can find you a pair of chaps and a bridle." I rode Fancy Heels for an hour that evening, just to get the measure of him. The following morning, I again rode him for half an hour to warm him up. In the arena, our herd work was pretty good and Fancy Heels led going into the single cow-working phase. That part was only acceptable. After this came the dry work—stops and turns. In the end, we took second.

After a week at home working with Fancy Heels, I gained a lot of respect for Randy Bunch. The changes necessary were going to be harder to effect than I had realized. This was a mature, well-established working horse, and I could not find my way forward with him.

After a month, Fancy Heels was ten percent less effective than he had been at the Elko show; after two months, twenty percent less effective. I was, I told myself, a major trainer of Thoroughbred race-horses as well as several world champion working horses, including the legendary Johnny Tivio. I can get this job done.

After four months, I conceded defeat. I had taken Fancy Heels backward so enormously that the kindest thing was to sell him to a good ranch where he could go back to the work he enjoyed. An amateur bought him, and when I saw them compete, I saw a rider who did not notice every mistake the horse made and a horse who tried his heart out. They won often.

During the many hours I rode Fancy Heels, that old adage "You can't teach an old dog new tricks" took on new life for me. In fact, you *can* teach an old dog new tricks, but all in due time. I had been so keen to get to work on Fancy Heels that I thought I could force rapid changes on him. I pressed for a standard of excellence without taking the horse's feelings into account. It did not work.

Given the chance to work with Fancy Heels again, I would not set a time frame for making changes and demand that he stick to it. That horse taught me to respect horses and not to demand immediate perfection. I had failed him, but I did learn from the experience. In the twenty years since, the hundreds of remedial horses I have worked with have benefited from the lessons he taught me. Certain horses in my life have humbled me, and Fancy Heels was one.

———

In 1974, I got the kind of telephone call you dread.

"Crawford's taken a bad fall. He broke his neck."

My old friend Crawford Hall had been riding a young racehorse when they both fell hard to the ground. Dave Abel, a classmate of Crawford's, was with me at Flag Is Up when I got the news and we raced north to Fresno, where Crawford lay in an intensive care unit.

Crawford is the son of Clark Hall, who owned a sizable cattle operation in Shandon, not far from where James Dean was killed. In the late 1940s, Clark was a good team roper who competed in the major rodeos. I roped with him when I was ten years old, got to know him well, and went to his ranch several times. Crawford was an active boy around the ranch and would work cattle with his father. There was some devilment in him, which only made him more charming. In the early to mid-1950s, while I was at Cal Poly, only fifty miles from Crawford's home, I saw him often. He was then starting to show horses in competition and in junior rodeo. Some ten years later he took a shine to a student who was working for us at San Luis Obispo. When they married it felt like a family event.

Sadly, they drifted apart, and Crawford took a job in Tulare in the San Joaquin Valley with Greg Ward, my close friend and ex-classmate who had set up a business there training cutting horses, reined cow horses, and quarter horses for racing. Crawford was a rider assigned to all three departments.

Now he faced the reality of never riding again. I will never forget stepping into the room where Crawford was being treated for severe spinal cord damage. He had an eyebolt embedded in the top of his head and screws through his heels, and from these points he was wired to a device that looked for all the world like a barbecue spit. It provided the necessary traction and rolled his weight around, reducing damage to vital organs.

The doctor took us to one side. "Crawford can't feel anything from the shoulders down," he said calmly. "That means he is going to be a quadriplegic, with maybe five to six percent use of his arms. I'm afraid there's a long road ahead for him."

Crawford struggled with the trauma. His emotions were a tangle of hope and despair, but shock was what he felt more than anything. "If I can't be involved with horses," he told us as we stood by his bed, "I'd just as soon not live."

"I'd say the same myself," I replied. "Don't you worry, we'll find a way."

"You promise me something? If I'm good for nothing but selling pencils somewhere, you all agree to give me enough pills to put me to sleep, do you hear?"

"You won't be selling pencils, Crawford."

"Hell, I probably won't even be able to do that. I sure as hell won't be able to lift the pills to my mouth, so do it for me if I ask you."

Then hope would surge in him. "I'll do something," he said. "I'm telling you, I'm not just lying down and doing nothing. There's a spot for me somewhere."

He was a desperately unhappy sight, and our hearts went out to him. Driving back with Dave, I wondered out loud about finding a job for Crawford on our farm. The main buildings and offices are on level ground, with good surfaces between the barns, the covered riding school, the round pens, and the track.

If Crawford could learn to operate an electric wheelchair, he could be another set of eyes and oversee the operation. I scouted and found a spot on the grounds where we could locate a home specifically designed for a quadriplegic. The idea took shape: he could be employed as an observer and help me where possible. He would find his own role and cultivate his position as his abilities allowed. Crawford might have a chance, after all, to stay involved with horses and the life he loved most.

Days later I called the hospital and talked to Crawford about the potential job. Only four months after that, he and a friend came to Solvang to look the place over. By that time, they had a special van to transport him.

The transition from young and athletic to wheelchair-bound was strenuous and difficult. But Crawford would learn to operate the chair more effectively, and the future would undoubtedly bring better chairs. He was convinced that in time he would navigate the farm as well as anyone.

Doctors and therapists involved with Crawford's rehabilitation came to the farm. They cautioned us that as prospective employers, we were taking on a near-impossible task. Only with great difficulty does the human body adjust to the quadriplegic state, and we were not to underestimate the challenge Crawford faced. An initial rush of sympathy might create false hopes for him.

The prognosis looked grim. Therapists listed dozens of potential physical problems (many of which came to pass), and warned that Crawford would likely only live another three to five years—with the prospect of a more normal life expectancy if he could get past the five-year hurdle. Within a few months, Crawford was living at Flag Is Up Farms in a custom-built modular home provided by his family. He found himself a good vehicle that could get him to every corner of the farm. Crawford had a job now, and he began to shape it around horses.

"The horses themselves were therapeutic," Crawford says now, looking back on that time in his life. "When I was in rehabilitation in the hospital, there were guys there who didn't want to get up in the morning. They were looking for ways to die. I wasn't like that. I had something I wanted desperately to do—work with horses. It has never *felt* like work, though; it's always been fun. An engineer or an architect might have the same passion for building bridges or houses. Mine was for horses, and they have never stopped teaching me. The setting of the farm, the climate, being outdoors most days of the year—all that is conducive to being healthy, and I love it. But the possibility of a life with horses: that's what inspired me."

From the outset, Crawford insisted on complete cooperation from me as he commenced his education in Thoroughbred racing. A voracious reader, quick to learn, he became extremely proficient at understanding the needs of the horses. Without my realizing it, he had already taken over the operation.

After only one year, I concluded that he should manage the training operation on a daily basis; I would step back and be the overseer.

That year, 1975, I purchased a yearling I named An Act. A good horse for Crawford to begin with because he set such a high standard, An Act was a first-class prospect who went on to win the Santa Anita Derby. The next year I bought two other horses, Alleged and Super Pleasure. Super Pleasure had as much talent as any horse I have owned or trained, but he was beset by a throat problem that relegated him to being a sprinter, so we will never know how he would have turned out.

As for Alleged, Pat conceived of that name for this extraordinary horse, and we still have it as the license plate on our car. The name began as Allegiance to the Flag (his sire was Hoist the Flag) but it was later shortened to Alleged. Eventually owned by Robert Sangster and a consortium of investors, Alleged was twice the winner of the Arc de Triomphe—the most prestigious racing event in the world.

One of my favorite clippings from the *Santa Ynez Valley News* dates from October 5, 1978: "Monty and Pat Roberts of Flag Is Up Farms here in Solvang have good reason to feel proud this week as Alleged won the 57th Prix de L'Arc de Triomphe at Longchamps, France, last Sunday. Alleged, ridden by Lester Piggot, won easily by two lengths ahead of Trillion in a time of 2:36.5."

With Alleged, An Act, and Super Pleasure, Crawford had a solid foundation to build on and a standard of excellence for the horses to follow. The years have enriched his education, and he has become invaluable to the farm—as good as anyone in the racing industry. His life revolves around operating the training center, and owners take comfort in knowing that he is there, on the job, virtually all the time.

When Crawford came to me, his approach to training horses was conventional. Although a thinking horseman, he had been trained in the mainstream. Over the years, however, he has come to embrace a set of philosophies more aligned with my own.

Crawford is a character, and well known in Thoroughbred racing for his clever pranks. "I decided a long time ago," says Crawford, "that serenity is a valuable commodity and that no one should get too much of it." On the farm, an asphalt sidewalk parallel to the track opens onto a grassy area where you will often find Crawford strapped neatly into his chair, facing the track, and looking studious in his glasses and white fedora, habitually rubbing his hands as he watches a horse and jockey breeze past. You hope he is assessing the horse; you fear he is plotting mischief.

Crawford, naturally, was part of an elaborate prank pulled off in 1986. An office manager named Corky Parker—who took his job very seriously and who had a birthday coming up (a dangerous combination at the farm)—was told that an Arab sheik was coming for a barbecue, a precursor to a major horse deal. "*Don't* lose him," I instructed Corky before supposedly leaving on a trip and putting him in charge.

From my hiding place in the bushes by the house, I looked on as the theatrical conspiracy unfolded. Behind the sheik's robes, beard and sunglasses was Satish Seemar, a farm employee, whom Corky would have worked with daily. The sheik's interpreter and the suspicious, gun-toting bodyguard? Both neighbors. The stretch limousine they arrived in proved a nice touch.

While Crawford and the sheik talked horses on the terrace, rider and appointed barbecuer Sean McCarthy drank beer and feigned inebriation. "I don't give a *damn* if he's the sheik," he said too loudly, "just tell me how he likes his meat!" The increasingly distraught Corky begged Sean and pleaded with the other riders to stop imbibing. When they finally all sang Happy Birthday, the tears began to flow down Corky's face and he was hours recovering. The acting troupe spent at least that long laughing and recapping.

Crawford has also gained a reputation for the way he works with the young people who come to Flag Is Up Farms and ride for us. "Leave the horse alone," he will say to the rider. "Let him go on, let him explore a little and then correct him. He'll be all right. Let him go in the direction he wants for a few steps, and then bend him more toward what you want. Don't hammer him."

The youngster struggling with the horse will inevitably retort, "But he's going to run away." Crawford's reply is invariably laconic: "How can he do that? You have the Atlantic on your right and the Pacific on your left. Where's he going to go?"

Another Crawfordism goes: "You can't be liberated in your thinking if you're conservative in your approach." As I write this, Crawford is in his twenty-first year with us and as healthy and active as anyone in his condition could be. Hospitals and therapists have used videotape to chronicle his career. Institutions use his example as an educational tool in treating similar cases. To anyone who faces what he faced, and to anyone who meets him, Crawford Hall is an inspiration.

———

After a day at the track in 1981 I headed straight for the farm office. It was April 24. Every year on that day I feel a twinge of sadness all over again. When I walked through the door, Pat immediately stepped forward and embraced me. "Johnny Tivio," she said through tears, "is dead."

Seeing a mare being taken to the breeding barn, he had stepped up on his toes, lifted his tail, and was coming over to try to get her phone number, as usual. In the middle of the field, he dropped like a stone. Dr. Van Snow, then our veterinarian, confirmed that the old horse had suffered a heart attack. Through my sadness, I was relieved only that he had not suffered. We were just beginning to have trouble with his feet, and I had dreaded a painfully slow demise. He was sound to the last.

"We left him where he fell," said Pat, "so you could see." As I walked toward his body lying there, saw the eye empty, the life gone, all those philosophical notions about his being spared a lingering death vanished. His death hit me hard. I stayed there with Johnny Tivio, and I remembered.

By then, he had retired. He was twenty-five years old, and no one had wanted to breed to him for some time. He enjoyed the best of care, with a warm box stall of his own and a field with plenty of green grass in the daytime. He could watch everything going on from his paddock. Mares moving to and from the breeding barn had to pass by him, and every time one did Johnny Tivio acted the big, bad stallion again, calling out to them and prancing the length of the fence like a three-year-old.

Early in our life together, I showed him in Salinas in a big competition, one of the most important on the continent. Johnny Tivio was so good at everything, and so willing, that I could not decide whether to show him in the cutting division or the reined cow horse division. Pat had said, "Why not show him in both?"

It was unheard of. No one had done it before. It was impossible....

We entered him in both events, and the official response was instantaneous. "Monty, have you lost your mind?" It was our old friend, Lester Sterling, chairman of the event, calling from the grounds office. "We can't let you show Johnny Tivio in both divisions. It's just ridiculous to think he could perform that way."

"Is it against the rules?" I asked.

"Well, no. But I don't think you ought to embarrass yourself."

Eventually I persuaded Lester to agree. As I was preparing Johnny Tivio, I would fit him with one type of bit and bridle when we were training for one event, and a different one for the other. He was intelligent and read the situation perfectly: he won both divisions, a feat not attempted before nor duplicated since. In his time, Johnny Tivio was undefeated in the stallion sweepstakes—a kind of pentathlon for stallions. He was four times a world champion working cow horse. In Western riding, a form of Western dressage, he was undefeated in fourteen consecutive competitions.

More than that, though, he was a sterling character possessed of superb intelligence, uncommon pride, and an inspiring work ethic. He made it a pleasure to shrug on a coat and walk down through the early-morning mist that often blankets this valley to begin the hours of work that an establishment like this demands.

Now he lay collapsed on his side, with that heavy, final weight that only death brings. I knew where to bury him. For some time, I had it in my mind to make a special graveyard just in front of the office, where I would give each horse his own headstone. The horses' names and dates and a line or two expressing some of their qualities would be engraved in bronze plates set into the blocks of stone.

Johnny Tivio would be the first.

With some members of our staff, we went over with a low-boy trailer to where his body lay. We fitted straps underneath him and lifted him onto the trailer. Towing him across the field, I remembered eleven years earlier riding him out of the farm, down the drive in front of us, when Hastings Harcourt was casting a long shadow over our lives. Johnny Tivio had been as confident as ever, and I remembered how I took sustenance from that.

That day, when we arrived at the Gardner Ranch, a notoriously eccentric woman, Marjorie Merriweather Post Dye, had come by. She pointed at my horse in the stable and said, "Johnny Tivio."

"What about him?" I asked.

"Well, I hear you're in trouble. You need money for a legal defense. Now, I don't give money. No one gets money out of me. But I'll give you anything you want in return for that horse."

I thanked her for the offer, but it was out of the question. "No!" she corrected me, annoyed with my stupidity. "I don't mean I'd take him away from you. I'd never take him away from you. But I want to buy the ownership documents."

"The papers?"

"Yes, just for a while. For safekeeping. Just give me the papers so I can hold them, and point at them, and say I owned Johnny Tivio for a little while."

We walked up to the house and I gave her the papers, shaking my head in wonder at this courageous, strong woman who had so much her own way of doing things. In return, she made us promise to call her if we ever needed a loan toward our defense fund.

Now, as I prepared to bury the horse she so clearly adored, I hoped that Marge had enjoyed having those papers. They were all that was left of him. I dug his grave myself, using the farm's backhoe. I am not a capable hand at that machine, and it took me longer than it should have. By then it was dark, but the hole was dug and Johnny Tivio's body had to be lowered in.

This was the tough part. I knew I would never again have a friend the likes of Johnny Tivio, and I could not bring myself to cover him with earth; I had had enough. Our veterinarian volunteered to carry on while I went up to the house and crawled underneath the covers.

The plaque on his gravestone reads: "Johnny Tivio, April 24, 1956 to April 24, 1981. Known to all as the greatest all-round working horse ever to enter the arena." He died on his twenty-fifth birthday.

———

I was walking up the steep southern slope toward the house when I took, as they say in the horse world, a bad step; my lower back suddenly locked, and my legs gave out on me. I was on the ground and helpless, unable to move the lower half of my body. All sensation ceased to exist. I conjured Crawford Hall lying in traction in his hospital bed. Now, seven years later, it was my turn.

I pulled myself up the slope with my arms, in excruciating pain. Stunt riding, football, team roping, calf roping, bull riding, bulldogging: all that impact on my spinal column had ruptured the discs, and I was about to know the cost. I was forty-six years old.

A doctor declared me too critically injured to move to the hospital. He wanted to stabilize me first, and to win back the feeling in my legs. He arranged for delivery of a rack—truly an instrument of torture— and for thirty days I was strung out on this device like a rabbit on a spit. I am as strongly opposed as anyone could imagine to the indiscriminate use of mind-altering drugs. But doctor-administered morphine is truly a miracle drug for one beset by debilitating pain. I was able to function somewhat in the business-management aspect of my life while being stretched on that awful rack.

After a month, much of the sensation returned to my legs. During that time I had educated myself in the world of back woes, and settled on Dr. Bob Kerlan as the man most likely to keep me out of a wheelchair. In a friend's motor home, I was taken to Dr. Kerlan's clinic in Los Angeles. After a CAT scan (a computerized axial tomographic X ray) was taken, he and his team presented their report. They brought in a plastic model of a human spine and used it to terrify me.

Dr. Kerlan pointed to the model. "You see here, the lower back? The soft material in the core of these five discs has ruptured—due to constant heavy impacts on the spine—and leaked out, causing stalactites of invasive material. That's thirty percent of your problem. The rest is due to fractures and spurs throughout the spinal column. This is what's causing you the pain and the nerve impairment. We can get in there and clean up that stuff, and remove the spurs and you'll be left with five discs which are like doughnuts—the soft middle sections will have been sucked out of them."

I offered a hesitant "OK," but the news just got darker...

"Normally, we find just one or two gone; but all five are ruptured in your lower back. It's going to be a long operation, and we won't find out how successful we've been until it's finished."

... and darker.

"You have very extensive damage to the spine, Monty. Forget riding—don't even think of riding again. You won't be lifting a weight more than forty pounds either. You'll probably just be able to walk around under your own steam. But be happy with that, because you are on the verge of living the rest of your life in a wheelchair."

For two or three days I went through preparation. They took me off the morphine, and when the pain roared back I roared with it. I wanted to scream "Fix it!" every second of every minute. Then I went under the knife. Ten hours later, I woke up to see a smiling black woman in a perfect white uniform. She looked like an angel: had I died and gone to heaven? Or was this the other place?

"OK, Mr. Roberts," she said, "shall we visit the bathroom?"

Surely she jested. "I can't move."

"Oh yes, you can. Time to sit up now."

Was she aware I had only just come around from the anesthetic? She started to pull my feet out from the bed and sit me up. The pain shot through me; iron bolts were being driven into my back by Satan himself. She held my shoulders, but every time she let go my body would flop, as if a new hinge had been inserted somewhere in my middle.

"Wow," she said admiringly, "they must have done a good job on you." Later, they hung me in a wheeled contraption that suspended me in mid-air like a wicker chair hangs from a tree limb in a garden. I was in a sorry state.

The video of the operation was one of the more grotesque movies I have seen. The surgeons looked like a gang of carpenters with muscular forearms arriving for work; their toolboxes were filled with hammers and chisels. After cutting through and peeling back muscles and soft tissue, they went at my back like they were mending a broken house.

Following my recovery, they sent me home and told me to keep moving, to walk a minute or two more each day. I was in a wheelchair for twelve days, then on crutches for several months. I have a scar down the middle of my back from my bottom rib to my tailbone, and my lower right leg is virtually dead: you could stub a cigarette out on it. Dr. Kerlan and his gang of carpenters did a better job than he thought was possible. I can walk fine, and I can ride.

———

The horse I would ride, and still ride, is a registered quarter horse gelding, a bay. He has a white pastern on his near hind leg and a white, irregular star between the eyes with a strip that runs down to his muzzle. It forms an inverted question mark, which seems apt for this horse.

Dually was a cull from the Greg Ward Ranch, a throwaway horse whom no one would buy. He had crooked hind legs six inches shorter than they should have been, pigeon-toed feet, and was bow-legged behind. Greg and I treated him as an experiment: we tied the reins to his saddle horn and let him have his way. He *still* has his way, he's jealous and possessive of me, and he is still funny-looking, but he has also become a superb horse.

He's fourteen hands, three inches high and weighs 1,200 pounds: a solid guy, this Dually. His name refers to a type of pickup truck, called a dually (as in Dooley), with a beefed-up rear end and twin tires at the back. We use them to haul horse trailers. Such trucks look massively broad and strong if you stand behind them, and that is how Dually looks.

His rear quarters are like two small hills jammed together, and the power they give him is mind-boggling. He is a turbo-charged, twin-engined type of rocket horse, with the balance and coordination now bred into the breed. There is no way he can replace Brownie or Johnny Tivio, but Dually is a natural successor to them—both in terms of my affection for him and in his achievements. He too is a world-class, championship-winning animal in his own right.

From my first day with Dually, I felt he was at heart a near-perfect working animal.

After join-up, Dually bonded with me very strongly, and like Johnny Tivio, he will follow me around the farm without any headgear on. I can wander up to the promontory that overlooks the farm, and he'll walk alongside as if there were an invisible thread connecting us. He has been schooled from start to finish using only the methods described in this book.

Now seven, he is in the prime of life. The understanding between us is mature and well-founded. I have not so much trained him as created an environment in which he has wanted to learn. I have never pulled at his mouth, ever; in fact, I could use cotton thread instead of leather reins. Yet, on a totally loose rein, he will slide to a blinding halt from a full gallop just hearing a single word, "Whoa," and at the same time feeling my weight settle back in the saddle. Again on a loose rein, he will spin like a top, just feeling the gossamer weight of the rein against his neck and a slight pressure applied to the inside leg.

Dually has an immense heart, which is just as well because to train him using these experimental methods takes patience and hard work from both of us. However, having learned from my experiences with Brownie and Fancy Heels, among hundreds of others, I have taken care not to dull his appetite for work by repetition or excess; it has been essential to our progress together that he remain fresh and keen.

———

The "crazy horse" is almost never born, but made. And it pains me to hear the term. If we could somehow see for ourselves all the events in a horse's life that together account for his malicious behavior, we would be astonished. Some horses will take so much, then finally take no more.

Few people still think humans are born crazy; but in the world of horses the "bad seed" myth endures. "His sire was that way, too," trainers will say of a troubled horse, and they have been saying that for 6,000 years. They are wrong: maybe two percent of horses are born bad; the rest are put on that path by people.

Stories abound about truly nasty horses. Native Dancer, who sired the fleet Northern Dancer, would pick up a groom by the teeth and toss him in the air like a stick. He would haul riders off his back by their boots. I once read that his groom, "who loved him like a son," freely admitted that had it not been for careful handling, Native Dancer would have killed someone. In his paddock, the horse would see the groom and, in his own time, come to the gate to be led away. If the groom entered the paddock before that moment, the stallion would run at him with murderous intent.

Flag Is Up Farms has also had its share of stallions requiring great vigilance, but none so dangerous as a Thoroughbred called In Tissar.

He was by Roberto out of Strip Poker, as fine a pedigree as you can imagine. It made him a half brother to the champion Landaluce. He was purchased as a yearling at Keeneland in 1979 for $250,000 by Buckram Oak Farm, and sent to France to race. He was a good winner early on, but then he was injured and offered for sale at the reduced price of $220,000.

The horse struck me as a good prospect for syndication, so along with partners Albert A. Katz and Ronald Semler, we bought him to put together a syndicate for breeding. He was a handsome, proud stallion, a "blood bay" horse—red tones with black mane and tail. In Tissar was tall, strong and muscled, especially through the neck and shoulders.

In California, we offered him at $16,000 a share, which is like arranging time-share leases on his capacity as a father. The twenty-five shares sold within two weeks, yielding the partners a gross of $400,000, which meant we were already $180,000 to the good and had kept back five shares each to be used on our own mares. This was a good piece of business.

In Tissar started covering mares in 1983 and bred without incident for the first half of the season. Then came reports that he was being aggressive with his handlers. I spent time watching him. If his handlers took him to the breeding room, he covered his mare and all was well. If, on the other hand, they turned toward his paddock instead of the breeding barn, he became aggressive.

Since the aggression seemed to be a function of his sexuality, I brought his handlers a metal noseband stallion halter to use on him, which seemed to solve the problem for a day or two. Then it recurred in the breeding room, where he had previously been willing and cooperative, if a touch overenthusiastic.

At the same time, rumors reached me that a young man on our night staff had taken it upon himself to school In Tissar. I am sure he had good intentions, but he had likely mistreated the stallion, at least in the opinion of the horse. In Tissar became dangerous, and he bit two men quite badly. I huddled with Dr. Van Snow, our resident veterinarian, and his assistant, the breeding room staff, and Darryl Skelton, who was handling the stallions.

Our solution was to create a safety zone around the stallion. Two eight-foot staves (one-and-a-half-inch-thick dowling) attached to In Tissar's halter would keep his handlers at a distance. They bred two or three mares that way. In Tissar was happy and did not object to this careful handling procedure; he even seemed proud of it.

The next time a romantic appointment was booked for him, I once again came down to observe and offer help if necessary. We brought a mare into the breeding room, cleaned under her tail with soap and water, bandaged her tail in gauze—all precautions to minimize infections and injuries to both stallion and mare—and had her standing in the center of the room.

Two men put the wooden staves on In Tissar and led him toward the breeding room where the mare waited in full heat and well "let down"—meaning that she was receptive to the stallion.

The two men led In Tissar through the large door in the center of this forty-foot-square room. Six feet into the room, he planted himself, lordly looking the situation over. In the room were seven people: two men on the staves, one man with the mare, the veterinarian, his assistant, Darryl Skelton, and myself.

I closed the door behind the stallion and Darryl and I walked over to join Dr. Snow. In Tissar stood stock-still, just looking at the mare and around the room.

Without warning, he struck out with his left front foot, reaching over the top of the stave and slapping it out of the man's hand and onto the floor. The weight of his body snapped the dowling in two. The man on that side was left holding one broken portion, while the jagged other half hung dangerously from the stallion's halter.

A second later, In Tissar reached up with his other foot and, without breaking it, slapped the stave out of the other man's hand. The horse was deadly accurate; no question, this was a calculated move.

Moving fast, he attacked the mare with his mouth wide open. He sank his teeth into her left flank, ripping at it like a wolf would a rabbit. When his shoulder struck her, she fell heavily to the floor, landing on her side. The man holding the mare fled for his life.

With a hunk of her hide in his mouth, In Tissar was now kneeling over the mare, squealing and pawing. The noise in that room was deafening, the excitement and enormous power of it overwhelming. My time in the rodeo arena with bulldogging and bronc and bull riding had given me the greatest schooling I know to cope with tense and dangerous situations, but it was little use to me now.

I moved to my right. In Tissar had knocked the mare down near the south wall, and as I moved to the corner he wheeled and took a run at me. I ran back along the wall to gain the protection of the examination chute.

Dr. Snow, who had moved along with me, held a shavings rake in his hand. His intention was to protect the mare and the rest of us by holding the stallion at bay with the rake. In Tissar went straight for him and ran into the end of the rake as if it were made of papier-mâché.

When Dr. Snow fled toward the lab in the northwest corner, he crashed into his assistant standing in the doorway, and both fell into the lab, and safety. Darryl and I both ended up in the examination chute. I never felt more vulnerable and less in charge.

The two men on the staves had sought refuge outside the north door, which was open a foot, and I am sure they were prepared to close it if the horse came that way. The man who had been holding the mare stood outside the south door, also open a foot. Having terrorized us all, In Tissar now faced the lab, weaving back and forth as if to say, "I control you all. I'm in charge now."

He turned slowly and walked on the tips of his toes with his tail stuck out and his neck arched high. It was a beautiful, terrifying sight. He went straight to the mare, who was still lying on the floor, and he stood over her flank. He pawed and squealed several times, as a stallion does when courting a mare, and the mare slowly got to her feet. Blood dripped onto the floor from the large gash on her flank.

In Tissar rooted at that flank with his nose a few times, and was fully erect. Incredibly, the mare lifted her tail to display her receptivity. He mounted her, and every one of us there stood frozen and watched in fascination: it was a primal, powerful experience.

After covering the mare, In Tissar walked slowly to the north door. He stopped there, the aggression clearly gone. The men outside slowly opened the door and walked him down the alleyway to his stall. He went quiet as a lamb.

As Dr. Snow, Darryl, and I walked along behind him, the doctor shook his head. "I'm going to carry my pistol with me from now on, and if he ever does anything like that again he'll have to die. I'm not going to risk losing somebody's life."

I agreed. Something dramatic had to be done before someone was killed. We concluded that the horse was perhaps overfed and underworked. If he was ridden in the hills, really put to work, maybe we could change his attitude. Darryl offered to ride him each day, but Dr. Snow and I insisted that one of us be around to offer help should something go wrong.

On the day set aside to try this new strategy, we took In Tissar to a place on the farm with strong corrals and cattle-handling facilities— a loading chute and a squeeze gate. Once in the gate, we would get his tack on and take him for a ride.

In the stall, Darryl managed to get a shank on In Tissar and lead him toward the corrals. Halfway there, the horse spotted a mare in a field a quarter mile away and started to play up. Darryl tried to soothe him, but the horse made a move indicating he was going to attack him. We all stood in a small half-acre area while In Tissar made some very aggressive gestures. Moments later, Darryl lost control of the shank and In Tissar was loose. We managed to avoid being attacked, but if he spotted one of us—even from a distance of 200 or 300 yards— he would go for us. He was really angry, and we ran around like Keystone Kops.

Eventually we set some gates to trap him near the heavy-duty cattle apparatus. Darryl was able to get him in the squeeze, and we swung the gate over to him until he stood in an area twelve feet long and three feet wide. When we closed the gate to move him over, he kicked it and then held his near hind leg off the ground for about twenty seconds. We held our breath, thinking he had broken his leg—the kick was that fierce. Then he put his leg down and stood on it as normal. There was just a bit of hair off, about mid-shaft on the cannon bone.

Once he was in there, Darryl tacked him up and mounted him. He took him up a hill where he could ride for about fifteen miles with no gates to open, and they were gone about three hours. When he returned, he rode him into the stallion round pen, took his saddle off, and led him to the wash rack to give him a bath. In Tissar was fine. He looked a picture of health, a fine example of a stallion in the prime of his life. You could have sold him to a schoolgirl, unless her father noticed that iron-hard, disinterested look in his eye.

We were all pleased, and Darryl started a program of riding the horse each day. On about the fifth day, Dr. Snow agreed that In Tissar was calm enough now for us to get an X ray of that still slightly sore hind leg. When this revealed a significant fracture of the cannon bone, we faced a dilemma: how long could Darryl ride him before the exercise became cruel?

Darryl cut his work right down. On the second day, when Darryl came back to the round pen and took off his saddle, In Tissar attacked him. That was the last straw. In the normal course of events, a horse with a history like this one would be destroyed. Around the world many stallions have been killed for less.

I could not bear to have him killed, however. It was dangerous even to try helping him, but we would have one last go at saving his life. In the end, I devised a complex system of gates, small enclosures and squeeze chutes that would allow In Tissar to be groomed, shod, clipped, bathed, and exercised, and to have his stable cleaned and serviced—all without having anyone in the enclosure with him.

He could also breed a mare without having anyone in the enclosure as well. He was bred in this fashion for twelve years without any injury to a mare, himself, or anyone working with him.

We now have another remedial stallion, Court Dance (by Northern Dancer) who stands in the same facility. Court Dance was owned by Robert Sangster and John Magnier when he was sent to our farm. They hoped I could sort out his problems so they could sell him, but

I quickly learned that he was another dangerous stallion beyond fixing, even beyond transporting or handling.

For the past three years, he has been breeding here under the same system we used with In Tissar, and he is getting along very well. I always prefer to come to an understanding with a horse through communication and dialogue, but that was not possible with these two stallions.

From the accounts I have read about violent stallions, such as Ribot and Graustark—and even In Tissar's sire, Roberto—I have no doubt that there exists a significant number of incurably aggressive stallions. On a scale of 1 to 10, In Tissar was a 9.9. He was intelligent and cunning and he wanted to harm people. Something in his environment had turned him mean, and he had no intention of listening to anyone.

———

Beauty may well be in the eye of the beholder. But while conformation is, in part, subjective, there are roots of realism when assessing the qualities of the equine athlete. And if, during an eighteen-year career buying and selling Thoroughbreds I showed that I had an eye for a horse, that owes something to sculpture.

Early in the 1970s, when Pat took up painting and equine sculpture, she began by studying horse anatomy. You have to know the *inside* of a horse before you can begin to capture the *outside*, and I tried to help Pat as best I could. I recall one time watching one of her teachers sketching horses by one of the paddocks. He was using a triangle to help maintain correct proportions.

To get a sense of what I saw that day, imagine a horse seen from the side, and over that horse lay a triangle, its apex sitting as high as the horse's head and midway between head and tail. From that high point, one line angled down at forty-five degrees through the shoulder; another angled down at forty-five degrees through the hip, and the baseline ran horizontally through both knees and hocks.

In a well-balanced horse, the apex is right in the middle. In a Thoroughbred racehorse, the two sides of the triangle are equal, but the baseline is considerably longer.

Using triangles to judge conformation is so simple, yet so profound.

Pat still works in bronze and it's rare *not* to have one of her equine sculptures taking shape in our kitchen. And when I look on as she subtly molds and adjusts, I think of that day by the paddock when an artist's sketch reduced the tangled business of horse conformation to a bit of basic geometry.

From the mid-1970s until 1989, sometimes with partners, I bought yearling Thoroughbreds at one public auction, in Kentucky, say, and then sold them as two-year-olds at another public auction, perhaps in California. It's called "pinhooking"—an awful name for a demanding and risky test of horsemanship in which an eye for conformation is critical. The term *pinhooking*, it is said, comes from England, where a woman whose husband bought and sold young horses likened it to crocheting—you reach in and pinhook an animal, then put him back in.

A lot can go wrong. If you select badly, if the horse gets injured, if the market declines, the pinhooker can get pricked. The aim, of course, is to sell the horse for a lot more than you paid. My aim always was to get twice for a horse what I spent, and between 1973 and 1990, I came remarkably close: Pat and I purchased 195 yearling Thoroughbreds for $6.9 million and sold them for $13.3 million—a return on investment of forty-three percent. Every young racehorse we purchased was also sold—a rare accomplishment in a business where many operations lose five to ten percent of yearlings for one reason or another.

The numbers are impressive: eighty-two percent of the horses we sold during those eighteen years would start in races, and of that number seventy-nine percent were winners—thirteen percent of them in highly competitive stakes races. Consignors, or sellers, of horses are ranked and during our years in the business, Pat and I were ranked first ten times, second three times and third three times—for sixteen of eighteen years, then, we were in the top three.

You will likely sell well if you buy well. But that presumes an intimate knowledge of pedigrees and smart bids at the sales ring. America still uses the old tobacco auctioning system of fast chatter; it took me years to master its tricks and psychology. Shipping horses is another major challenge—for me especially since 2,500 miles separated the auction ring and my training grounds. Conditioning, foot care, nutrition, marketing, and promotion: all matter, and the trainer who falls down in just one category will suffer in the long run.

A sleek, impeccably groomed young Thoroughbred is as graceful and desirable as any animal on the planet. But letting him use his gift of speed while also keeping him sound and healthy, and starting him so he remains keen to work—there is art in that, and the record of Pat and Monty Roberts, Agents is unmatched.

In Kentucky in the mid-1970s, I bought a registered Thoroughbred yearling stallion, fourteen hands, two inches high, less than 900 pounds in weight, by Hoist The Flag out of Princess Pout. A bay horse with two rear white pasterns, he was in horrible condition and not many people gave him a second glance.

Precisely because he was so thin, I could see that he had the best skeletal balance of any Thoroughbred I had ever seen. And history would suggest I was right.

Ten years later, in 1984, I attended a Thoroughbred symposium held by Dr. Michael Osbourn, a world authority on Thoroughbred conformation. Toward the end of his lecture, he flashed a silhouette of a Thoroughbred onto the overhead projector. "This animal," he said, "is perhaps the most perfectly constructed Thoroughbred I've ever studied." He gazed out to his audience. "Can anyone name this horse, by any chance?" I raised my hand.

"Aha," said Dr. Osbourn, "how did you identify your horse in silhouette, Monty?"

I said, "You have your system of circles. You test to see if certain anatomical features meet or fail to meet the various points on the circle."

"That's correct."

"Well, I have a similar system involving a triangle." Dr. Osbourn invited me to the overhead projector to explain. My triangle, I said, seeks to discover the balance between the two major skeletal structures in a horse: the pelvis and the shoulders. These two "engines" propel the horse over the ground and their engineering determines the efficiency with which the rest of the body responds to brain signals.

Dr. Osbourn finished by saying, "For those of you still in the dark, this horse was owned by Mr. Roberts very early on in his life. That horse, twice the winner of the Arc de Triomphe, is...Alleged."

———

My mother had not long to live, and knew it, when she set about trying to reconcile her husband and her elder son. Intuitively she hoped that through horses we might connect.

My parents' visits by this time, 1986, had become rare and short; suddenly, they were coming to the farm for an entire week. It was clear to me that my mother's cancer had gotten worse, and that this visit was both a final farewell and a peace mission.

She engineered and cajoled, pushed and prodded. She arranged for my father to watch me work with horses in the round pen, ensured he had a stool to sit on, made it so he could not wriggle free. She came close to telling him he had to sit there and take note of what I was doing and acknowledge that it was working.

On the day my father sat down, finally, to watch me start a raw horse, he was well into his seventies. I was no longer desperate for his approval, though I was still a son who would have welcomed his father's belated blessing. I was also a man in his fifties who had by this time started more than 6,500 horses. Apart from all the working horses, I had trained Thoroughbreds who had gone on to win major stakes races all over the world.

The irony of that day was not lost on me: when I began to learn the language of horses at the age of seven, my father was the one man I first wanted to impress with it. And when he turned so savagely on me, and so furiously rejected my ideas, I determined he would never see me gentle a horse. No one would.

The round corral had been a feature of European farming and Western ranching for centuries, but the one I designed was built with solid walls—partly to keep the horse's focus on me, and partly to keep out a world of disinterest and rejection. I remembered too vividly the scornful words of Ray Hackworth after seeing me gentle a horse. "That was a fluke!...You're wrong to go against your father."

I had spent my life going against my father, and now, finally, because my mother had made it her dying wish, he would see where it had taken me. Only recently had I added to the pen the skirtlike structure that let people see me converse with horses.

This day I would start a gorgeous young chestnut filly, a horse whose character I would have to discover. I could see immediately that she was a "fast" type—quick to respond, nervous, but intelligent.

I stood in the middle of the ring and coiled my light sash line. Moving slowly, I squared my body to hers, lifting up my arms a touch and opening my fingers. I locked my eye onto her eye. The result was dramatic. She fled to the perimeter of the round pen, running counterclockwise.

"OK, Dad," I called, "I'm going to explain the sequence of events so you can understand what's happening."

I hardly needed the sash line to keep this filly going comfortably. I could control her speed by choosing where to look at her: if I kept my eyes on her eyes, I could increase the speed of her flight from me; if I moved my gaze back to her shoulder, she slowed. At all times, I kept my body squared to hers.

"The first thing I'm looking for is that inside ear to lock on to me," I called to my father, who sat still as a post on his stool. "It'll happen maybe within a minute." The words were hardly out of my mouth when the filly's ear settled on me. "Course she's going to listen out for you," my father called out.

"It's more than listening out for me. She's keeping the ear on me as a mark of respect. She's allowing me some importance here." I pitched the sash line ahead of her, causing her to turn sharply and flee in the opposite direction. Despite the switch, the ear nearest me was turned in my direction, constantly. She settled back to a steady trot.

After another revolution of the round pen, I said, "Next you'll see another mark of respect she'll want to offer me. You'll see her licking and chewing. You'll see her tongue come through her teeth, then she'll pull it back and demonstrate a chewing action."

Sure enough, she began to lick and chew. "There it is. She's saying that she's a herbivore, that if she can be allowed to eat safely, if she can be allowed to stop running away, then we can come to an agreement. We can settle our respective positions, live and let live, let's talk."

We were now five minutes into the starting procedure, and I explained to my father the final signal before join-up: "I'm looking for her to drop her head, to run along with her nose a couple of inches from the ground." Within a few minutes, the filly was trotting around blowing at the sand in front of her feet, her ear still on me.

"She's telling me it's OK, she can trust me." Turning my shoulders to a point slightly beyond the filly, I allowed my eyes to trail there, too. Immediately, the filly stopped. I waited, perfectly still, standing at an angle to her, showing my flanks and avoiding any eye contact, even out of the corner of my eye.

I sensed a reluctance in her; she found it difficult to believe I knew her language, but she was forced to acknowledge that I had responded to all her signals.

Join-up is always the most thrilling part of the process. Not because I ever doubt it will happen, but simply because it proves the possibility of communication between human and horse. A flight animal giving her trust to a fight animal, human and horse spanning the gap between them, always strikes me as miraculous. The moment it occurs is always fresh, always satisfying.

The filly took a tentative step toward me. I was not looking at her, but I knew she was weighing her next move, and deciding to join-up with me. Moments later she was standing next to me, her nose at my shoulder. I walked slowly in a circle to the right, then to the left: both times she followed me. Join-up with this filly was complete. "That's what I call join-up," I said to my father.

"How many times has that one been ridden?" my father asked doubtfully.

"Never, Dad."

"Paah."

The chestnut filly waited for what would happen next on this extraordinary day when everything would change for her. As I always try to, I reminded myself that this was possibly the most nerve-racking moment in her whole life. I called to my father, "Now I'm going to investigate the vulnerable areas, to confirm that she trusts me completely."

I walked to the center of the pen, with the filly following me. I dropped the sash line on the ground and stood at her shoulder. "The vulnerable areas are where her predators will attack," I said aloud.

Moving slowly and quietly, I ran my hands over her withers and her neck. "The big cats will jump up here, clawing into the back of a horse, biting into the top of the neck in an attempt to damage the spinal cord, paralyzing the horse or causing it to fall just from their weight.

"If the horse is paralyzed, it's easy for the cat to finish him off. If the horse isn't paralyzed, then the cat will go to the ground with him and slip his teeth around under the neck, in order to collapse the trachea and shut off his air supply. So it's important she lets me into these vulnerable areas."

Next I moved my hands slowly across her flanks and under her belly. "On every continent one type of wild dog or another preys on horses. One in the pack grabs the tail, another hangs off her nose, but the majority head for her soft flanks—another sensitive area."

She stood reasonably firm, sidestepping only once or twice. I continued until I found an absence of rejection and tension in her. Then I picked up each of her hooves, sliding my hand down from the knee or the hock over the tendon and then to the rear of the fetlock joint, before asking her to lift her feet one by one, just holding them off the ground for a second or two.

"You see, she's a flight animal and she's just allowed me to pick up her method of propulsion, her feet. She's trusting me, pretty much from top to toe, now." By this point, we were about twenty minutes into the starting procedure.

Hector Valadez now entered the round pen carrying a saddle, a saddle pad, a bridle, and a long stirrup leather as well as a second driving line. Hector had been sent to me by another trainer in 1969; then eighteen years old and weighing about eighty pounds, he looked as if he might make a jockey.

I put him on his first horse that year and he has been riding eight to twelve horses a day for me ever since, save for several short periods when he worked for friends of mine. As it turned out, he was not motivated to be a jockey: he would be a better father instead for his two sons.

Hector has spent more time with me in the round pen than any other person. While his size kept him useful on the training track, he has probably been the first rider up on about 1,500 horses during the thirty years he has been with me.

Hector positioned the equipment in the middle of the round pen, then left. The arrival of this new person in the round pen—and more alarmingly, a pile of odd-looking equipment—caused the usual consternation in the young filly. She snorted, blew at the saddle, stared hard, wandered around, and generally came to terms with it.

If anything, however, the equipment heightens join-up because the perceived danger makes the horse seek her safety zone: me. This one stood by me as I lifted the saddle onto her back, took the girth under her belly, and buckled it up the other side. "I want her to get used to the saddle for a while," I told my father, "before Hector gets on her."

I stepped back from the filly and squared up to her, driving her away again. She went into flight, cantering with an odd, skewed gait as she coped with the strange new feeling of a saddle on her back. As she cantered, then trotted around the ring, I waited for the same signals— the inside ear settling on me, the licking and chewing. This time I would not expect her to lower her head. She could not trust herself to do that with this new weight on her back. That was too much to ask so early.

"Now I'm going to try a little experiment," I announced. "You'll see she has a sweet spot just there in the ring." I had noticed a particular place where she gave me her full attention. At other points around the circle, she was distracted by something—my father, the pen door, the light above. I knew from long experience that most "babies" (young green horses) have a sweet spot and that it is best to wait until they are in it before trying the more subtle signals of Equus.

"I'm going to hold my hand across the front of my body, and when she reaches her sweet spot I'm going to do nothing more than simply open my fingers. You'll notice her pick up speed considerably."

I held my hand across in front of my chest, and when I opened my fingers she broke into a canter. "See? That's how much she's reading me. She knows she can let a cat walk right past her, but if that cat has its claws open she has to flee, and pretty quickly." I set her going in the opposite direction, allowing her to become familiar with the saddle; and after three or four revolutions, she was asking to come back in to me. I tightened her girth a notch.

"Now for the bridle. Once join-up is achieved, it's pretty much of a formality. The join-up tells me she trusts me. And with horses, that's not too big a step away from her offering to work as hard as she can for me."

She was now wearing her first bridle, standing there unconcerned, chewing at the bit that sat across her mouth for the first time. "Now that the bridle's on, we can long-line her." We were now twenty-five minutes into the procedure. I long-lined the filly in both directions; this marked the first time she had ever walked into the reins and I wanted to get her used to them before Hector got on her back, just to give him something like a steering wheel.

After the long-lining, I backed her up a step. As soon as that backward step was taken, I released the pressure on the long-lines, rewarding her immediately. Then I pulled her girth tighter by a further notch, ready for Hector to ride her. Hector came into the ring and made himself known to her. He too rubbed her vulnerable areas, until she was happy with his presence. He brushed her new saddle lightly with his hands.

Then I lifted him on to her back and he lay across her for several moments, while I turned her head this way and that to make sure she caught sight of him draped over her middle. Carefully, slowly, Hector lifted a leg over her back, and rode her for the first time.

Hector walked her around the ring, not bothering with her mouth or whether she broke into a trot or anything else. The aim was simply to let her take stock of what was happening on her back. I checked my watch. "Half an hour," I called to my father. "About average."

My father went off to quiz Hector, then returned to the viewing deck and his stool. Because my mother had so carefully chosen the day, I had started ten young horses by the time darkness fell. Each time the same process repeated itself, each time Hector was in the saddle and riding them comfortably around the ring within half an hour. No restraints, harsh words or whips.

By the end of that day, my father had seen me start more horses than he could have broken in six weeks. He came down from the viewing deck and we stood outside, hardly able to see each other's faces in the dusk.

"What do you think of that?"

"Keep doing it that way," I heard him say, "and they'll get you."

Up at the house that night, my mother seemed especially anxious to know what he thought. In her mind, much hung on this. It was a question of justice for her son and a truce between the two men she loved equally. She skirted the topic for a while, then finally she asked, "So, Marvin, how'd you enjoy what you saw today?"

"Fine."

My mother pressed. "What do you think of it all?"

My father replied, "It's suicide."

There would be no end in her lifetime (or his, for that matter) to the rift. My mother had hoped that with the passage of time, the changes in circumstances, our common interest in horses might at last help us connect. But the horse remained a towering symbol of the space between father and son.

My mother's intestinal cancer took her away from us soon afterward, and we journeyed to Salinas for her funeral. We arrived at their house, where my father had some years ago built a block of stables and created a few paddocks. Until recently he had given riding lessons and had still been involved with horses. Now, with the death of his wife, he was in a sorry state. He greeted us upon our arrival with the words, "Come on in, your mother'll be back in a while."

Pat and I looked at each other, as if to verify what we had heard him say, and then I walked inside with him. "Dad, she won't be back; she died." He waited a long while and then admitted, "Yeah, I suppose she did." Half an hour later, as we were leaving the house for the funeral service, my father stopped in his tracks and said, "Hold on, we have to wait for Marguerite. She's not back yet."

Again I jolted him back. "Dad, she's waiting for us at the funeral home. This is her funeral."

"Yeah, OK."

By a strange coincidence, the Struve and LaPorte Funeral Home was located four doors down from our old house in Salinas, 347

Church Street. It seemed to me now such a small neighborhood com- pared with what I remembered. The houses had shrunk, the road a thin strip of pavement.

The funeral home was operated by Jim LaPorte. In the 1940s, the whole LaPorte family, including Jim, had been our riding students at the competition grounds. Now this gray-haired man, whom I remem- bered as my young pupil bouncing around on the back of a horse, was greeting us. As we headed inside, my father again wondered about my mother's whereabouts. Jim told us that this often happened when el- derly people long together are suddenly separated.

Only a few people attended my mother's funeral service at the local Catholic church. Her life had been spent entirely in the service of her husband and her children.

Larry and I were concerned about how fast our father was now de- clining and whether he could cope. Any suggestion that he move in with us was firmly rejected. Even his doctor advised against it. My fa- ther, the doctor said, was healthy as a mule, with no desire to move anywhere. The doctor had someone to check on him regularly and to ensure that he was eating well. Larry and I set up a program of regu- lar calls and visits. If I asked my father on the phone how he was, he would say, "Fine. Got that filly going nicely now, you know, and the palomino colt is a good horse."

"Dad, you're not doing anything with those horses."

"I certainly am!"

"Well, OK."

After one visit, Larry called us to say that my father had stopped eating and was fading fast. I agreed to come the following day, but next morning—forty-two days after my mother's death—Larry found him dead.

On a hunch, Jim LaPorte politely called me to say that my father's body was lying in a room at the funeral home. Did I want to see him? Jim ushered me into a small room, clean and bare but for a stand of flowers and a trestle at one end holding the coffin. The only light in the room, a soft glow, was aimed directly on my father.

Jim left me alone and I walked forward to look into the coffin. Larry's words came back to me: "He's shrinking to nothing in front of my eyes." My father seemed only five feet tall, and the flesh had almost disappeared from his bones. I had waited for this moment most of my life. When I was ten, I knew that one day there would be a funeral, and then I could touch him. Only then. I could finally shake his hand.

For most of my life I had longed for the moment when I would stand over my dead father. This was precisely the picture I had had: he in a wooden box, me looking down on him. Through his punishments and beatings, that image had sustained me. Cowering under his blows as a child, I knew that one day he would not be able to hurt me anymore.

It was a cathartic moment, and though I have shed many tears in my life, I did not shed one as I gazed into that coffin. The anger lived on, as if he had thrashed me yesterday, not more than forty years earlier.

He, at least, was relieved of whatever made him like he was. I will not forget the triggers that set him off—when I forgot one of his orders, or defied him. Once he had for many hours tied up a horse's hind leg, and I could bear the horse's pain no longer. I released him, intending to retie the ropes later, but when my father returned home earlier than I expected and saw what I had done, he chased me around the barn and flung me from a haystack. Another bloodied skull, another trip to Dr. Murphy.

I knew the triggers that led to violence. I, too, have felt that anger rise in me, felt the urge to strike out at someone in my family. But I put my grip on that anger. I swore that this man in the box would be the last link in the chain of violence and anger aimed as much at humans as at horses.

What stopped me, what still stops me, was the man my father killed. At that moment in the Golden Dragon saloon, I had sworn I would not be cast in my father's image. My father's death put a final seal on that pact with myself.

———

After leaving the funeral home, I was moved to drive to Chinatown and find the bar where all those years ago I had watched my father's cruel arrest of the black man. It was still a downtrodden area and now there were drug addicts lying around as well, which was not the case in 1943.

The Golden Dragon was not where it should have been. As I searched, a police car swung by and parked right behind me. My Lincoln looked out of place in this area. The officer carefully approached the passenger-side window carefully, and I lowered it so he could speak.

"You're lost, right?"

"No, I'm not lost. I'm back here to visit. It's more than forty years since I last sat in this spot." Because I had not immediately asked for his help in navigating my way out of this dangerous neighborhood, he perhaps suspected I had come to buy drugs and his manner became more guarded.

"Oh yeah?"

I went on, "There used to be a saloon here called the Golden Dragon. You know what happened to it?"

"It was torn down a year ago maybe."

"My father made an arrest in there forty years ago. It was a bad night. I came by just to remember it."

The officer brightened. "Your father was a policeman?"

"For twelve years, as it turned out. He retired from the force quite a few years ago now, though."

"What was his name?"

"Marvin Roberts."

"Oh yeah. There's a big funeral for him tomorrow. A lot of officers are going to that."

He was right. At my father's service the following day, an enormous contingent of Salinas policemen added to an already packed church. At my mother's funeral only six weeks earlier, the church had been virtually empty.

———

One day a ghost called me on the phone.

"It's Lyman Fowler here."

I could do no more than echo his own name back to him, but with an exclamation mark at the end of it. "I wonder if you remember, but I used to teach you in high school?"

"Of course I do."

"You might also remember, I had you do a paper?"

"I remember it distinctly."

"I'm retired now as you can imagine. But I have a favor to ask of you. I'm the social director of my church group and every year we try to go somewhere pretty. Somewhere civilized. No muggings or any of that, because we're quite a geriatric group as you might expect."

"What can I do for you?"

"I thought it might be possible to bring them out to have a look at your place. We wouldn't be any trouble; we'd only take up an hour or two of your time, but we've read about you in the papers, of course, and it occurred to me that it might be possible."

After agreeing on a time for the tour, I put the phone down and shook my head in disbelief. I remembered Mr. Fowler all right, and that "life's ambition" project with the big red F written across it. He was coming to visit the establishment that bore quite a resemblance to the plans I had submitted in that paper, plans he had initially rejected as impossibly extravagant.

On that perfect summer's day when the bus arrived at Flag Is Up Farms, Mr. Fowler—he would always be *Mr.* Fowler to me—was the first to step out. Despite his age, he did not stoop. He was still very tall, still smartly dressed, and with the same olive complexion and prominent eyes that I remembered. His hair had turned completely white, and his face was lined; otherwise, it was the same man.

He offered me a long, graceful hand and spoke in his precise way. "Monty, hello." Then he kept coming and gave me a heartfelt embrace—which seemed unlike him. People were filing off the bus and now stood in a semicircle; fifty seniors looking expectantly at me.

Lyman Fowler made his introductory speech. "Ladies and gentlemen, this is Monty Roberts, whom I've told you about, and he's kindly offered to show us his establishment, Flag Is Up Farms." Given the advanced years of many of these people, much of the tour had to be conducted from the bus. Like a proper tour guide, I used the bus's microphone to explain the sights as we drove around.

My guests had all lived in agricultural communities, so were genuinely interested in the planning of the farm. I had arranged for some horses to be on the training track; parked alongside, we could watch the Thoroughbreds breeze by. Lastly, we drove up the slope to the house, where everyone came inside to look around. Out on the terrace, refreshments in hand, they could see the whole farm spread out below.

Mr. Fowler then gave a speech I will always remember. We stood side by side as he began, "As you all know, I taught Monty when he was a young man. However, he taught me something, and it's possibly the most valuable lesson I ever learned."

He paused, then articulated a notion—almost word for word—that my mother had voiced to me almost four decades ago and that I had written down in a brave little note appended to the paper I returned to him. "A teacher does not have the right to put a cap on the aspirations of his students, no matter how unreal those aspirations might seem." He held out his long arm, indicating the buildings and paddocks below us. "There was a time when I told Monty that this was unattainable. Now we've all had a good look around, and seen how he proved me wrong."

Lyman Fowler clearly enjoyed telling this story, and I felt a great warmth toward him.

━━━ 🐎 ━━━

CHAPTER 6

Deer Friends

One cloudy day in November 1977, I was riding Johnny Tivio around the farm as I often did to check on pastures, fences, and horses. I would ride over the farm itself and then up a hill north of the property. From that vantage I could see much of the valley.

I was on one of those high trails in a canyon when I noticed activity on the face of the hill. A group of coyotes was frantically darting in and out of the brush. When I got closer, I saw that they had a deer down and were in a feeding frenzy, ripping at her hide with their sharp incisors. I ran at them with Johnny Tivio and used a rope I happened to have on the saddle to drive them off.

The coyotes ran to a higher position on the hill before turning to look back. I chased them further still before returning to have a look at the deer. She was an old doe, thin and toothless, and probably only half her normal body weight. She had severe lacerations from the coyotes' attack. Scouting around for offspring, I spotted two half-grown fawns, obviously hers. I hoped they would fare all right; they were old enough to survive once they found their way back to the herd.

The task now was to save the life of this old doe. I cantered down the hill to the shop area where I got my pickup truck, woven fencing, and steel posts.

With several farm-hands, I drove as close as I could to the doe. The coyotes, meanwhile, had inched back down the hill toward her. I started up the hill yelling at them, rope in hand and slapping my leg to divert their attention from the doe while the farmhands unloaded the fencing and posts.

Eventually, the three of us built a coyote-proof cage over the doe about fifteen feet in diameter and closed at the top. I put some grain and alfalfa hay in there and a bucket of water. As we worked around her, the weak doe struggled vainly to rise. I was certain that she would be dead the next day, but I had to give her a chance.

When I arrived the following morning, she was up on her keel and had eaten and taken some water. This itself was amazing; wild deer rarely allow themselves to eat or drink in captivity. I disturbed her as little as possible, and for the next four or five days I returned only long enough to ensure she had food and water.

By the fifth day she was standing and taking a few steps around her enclosure. Fortunately, she lacked enough strength to run at the fencing and bash into it as a healthy wild deer would. Before she recovered and began doing just that, I decided the best course of action was to try to accustom her to my presence so she would not panic at the sight of me.

I started by entering the cage, bending over, and working gently with her, making the same subtle and nonthreatening movements I used in starting horses. Amazingly, I was to find that the two languages are almost identical. Saving the doe launched me on an adventure that has spanned nearly twenty years. It has been one of the most gratifying experiences of my life.

———

Grandma, as I called her, was only two or three weeks in the cage before she was strong enough to take a chance on going outside. When I opened the cage, she walked off in that stately fashion that deer have, but you could tell she had no desire to put much distance between herself and me.

Next morning, I found her a hundred yards or so away from the cage. I put more grain and alfalfa inside and fashioned a watering device. Each day I worked with her, using the concepts of Advance and Retreat. Whenever she acted as though she preferred not to be with me, I would deliberately push her away and walk behind her for up to three miles. When I saw her circling and showing me her flanks, thinking about renegotiating with me, I would turn and walk away in the opposite direction.

I was squaring up, looking her in the eye, driving her away, then dropping off and turning from her, just as I did with horses. I could coax her back toward me. But join-up with Grandma seemed more tentative, not as solid. In fact, it would be several years before I could entice her from the herd and have her stand as close to me as I was accustomed to with horses.

Finally, one day, it happened. I had been pressing her away from me for some time, watching for the signals that said she was seeking relief from this disciplinary action. She showed me her flanks, locked an ear onto me; she mouthed at me, a silent whisper that she was a herbivore and wanted to try trusting me. Then she dropped her head and walked along like that, with her mouth inches above the rough terrain.

I backed off, turned at an angle and no longer looked her in the eye. We were in a beautiful spot on a promontory overlooking the farm, so I lay on the ground and turned my face to the sun. I watched as Grandma came closer and closer. I realized my dream of join-up with a deer. She trusted me. The warm sun seemed to bless that moment: the deer chewing her cud, the man with the grin, the eagle overhead catching the updrafts from the valley floor.

I learned a great deal from Grandma. I discovered that the flight mechanism of a deer is many times more sensitive than that of a horse. When I made a mistake in one of my movements, I would pay, sometimes for weeks or even months. This hypersensitive flight mechanism taught me subtle lessons that proved invaluable as I continued to refine my understanding of Equus, the language of the horse.

Consider this example. On one occasion, I was encouraging Grandma to come to me: I had my shoulders at a forty-five degree angle to her, looking away. However, I wanted to see what she was doing, so I glanced at her out of the corner of my eye too quickly. Grandma saw that I had broken the rules, and she walked 500 yards away and would not let me close to her for three days.

I realized I had been making the same mistake with horses; I quite often glanced quickly at them out of the corner of my eye when I was not meant to. In the round pen, I started working with a horse, experimenting with the speed with which I moved my eyes. I also tried different ways of reading the image of the horse out of the corner of my eye without actually looking at the horse.

By moving my eyes more slowly, I found I could temper the flight impulse. As soon as I understood that, Grandma was much easier to work with. I also found that spreading my fingers, moving my arms or going too quickly from retreat to advance all set her off, slowing the process of communication.

Again, I experimented with the horses I was starting. When I held out my arms as part of squaring to send the horse away, open fingers set the horse going quicker and faster. To the horse, the opening fingers were like a cat opening its claws, a clear sign of aggression.

Without Grandma's help, I would never have learned this more refined aspect of the language. It was as though this frail old lady was giving me advanced lessons in Equus; she was fine-tuning my responses and taking my qualification to a higher degree. Perhaps it was to repay me for saving her life back in the canyon. When Grandma died of natural causes on December 2, 1995, we buried her on the hill near the house.

While I worked with Grandma, I was thinking how fruitful it would be to start with a young deer, one with a malleable mind and not yet traumatized by life. I wanted to see if such a deer would respond faster than Grandma, who carried her life's baggage with her.

There were not many deer to be seen when I came to the farm in 1966. By the time I encountered Grandma, I had lived on the farm for eleven years, and throughout that time I never saw more than three or four deer in a group. But during the first four or five years I worked with Grandma, the number of deer making their home on the farm increased markedly.

I picked out a young male and began to work with him. Later on I called him Yoplait, from the brand of yogurt he enjoyed. He was a better student than Grandma; but then, by this time, so was I. Within six months, his behavior had changed significantly. I could draw him from the other deer, give him a rub around the neck and head, and stroke him. He always seemed a rather indifferent character, and I assumed that in general deer were like that. I later came to understand that they all have different personalities.

Yoplait would ignore me for long periods of time, staring in the other direction. I assumed I was making mistakes, and no doubt I was, to some degree.

Ours was not always a perfect relationship, but it did endure for twelve years. During his life, Yoplait came to believe that Flag Is Up Farms was his property. He would often go to the highest point north of the farm and lie there regally, as if surveying it. He would become aggressive with people and other animals who he thought were intruders. When strangers came, he would jealously position himself between them and me, brushing them away. Yoplait's indifference was unique to him; his possessiveness, however, is a trait I now know to be pervasive in his species. My employees told me that when I left the farm he became uneasy; he would look for me, and at night he would lie outside my bedroom.

Later, I tried an experiment. On the day of my departure, I put one of my worn undershirts near a tree. Instructed to watch for his reactions, staff later reported that he would lie near the undershirt for inordinate periods until I returned.

Later still, I put undershirts in plastic bags and tied them in knots to hold my scent, leaving them with my employees to set near a tree and change every three or four days. I was conditioning Yoplait to think that I was still there. This seemed to work. Without the undershirts he would get restless, often leaving the farm. When I was away for extended periods, Yoplait would walk into nearby Solvang, which posed a danger to him and created a minor brouhaha in the town.

It remains a part of my routine to organize some dirty undershirts for the deer. On extended trips, I mail used clothing back to the ranch, to keep my deer friends happy.

During his formative years, Yoplait took a dislike to both Pat and her dog, Jay. He regarded them as competition and made this much abundantly clear: the dog was to stay in the house, and Pat was to stay away from me, at least while he was around. Yoplait had the dog, a Queensland Heeler, completely intimidated. At the slightest provocation, the deer would lower his head and drive the dog back into the house.

Once, when I was away for an extended period, Pat decided to plant some flowers in the back garden. By now the deer had increased to sixty or seventy in the family group; several of them spent most of their lives close to the house, and there were only a few plants they would not eat.

Pat, however, had discovered that the deer declined blue flowers. Working on hands and knees, outside the kitchen and laundry room, Pat was planting blue flowers when she discovered that Yoplait was coming along behind her, uprooting each plant and dropping it un-eaten. Pat picked up a broom and waved it at him, driving him off the hill and down toward the farm.

But Yoplait was not finished. Pat warmed up her Jaguar, opening the garage door to let the exhaust fumes escape. She then went into the house to get some things to take to the office and returned to find Yoplait in the garage and on top of the car. Pat had only recently bought the car and was proud of it, naturally. Yoplait had danced on the trunk and hood and used his antlers to rake the sides. The whole car had to be repainted.

I am sure the following is *just* coincidence, but Yoplait had also knocked down a photograph of Pat and Jay that hung on the garage wall. The garage is a kind of gallery, with some fifty photographs hanging there. Yoplait had seemingly chosen his target carefully, if not vengefully, and the glass in the frame was shattered. Crowning the photo now was a neat little pile of deer dung. There was no need to probe the pile for yogurt traces. The culprit was abundantly clear.

Pat telephoned me that evening and recounted all this, and just before she broke off she said that for dinner she might be having... venison.

Yoplait's gypsy ways would cost him. One time he crossed the highway in front of the farm and got hit by a car. He broke his right hip, and his right hind leg swung like a flag in the breeze. I found him on the front lawn of the house, as though begging for help. With assistance, I lifted him into the bed of my pickup truck, then took him to one of the stables and put him in a box stall. If I could put the leg in a cast, perhaps I could save his life. The vet tried, but Yoplait would abide no one other than me working on him. Because of his resistance, the cast would have done more harm than good.

With no other choice, I continued alone. He settled enough to lie on a very deep bed of straw with his broken leg propped in place. I put grain, hay, and water within reach. He lay there for two weeks before I finally saw him stand, and I noticed that the leg had started to mend and was fairly rigid.

He put no weight on it for another two or three weeks, and it healed. Ultimately Yoplait walked without even a noticeable limp. The healing properties of deer are astonishing; many times Yoplait and other deer have overcome injuries that would have been fatal to any horse.

Another time, Yoplait broke his jaw in many places and had several teeth knocked out in another altercation with a car. That time, I had to feed him hot gruel to keep him alive. His jaw healed, and while he had a funny smile on his face thereafter, he was able to live comfortably and eat normally. Yoplait finally succumbed to a third highway accident.

By then, I had begun to work on another male deer, Bambo. He was a dramatic success and joined up strongly. He is so tame now that I can run at him, slapping my thighs, and all he does is ignore me and come closer. Now twelve years of age, he has displayed the same jealousy I saw in Yoplait and other deer I have worked with, but to a lesser degree.

More kindly disposed than Yoplait and less inclined to take offense with strangers, he is still possessive. He frequents our house and is diligent about greeting me in the morning and coming around at dinnertime when he knows I am home. Were I to walk, say, five miles up into the hills, I could literally take Bambo with me and bring him back to the house again, controlling his movements by using communication skills.

It was only in 1990 that I started to work with a young female we call Patricia. Like Yoplait in character, she is distant and cold and will ignore me for long periods of time. She is also virtually expressionless in her communication. But unlike Yoplait, she is in no way surly. She bears no ill will to anyone; strangers are simply ignored. Patricia is by far my greatest challenge: she tests my ability to communicate each time I work with her.

Some years later, I took on another female called Feline (pronounced Fa-*lean*). She is one of the sweetest, kindest, most attentive deer I have come across. She never ignores me, and her responses are dramatic. When I ask her to go away, she expresses great displeasure at this horrid discipline. She shakes her head and will actually balk, round her back, and jump up in front. A horse who roots his nose out in a circle is making a very different motion but saying precisely the same thing: "I don't want to go away. I didn't mean that. I'm sorry for what I did." When you invite her back, you can almost see her smile. She returns fast, full of reaction.

One morning I noticed that Feline's muzzle and the bridge of her nose were swollen to almost double their normal size, the result, perhaps, of an insect bite. Almost all the deer I have chosen as subjects have come to the house quickly when injured and presented themselves on the lawn, as if to say, "I need your help and attention."

Feline's swelling subsided in a few days. She has been a joy to work with; her responses are keen and more sensitive than any horse I have dealt with. It is hard to compare animals, but the intelligence of horses and deer seems on a par. Both share a highly developed flight mechanism. But if you were to release horses and deer and mountain lions in Santa Barbara County—devoid of human interference—I think the horses would be wiped out before the deer. We have too long underestimated the intelligence and acuity of deer.

As commonly happens, a doe on the farm once gave birth to twins, one male and one female. She then proceeded to walk away from them and not return. I saw the twins several times on the hill 300 yards from the house. The first time they were still wet, newborn, and unable to stand. Four hours later, the doe was still nowhere to be found. And though up and walking around a bit, the twins were still weak and hungry.

Around sunset that day, the twins had moved down the hill and were starting to bump into one another looking for a way to nurse. Still no mother. If I were to touch the newborns, the mother might permanently reject them. And none of the deer I had joined up with were domesticated—they were wild when I started working with them, and remained able to function in the wild. I was concerned that these little ones would "imprint" on us as parents, and would lose their ability to live as deer in the wild. I decided to let them go, hoping that the doe would return and suckle them during the night. The following morning, they looked pretty sad. Though loath to intervene, I finally did take action.

I gave them each three ounces of goat's milk. A farm goat had just given birth, so I got the first milk and the colostrum that comes with it. Then I left the twin fawns where they were. By sundown the next day the mother still had not returned, so we took out adoption papers. We brought the two babies to the breeding barn and started to feed them with the goat's milk at four-hour intervals for about three days. A Thoroughbred breeding farm makes this easy; our night foaling attendant is trained for this kind of work. Then I brought in a female goat who was fresh with milk and fostered them onto her, and they began nursing.

Cyrus and Reba, as we called them, were successfully established into the wild at about three months of age. A joy to have about, they spend most of their time a few hundred yards from the house, and are acutely responsive to the communication process. Both are extremely friendly with the people around us as well as with strangers. I can take them with me as I wander the ranch or leave them at home at will. They will eat out of my hand and, if I am not careful, follow me through the door into the house.

I have learned a great deal from my communication with the deer, but it is important to keep in mind that, in one sense, these deer I have chosen to work with have received no great favors from me. Living in the wild is a challenge for them once they lose their full desire to flee from danger. Because I have assumed responsibility for their protection, I have also learned to keep things as natural as I can, except for the communication work.

When I speak with equestrian groups around the world and mention working with deer in the wild, the response is usually disbelief: The deer will run away, there is no way to communicate with them. Yes, the deer will flee, but if you follow and then read the curve they make, you will see that they often circle around to stay within a given area. They do not continue on.

If I create in my mind's eye a round pen several miles in diameter, and if I think about the deer as horses in a round pen, I do, in fact, communicate with them effectively. It has worked for me virtually without fail. I have to be twice as tenacious and twice as delicate in my responses with deer as I do with horses, but it does work.

Working with deer is a time-consuming activity, which few people have the inclination to pursue. If I have been silly enough to accumulate this knowledge, others can learn from me and avoid having to walk about on a hillside for weeks at a time.

I like to think of myself as multilingual: I speak English (quite well actually), desperately poor Spanish, a better than passable Horse, and I can get along quite nicely in Deer.

CHAPTER 7

The Invitation That Changed My Life

One December evening in 1988, when I was fifty-three years old, my longtime friend and neighbor, John Bowles, called me. "Monty," he said in his unmistakable southern accent, "guess what? The Queen of England wants to meet you." Her Majesty, he said, was intrigued by my claims of being able to communicate with horses.

John Bowles is not above playing a practical joke or two. I asked why he, plain John Bowles, was carrying royal messages.

He replied that an English friend of his, a certain Sir John Miller, the Queen's former equerry—her horse manager—had instructed him to locate me. Her Majesty had noticed articles in *The Blood Horse* and *Florida Horse* (she is an avid reader of these and many other equestrian magazines) about demonstrations I had given.

Not long afterward, Sir John Miller came to the farm for a demonstration and was excited by what he saw. On the way back to the house, he listed particular dates during the following year—Her Majesty's itinerary. It began to sink in that he was fitting me into the royal schedule. Some weeks later, I received a formal letter of invitation from Buckingham Palace: in April 1989 I was to spend a week at Windsor Castle.

"I wonder," Sir John had asked me in his upper-class accent, giving every syllable its due, "if a demonstration such as I've just seen could be accomplished for Her Majesty in the mews?"

I had no idea what a mews was, but I nevertheless assured him that we could make it work somehow. If the Queen was convinced that my work was worthwhile, said Sir John, she would arrange for me to tour several British towns and cities. Most important, she would want Newmarket (home of the largest racing community in Britain) and Gleneagles (site of a large equestrian center) to be part of that itinerary.

After the better part of a lifetime concealing from the world what I knew about horses, the interest of the Queen offered the prospect of a door opening wide. If I could prove to Her Majesty's satisfaction that my work was credible and important, I could bring my methods to the broadest possible audience.

On April 5, 1989, I was met at Heathrow Airport by Sir John. We drove directly to Windsor Castle, a distance of only ten or fifteen miles. Parked there were vehicles that looked more like Sherman tanks than passenger cars. I was told the Queen was having lunch with Russian president Mikhail Gorbachev and his wife, Raisa, and they had shipped in their own cars for the occasion.

The interior of the castle was a revelation. Behind these doorways and in these corridors, great affairs of state had been conducted for hundreds of years. The royal family had owned racehorses for hundreds more years than my own country had existed. Walking past tapestries and huge paintings, I had the feeling that a country boy from California was going as far up in the world as it was possible to go.

Sir John took me down to a meadow in front of the castle, where he showed me fifteen horses of all colors, shapes and sizes. In a separate paddock was a Thoroughbred filly, making a total of sixteen horses, none of which had been ridden. All green and raw but halter-broken, these were the horses I would communicate with during my week-long series of demonstrations here.

Then Sir John took me to the stable area on one side of the castle. This, I understood at last, was the mews. Next we toured the indoor riding school. It had the look of a chapel, with Gothic-style windows and a high, vaulted ceiling. At one end, fronted with glass and wood, was a balcony—a soundproof viewing stand for the royal family. In the center of the riding school was a fifty-foot wire-mesh round pen that Sir John and I had arranged to be delivered and set up.

I had never demonstrated my techniques in such a pen before, and I was unsure how the horses would react. They would be able to see through the wire to the outside, which would reduce their focus on me. There was, however, no other option.

The Queen had apparently invited up to 200 people to watch me during the coming week. She herself would spend only an hour with me on the Monday morning—prior commitments would allow no more time than that—but she would probably watch the days' events on video in the evenings.

After our tour, Sir John and I walked back to Windsor Castle. The Gorbachevs were set to leave. It was an eerie feeling watching the Russian guards mingling with British security officers, men carrying machine guns around the ramparts of the castle. Some small upset occurred between the two factions and, as I watched, a senior British officer—clearly a master grudge holder—turned away muttering loudly, "By God, we stopped them in the Crimea and we'll stop them at Windsor Castle."

At nine o'clock the next morning, we were back at the castle so I could introduce the horses to the round pen. Experience has taught me that my demonstrations work more effectively when the horse is not overly distracted by his surroundings. When I arrived, I immediately sensed a cold feeling from the grooms; the head groom, in particular, seemed to think I was treading on his toes.

I had asked several times for assistance in shepherding these horses, one at time, into the pen. While I tried to muster aid, a lady dressed in impeccable riding clothes walked through the riding hall and started talking to Sir John. She was an erect, obviously self-assured woman with a commanding walk and demeanor. His transformation was remarkable: suddenly his stance, even the tone of his voice, changed.

He was talking with the Queen of England.

For some days I had pondered the proper salutation to use, should I meet her. And should I bow, or was a handshake the order of the day?

Now she was coming toward me. Far from home, the guest of a foreign nation, I wanted to do the right thing. But the Queen made it easy for me by offering her hand. I shook it and said, "Your Majesty," and let it go at that. She was quick to put me at my ease. "Come, Mr. Roberts," she said, "and show me this lions' cage in the center of the riding hall. I want you to tell me about it."

Together we walked into the riding hall and looked at the wire-mesh round pen. "It appears," she said, "to be the sort of thing you should enter with a whip and a chair." I agreed with her, although the similarity only then occurred to me, and I worried that it would strike the horses as equally forbidding. I gave her a summary of what I intended to do the following morning. I was pleased that she wanted to know as much as possible beforehand. Then she was gone.

I hoped I had at least made a good start. The relationship between us was now relatively informal, and I had the impression of a straightforward woman who was making happen what she wanted to happen.

At midday on the Sunday, reinforcements arrived: Pat, my son, Marty, and my rider Sean McCarthy, came directly to Windsor Castle. Working with me in the round pen for nine years, Sean has been that first rider for more than 1,400 horses. Now, he and I went over our equipment in the round pen; then I showed him the horses in the field. He was surprised at the diverse range of animals. Standing in the separate paddock were two or three mostly Thoroughbred horses; the one filly was a registered Thoroughbred. There were two large Shire Piebalds who would go on to be drum horses in the ceremonial division of the royal stables, a few warm-blood crosses, a few other large horses, and some smaller types right down to the Fell and Haflinger ponies. I was reasonably confident that none would kill me.

Our preparation done, we spent the evening at Sir John's home, Shotover House, near Oxford, which has been in his family for more than a century. Together with Major Dick Hearn—who was Her Majesty's racehorse trainer for many years—and his wife, Sheila, we enjoyed a fine dinner that evening that went a long way toward steadying my nerves for the following day. The next morning, at nine o'clock, we were due to meet the Queen, Prince Philip, and Queen Elizabeth, the Queen Mother, at the riding hall.

Once they arrived, the event took on official, even ceremonial, overtones. The woman in riding clothes was now the Queen of England attending an engagement. She and her party were surrounded by security personnel and subject to rules of protocol. Sir John Miller introduced us as though she and I had not spoken the day before, and he again pointed to the glassed-in viewing gallery from which the royal party would view the demonstration, as if no discussion of all of this had taken place. The event began to take on a life of its own.

I was, I admit, nervous. As a rule I am a relaxed person; my work requires it. How disconcerting, then, to feel my pulse rate soar and my concentration falter. The royal family, accompanied by Pat and Marty, moved to the gallery and took their seats.

I was charged first of all with "breaking in" the young Thoroughbred filly—owned by the Queen Mother herself, who would be watching intently. As I entered the round pen, it occurred to me that unless I relaxed I would not be able to communicate with the horse as I normally do. The filly would then not be receptive and this could become the most embarrassing and humiliating day of my life. As I closed the gate, a sense of terror engulfed me.

The filly—adolescent, skittish, and wide-eyed with fear—was brought in by her handler and released. I recognized a raw young creature more frightened than I was and needing my comfort and assistance. The instant I saw this, my nerves settled and I got down to work.

In minutes, I could feel things come right. The filly gave me the signals I was looking for and behaved exactly as I would have predicted. She was following me around the ring within seven minutes. In her predicament, she trusted me. I was her comfort.

Within fifteen minutes, this high-strung Thoroughbred stood steady as a rock while I fixed her first saddle on her. After just twenty-five minutes, she quietly accepted the bridle and snaffle bit, and Sean was on her back riding around the ring. It was as if she had been looking forward to this all her life. Finally, Sean dismounted and she was led away.

As I left the round pen, the Queen, Prince Philip, and the Queen Mother rose from their seats to come down and join me. The Queen was the first to emerge from the door of the viewing gallery. With a smile on her face, she put out her hand to shake mine and said, "That was beautiful." She told me she was amazed how the filly had responded, that I should feel proud of the work I was doing.

How long I had waited to hear someone say just that. For most of my life, my ideas on schooling horses had been scorned and rejected, my work done in virtual seclusion because no one was ready to see it. To have no less a person than the Queen of England, a woman who knows and cares for horses and is herself a leading expert on horses, praise my work in such warm and genuine language marked a profound and deeply satisfying turnaround, and I cherish it to this day.

Shortly afterward, Prince Philip shook hands and asked me if I could work with the young men who were "breaking in" some of his Fell ponies that week. I was delighted by these responses to my demonstration, but I confess I was waiting especially for a reaction from the filly's owner, the Queen Mother. Then she too appeared, and I was bowled over by the warmest appreciation I could have hoped for. With tears in her eyes, she quietly and firmly said, "That was one of the most wonderful things I've ever seen in my life." She was visibly moved by what she had seen her filly do, and by witnessing what communication is possible between human and horse.

Seeing her emotional reaction, I was caught up in the moment and I forgot who she was and where we were. It felt right to put my arms out and give her a gentle hug. The security guards stiffened with surprise and stepped forward. It hit me that no one was supposed to touch the royal family in this intimate way: I dropped my arms and stepped back a full stride.

However, the Queen Mother did not seem in the least offended. Still talking in a soft voice, she told me she hoped I would continue my work and bring about a different, more humane relationship between humans and horses. I think back on her reaction as being the one that would satisfy me for the rest of my life.

Imagine the impact of all this. It was as though I was finally allowed out into the daylight, blinking a bit in the fierce glare of publicity, but with my work recognized as valid and genuine. The Queen, one of the most important figures in the horse world, would actively promote public demonstrations of my work. But if I needed the royal seal of approval, so did some other doubting Thomases still need convincing.

After the first demonstration, we went with Sir John and twelve others, most of them journalists, to the Savile Gardens Restaurant in Windsor Park. During lunch, Sir John changed positions several times in order to have conversations on his radio phone. On the way back to the castle to continue our demonstrations, he mentioned to me that the stable staff were making an unscheduled stop to pick up two new horses.

Much later, I would learn that some members of the Queen's staff had suggested to her that I had done something underhanded with the horses as I took them through the ring to acclimatize them. In short, they suspected skulduggery. The Queen had not agreed with their judgment. What, she asked them, would convince them? They had suggested a stiffer test, one they doubted I would pass. A truck would be sent over to Hampton Court to pick up two large, three-year-old piebald stallions that were very raw and had barely been handled.

Sir John wanted me to start these horses without acclimatizing them to the ring. Because my working methods were new to him, it did not strike him as much of a request. It meant that the horses, however, faced a double and coincidental threat: the most traumatic experience of their lives to that point in a frightening new environment.

This new plan concerned me; there was enough pressure on the event, and on the horses, already. Back at the Windsor mews, a small van was parked with the two piebald stallions shoehorned into it. They were sweating and banging around. When the first was taken off, the other screamed fiercely and the first one called loudly back. They had been kept together in a field at Hampton Court, and were obviously deeply attached.

Meanwhile, a hundred guests had come to see the demonstration that afternoon. The stable staff were lined up against the wall, some of them smiling, there to watch me fail and my work be judged as fraudulent. Sir John took the microphone and stepped into the round pen to introduce me. The huge colt came charging toward him and slapped his big front feet on the ground, displaying his anger. Sir John stepped quickly back outside the gate and made the introduction from there. One could hardly blame him.

I was not happy about these new circumstances, which were both unfair and dangerous. The aggressive colt was still distracted by the other horse calling him from just outside the building. Suddenly, everyone stood up; the Queen had walked in. She was not scheduled to be here, but she obviously wanted to see the outcome of this new test. From an area behind the seats, she gestured to everyone that they might sit down. Sir John continued with his introduction and explained what they were about to see.

I stepped through the gate into the round pen, picked up my line and began. The colt circled me, acting with an all-male arrogance. I pressed him a touch harder to go away, and he did just that. As he left me and went to work, cantering a good circle against the fence, he forgot about his partner outside and tuned in to my presence and what I was doing. He was working hard for me. After three or four circles of the round pen, I was getting a good response from him and my voice rose a few decibels in volume.

"I'm looking to have the same conversation with him as I'm having with you. And I can assure you, he will talk to me. Watch out for the inside ear. The licking and chewing. The head down, skating a couple of inches above the ground. Great! There he goes. . . ."

I wanted to drive it home—to the stable crew especially—that this was a legitimate process, that this horse was communicating with me. Indeed, I felt a good deal more comfortable conversing with this horse than I did with the skeptics in the royal stable. This unruly colt, after all, believed me within two minutes and trusted me after seven.

Sean rode him without difficulty and well before the thirty-minute mark. It was a perfect demonstration, and the Queen's reaction was one of pleasure and satisfaction. Her confidence in my work had been well-founded. As I waited for the big colt's companion, the stable hands started to filter back to their work areas. I politely asked them to come back and watch me start both horses from Hampton Court, not just one.

They returned to their old positions against the wall, but perhaps with slightly more open minds now. I started the second horse, and the demonstration went equally smoothly. For the rest of the week, I continued with demonstrations before different audiences. The doubt I had originally encountered was either gone, or had at least dissipated.

The Queen and others, most of them involved with royal horses, continued to ask guests to come to see what I could do. Each day brought audiences of 200 people. On the Tuesday morning, the Queen again arrived unexpectedly to watch the horses work. She returned on Tuesday afternoon, Wednesday morning, Wednesday afternoon, all day Thursday and Friday morning. It was an exhilarating feeling to have won her commitment to the extent that she changed her itinerary.

We share a genuine fascination with horses and it was a great pleasure to talk with her about them. As her support continued, my respect and feelings of warmth for her grew steadily.

At one point, my neighbor John Bowles arrived from California. When he entered the stable area, I was speaking with the Queen. John walked up behind her, off to one side and stuck his hand out with a big smile, ready to greet me. When he realized I was conversing with the Queen, a look of consternation fell across his face.

I had spent so much time with so many Sir Johns and Lady Annes by this point that when along came plain John Bowles, a good old boy from the deep South if ever there was one, I shook his hand and confidently said, "Your Majesty, this is Sir John Bowles." I had bestowed instant knighthood on an old friend for services rendered.

That week we started sixteen of the Queen's horses, four ponies for Prince Philip, the Queen Mother's filly and one show-jumping prospect owned by a friend of the Queen's—a total of twenty-two horses during the five days.

In addition, we decided to ride the Queen Mother's Thoroughbred filly each day and bring her on a bit, so that before we left the Queen Mother could watch her ridden in the open parkland surrounding Windsor Castle. There was the risk of embarrassment because a young horse going outside for the first time can do silly things, no matter how well started. I would take the risk.

That Friday in mid-April 1989 must be written in the record books as one of the most glorious, sunny days that England ever experienced. Only occasionally did billowy white clouds sail across those brilliant skies. Windsor, and England, looked as beautiful and civilized as only England can.

The Queen Mother was chauffeured in, and I stepped to an area near the car to greet her. Before the car had even stopped rolling, she opened the rear door with a big smile on her face and greeted me as though she had known me all her life. She gave her filly a rub on the nose and spoke with Sean, then greeted head groom Roger Oliver, Sir John and Pat.

With Roger leading on an experienced horse, Sean followed into the magnificent gardens on the filly and elegantly put her through her paces. On that day, in that setting, man and horse together seemed a thing of rare beauty, a scene that might have been taken straight from a fairy tale.

The Queen herself had an important engagement but she had asked to be informed when the filly was ridden in case she could slip away to see her. As we walked back up the hill toward the castle, we saw the Queen coming out of her apartments, dressed for her engagement. She greeted us with a warm smile and was generous in her praise of the filly on her first outdoor ride. Thanking me for spending the week at Windsor Castle, she went on to outline the plans she had for the countrywide tour on which I was due to embark. This day, this week, had been among the most rewarding in my life. The pressure had vanished, and our visit had been a success. For myself, my family, and for Sean, it had been a storybook week.

That afternoon, we went back to Shotover House to stay the night. Sean was looking forward to seeing Sir John's butler again, a man who went by the name of Horseman. Sir John called Horseman's wife, who also worked at Shotover House, Horsewoman. If Shotover House— that gracious, square-built manor—was as I expected, so was the English butler who came with it.

Horseman was probably no more than sixty, but he looked eighty-five. Stooped and gray, he had a sad, droopy face with big watery eyes. He was dressed properly, but his collars and cuffs had seen a lot of wear. His method was to move quickly, wobbling on his feet as if his joints were suspect. With each step he mumbled, and occasionally the mumbles got louder and took on a strangled quality. At first, I worried that he was about to die; then he would revert to his regular mumbling as if nothing had happened. He neither explained these outbursts nor sought any response.

When I arrived at the manor house, he trotted as fast as he could across the gravel and attempted to lift up my heavy suitcase, muttering away, "Oh-oh-oh-oh, I'll get that." It seemed unfair to ask him to carry anything, but he would not hear otherwise. While Horseman's arms were being pulled out of their sockets, Sir John introduced him: "Ah, this is my butler Horseman; he'll show you to your room. The Canopy Room, Horseman."

The shallow stone steps into the house were trouble enough, but now we faced several flights of stairs as well. Horseman soldiered on. Several times he had to stop and rest, clutching his chest and muttering. He settled me into my room and showed me the bathroom, made four more trips to fetch towels, and returned yet again with a pitcher of water and a glass. I feared each trip might be his last.

During dinner we saw his wife. Like Horseman but less disheveled, Horsewoman was apparently in charge of the kitchen; she helped him bring out the food and lay it on the sideboard.

When Sean arrived later in the week he came straight to me with disbelief written all over his face. "Did you see that butler guy?" He was entranced by this unique figure. Sean's room was a flight farther up than ours, so heaven knows how long it must have taken for him to be shown to his room.

One evening Sir John was expecting important company for dinner and he asked Horseman, "Can we have the sitting room in tip-top condition, please, for tonight? Give the room a thorough going-over." By day's end, Horseman had yet to reach this item on his list of duties, and we happened to see his version of "a thorough going-over." Conversing as usual with himself and carrying a feather duster, he batted anything that got in his way. Then he took the fifteen-foot-high curtains and flapped them against the walls, pushed a pile of newspapers to one side—and the sitting room was ready.

Before dinner, with all of us in the now tip-top sitting room, Sir

John got involved in a long telephone conversation. Horseman took orders for drinks, then disappeared.

Sir John remained on the phone and fifteen minutes ticked by. Still no Horseman. Fearing the worst, Sean volunteered to reconnoiter and found him leaning against a sideboard in the hall. Mumbling as ever, he was lifting each heavy glass decanter to his lips and taking long pulls, then shifting the decanters around as if they were pieces on a chessboard. Sean picked out enough words to understand that the butler was drinking from each decanter to determine its contents.

By the end of that evening, Horseman was flying. His manner became imperious; he played to the hilt the part of an English butler and announced new arrivals as though shouting over hundreds of people. He was magnificent. Sean followed him around like a puppy; a smile never left his face. Horseman and Horsewoman are both dead now, but they gave us much pleasure and many laughs, and I know Sir John must miss them. Sean and I were genuinely fond of that old man.

For our nationwide tour, Sean, Pat, and I had the use of a car loaned to us by the Queen—a rock-solid, bullet-proof Ford Scorpio. The response I got on the tour was remarkable. In Newmarket we faced five extraordinarily wild two- and three-year-olds. They were just a shade quieter than mustangs, extremely raw and green, but they were healthy and well-fed. The weather was hostile, with driving wind and rain on the second day, and I could not imagine that people would come. But 200 or 300 people braved that weather and the horses went well. One of them was filmed by Channel 4, which televised the event all over the British Isles. Sheik Mohammed and a contingent of people from the United Arab Emirates also came, and I am told they liked what they saw.

We stayed at Sandringham, on the Queen's property, with Michael Osborne and his wife. They arranged a wonderful dinner party where I answered many questions. Later we stopped at the Yorkshire Riding Centre, then pressed on to the impressive Gleneagles hotel and leisure facility in Scotland. Between 400 and 500 people attended and asked countless questions in Scottish accents so rich I really needed an interpreter.

In Scotland, Sean had just ridden a four-year-old stallion—an aggressive, well-fed animal, I remember, sixteen hands, two inches high and more than 1,200 pounds in weight. When the horse relaxed and forgot about being a stallion, he went beautifully. Up on his back for the first time, Sean could relax, and he called to me in a loud voice, "Fifty-first fluke in a row!"

I had to explain my laughter to the audience. "You know," I said, "every place we go, there's always someone who says that what they're watching must be a fluke. It's become a standing joke. New audience, new fluke! Well, as Sean mentioned, this is our fifty-first fluke in a row in this country, and I'm not even counting the many thousands of horses I've started before I landed at Heathrow."

We then flew to the Isle of Man, where we had perhaps our oddest experience. We were picked up at the airport by a woman in her late sixties who had seen much wind and sun and who went by the curious name of Dizzy Wriggle. Warmly gracious and hospitable, she told us en route that she and her husband lived in the cobbled stable block now; their old house was too big for them. Billy Wriggle got around in a wheelchair.

Pat, Sean, and I followed her into the most ancient house I have ever seen; it was close to a thousand years old. We would spend the night here. The smell in one room was deathly foul, and as I approached the fireplace I saw the source: a horse's foot on the mantel. After a favorite horse had died, Dizzy had someone saw off one foot and prop it there without curing it.

The mansion had not been lived in for a long time. Huge old toilets, their cracked wooden seats dating from the dark ages, sheltered spiders. Taps produced leaves and twigs. Dizzy disappeared into a bedroom and started shouting: she was throwing a tribe of dogs off our bed. Whippets and spaniels and setters tumbled past us, and we wondered if the mastiffs had the house to themselves.

That night, we dined in the main house—its kitchen kick started for the occasion—with the most stimulating company. They were far removed from our experience of life, yet they received us with much hospitality and genuine interest. Though the plates were chipped and the glasses leaked, everything was done properly. Billy Wriggle, his white hair greased back, sat at the end of the table, stoic in his demeanor, talking in a voice as loud as a bugle. He spilled generous quantities of food and wine down his canary-yellow sweater.

The lady to my right enlightened me on the history of personal hygiene. "Washing yourself," she began, "is unhealthy. All this soap—destructive to your skin. And our ancestors knew that. In former times, they didn't do all this silly washing. When they went to the loo, they merely dipped their hands in a bowl of potpourri and emerged fragrant and refreshed."

Following tradition, the ladies were then asked to leave the room. Billy Wriggle produced a box of Havanas that may have predated the house, and everyone proceeded to try to light the things. Port was served. There followed more questions, disagreements, discussions, and more to drink. We toasted the Queen. One by one, each man stood to deliver his own recitation—amusing or solemn, about Mother England and the Crown. After each pronouncement came another toast: "God Save the Queen."

When the ladies returned, the party began to break up. I helped Dizzy load Billy into the car to drive the short distance to the stable block. Convinced she would have to flee something in the night—spiders, ghosts, dogs—Pat went to bed fully dressed.

The next morning the three of us walked down to the stable block where the same pack of dogs all gathered in a circle, noses to the ground, tails wagging. They were lapping at a large pool of blood. It seems that Dizzy, while transferring Billy from the car to his wheelchair, had dropped him, and he had bled profusely onto the cobbles from a deep cut on his leg. He was at the hospital now, recovering. So this was old-fashioned, upper-class English life!

After the Isle of Man we went to Chichester, a country town in the south of England, and started some New Forest ponies and wild horses, mostly for people involved in the Pony Club and the horse-show circuit. Various other dates brought the head-count to ninety-eight horses and ponies. On average, each horse accepted saddle, bridle, and rider in twenty-seven minutes. Returning to Shotover House, we spent a day with Sir John and gave him an account of our tour. I also wrote a report for the Queen and left it with him to deliver personally.

When we flew home to California, I had the feeling that life would never be the same again. As the plane lifted off that beautiful, crowded island—"this sceptered isle ... this blessed plot," as the bard called it—I imagined all the horses down there whose lives we had briefly touched and I wanted to continue. I believed I would return to Britain many times in the future, and I was right.

It also looked as if my association with the Royal Family's horses would continue. The Queen had asked if she could send people to California to study my techniques and to start her young horses accordingly. Victor Blackman from Dick Hearn's yard, and later from Lord Huntington's yard, would do just that, and returned to take charge of starting the Queen's yearlings.

Corporal Major Terry Pendry, who oversaw the starting of horses for the Household Cavalry, and Richard Maxwell, also in the Household Cavalry, would also study extensively with me. These were new opportunities, and I was glad to accept them.

———

When Ireland beckoned in 1990, for example, I went. I found the Irish people down-to-earth and interested in testing me to the hilt. They brought me tough horses and demanded honesty and openness in my dealings with them.

My Irish contact was Hugh McCusker, who is famous for his hunter show horses. It put a different spin on my visit there and opened up a new world for me. Hugh is known on the English show-horse scene as "the flamboyant Irishman," and I would go along with that description.

Hugh had scheduled a demonstration in the town of Kill, near Dublin. The property we were to use had just been bought by the president of the Irish Draft Horse Association, Fenton Flannely and he was keen to use the demonstration as a launch for his facility. He asked me to start a pair of fillies and said there would possibly be a third horse.

As was routine by now, we arrived beforehand to introduce the horses to the round pen.

One of the horses, a flashy three-year-old Irish draft colt called Stanley, had feet the size of dinner plates and a neck you would have trouble encircling with your arms. This was the mysterious "third horse."

Shown the pen, Stanley seemed quite alert—an "all-boy" sort, aggressive and uncooperative. Hugh knew nothing of the colt's history, only that he was completely green. When it was time for Stanley to return to his stall, two boys came for him. This did not seem out of line at the time, but all came clear later.

That evening, before a near-capacity crowd of about 500 people, both fillies went extremely well, and we were, if anything, ahead of schedule. Hugh said the owner wanted to break for refreshments but would I then start the big colt, Stanley? Fair enough, I said.

When it was announced over the public address system that I would soon be in the pen with Stanley, a ripple of interest ran through the crowd. My experience in match racing and rodeos in small towns told me there was something in the wind. By ten P.M. there were more people in the building than *before* the break: every seat was filled, and many people were standing. Hugh McCusker explained: When people heard that Stanley was going to be started without a lead rope on his head, many in the audience had telephoned their friends to come and see this cowboy get eaten alive.

When Stanley was brought into the building, he was cautiously led by the two lads, each with a lead rope on either side. They kept their distance from him, and a third groom kept him moving from behind. When he was inside, they gently released the two lead ropes.

With the adrenaline surging in his body from being under the lights and having hundreds of people watching him, Stanley marched around the pen and appeared very much in charge. This was a colt with a well-earned reputation. I switched on my lapel microphone and announced to the crowd that I was ready to go ahead. As I walked toward the gate leading into the round pen, you could have heard a pin drop.

I opened the gate and stepped into the pen. At that time Stanley was on the far side, about fifty feet from me. As I closed the gate behind me and stepped away from the fence, he arched his neck and marched about three steps toward me. Then he pinned his ears back, bared his teeth, and came at me, full-speed. The audience gasped. I tripped the latch on the gate and stepped outside. The colt slammed to a halt inches from the fence and turned away to show off his supremacy.

"Wow!" I exclaimed to the crowd. "What are you trying to do to me here?" I shook my head and put my hands on my hips, looking around at the banks of people sitting and staring. "Surely the nice people of Ireland wouldn't set me up for something like this, would they?"

Not a word was spoken, not a sound could be heard. I stood there for a while; then I sat down on a chair near my gate and gave the impression that I was very worried about going into the pen and dealing with this horse. I addressed the audience again. "On this trip I've met a lot of skeptical Irish horsemen who feel that some of my work is less than believable. Now, I know that Ireland is filled with good horsemen—in fact, I'm sure there are a lot of them in the building right now. And since I'm a fifty-six-year-old man who's completely out of shape and has had half his backbone surgically removed, I'd very much like to ask for a volunteer to come and deal with this horse. It would be interesting to see what an Irish horseman could do with a horse as aggressive as this."

I sat there for a few seconds and listened to this deep silence. In truth, I wanted to see a few red faces. And then I said in a surprised voice, "No volunteers? Come on, think about it. Let's get some young kid down here who's in good shape, and he can go ahead and do this horse. I'll make some suggestions from outside the ring."

The silence endured. The only sound was of the colt's breath and his giant foot pawing at the floor of the round pen. Then I said, "Well, I guess I'm going to have to go ahead and do him." From my equipment bag I took my nylon rope, entered the pen and immediately started to swing a loop.

This young Irish draft horse had never seen a cowboy before, so he stood off and moved around the perimeter of the pen and looked me over. He was confused enough by this loop whirling around my head; he wasn't going to try to charge through it.

We circled one another for a few seconds and I started to close in on him. He went into a high-stepping trot near the fence. I continued to close on him, and he picked up speed. When the time was right, I threw the loop, which caught him around the neck. This was real western stuff I had been doing all my life.

The colt went crazy. He bawled and bucked and did everything he could do to shed this rope. Now he had a new concern: I was not the problem, the rope was. I would just give him a little tug now and then, and he would go into renewed orbit, expressing all the rage he had locked up in him. This went on for thirty or forty seconds; then he settled down and came to a stop.

At that point I slipped in near him, and I wound the rope around his head in a come-along—a way, remember, to apply pressure to nerves on the horse's head.

And then I started to school Stanley on the come-along. His aggressive tendencies were clearly obvious for about five minutes. Then he began to settle and respond to me; he started giving me the early signs of "join-up"; he opened up an ear to me, according me that much respect anyway. Then I observed his tongue come out from between his teeth, and he was licking and chewing. I was communicating with him pretty well within five to eight minutes.

Rather than go through the normal loose-horse or free-horse join-up, I continued to work with the come-along on him. He would have been a very dangerous horse to work with had I released him in the pen.

When he was comfortable, I put the saddle on his back and he had a few complaints about that, but not too many. He started to calm down a bit and have confidence in me. I put on the bridle, then long-lines, and I long-lined him pretty hard for about ten or twelve minutes. I brought in my rider, who was a game lad to climb on such a monster animal with the power of two normal horses. But the colt was acting well, and I was giving him plenty of encouragement. Once the rider was up and he was working in a controlled circle, we gave him about fifteen minutes of trotting and cantering. The colt performed well in what I still consider one of the best demonstrations I have ever done. The Irish crowd was amazed and full of questions. I could have stayed there for hours talking with them about what they had seen, but I was ushered away to a party at the owner's house.

There I finally learned the story. Stanley had been the champion in-hand Irish draft at the Dublin Horse Show the year before as a two-year-old, but he had become very aggressive and had been kept in a dark stall ever since. I was, more than anything, pleased to have plucked him from the darkness. With proper handling, he could now shrug off his reputation and put the trauma behind him.

In 1996, I returned to the same venue. They had put up some show-jumping fences in one corner of the arena, but I thought nothing of it. But after my demonstration, the organizers unveiled their surprise for me. "Monty," said one, "this is Stanley, and he's now Ireland's finest show-jumping Irish draft horse." They brought him in and a young rider put Stanley through his paces. All his power and grace were now controlled and fluid. The big colt was wonderful to behold as he jumped those fences.

Another trip to Ireland took me to the Irish National Stallion Show at Ballinasloe, in the very center of Ireland. The stallion festival was a large event held in the bowl of a valley, but the bowl seemed to be rapidly filling with water. It was a quagmire. We have drops of rain in California—sometimes big drops during a storm—but I had never witnessed these curtains of water that were now drifting across the countryside.

Why not cancel the event? Hugh McCusker pointed out that if they started canceling events in Ireland because of rain, there would be none left to go to. The brave Irish turned up and stayed. By the time we had rented a four-wheel drive vehicle and made our way into the grounds, there must have been 3,000 people there. The place looked like Woodstock, except that everyone was in oilskins.

The two stallions we would start were in a truck on a nearby promontory, so we slogged our way up there. They were squeezed into a tiny van where they banged and kicked; steam rolled from air vents set into the top. A young Irish fellow, soaked to the skin, was in charge. We agreed not to unload the horses to show them the round pen—the return swim to the trailer would have been treacherous. This was going to be a once-only effort. When the time came, the round pen was a mudhole with me in the middle of it.

In the absence of a lapel microphone, someone gave me a remote microphone the size of a cucumber. How to attach it to me so I had both hands free was a problem. They took my coat and shirt off, taped the cucumber to my chest, then squeezed the water out of my clothes and allowed me to put them back on.

The first stallion was sliding down the hill, towing the lad behind him like a dinghy behind a sailboat. The horse's neighbor in the trailer was screaming, and he was screaming back. When the stallion stepped into the round pen, his feet were sucked into mud a foot deep. He probably could not have run from me had he wanted to.

I started my usual introduction. "Ladies and gentlemen..." But with a fizz and a crackle, the cucumber died. By this time, I was too drenched to care. I was just going to go on, try to rescue some sort of demonstration and get out of there.

Hugh ran to the announcer's stand. Seconds later I heard his voice come over the public address system, loud and clear: "Monty Roberts's microphone has been drowned out, so I'm going to take over, and I know he would have said something along the following lines: "Good afternoon, ladies and gentlemen, my name is Monty Roberts and we're here today to..." Hugh McCusker was my voice that day, and he did fine.

Perhaps the horses wanted out of the rain as much as we did: they were begging to join up with me. They seemed to understand how important it was that they cooperate. Together, they were two of the best demonstrations of the language of Equus that I have ever undertaken.

Afterward, Hugh McCusker and I headed straight for the nearest supply of best Irish malt whisky.

CHAPTER 8

When a Racehorse's Worst Nightmare Is a Starting Gate

I look back on my life and clearly see that certain events were more than just points on a calendar: some actually changed the pattern of my life altogether.

The first of these occurred in 1943 when my father killed the black man; my conversation with Brownie in 1948 also looms large. In 1956 I married Pat, and I now know how fortunate I was to find her, how essential is her support and tolerance for my shortcomings and maniacal approach to work. The births of our children—Debbie in 1957, Laurel in 1959, and Marty in 1961—also profoundly influenced my life.

There is the Monty Roberts before 1989, when I spent my first week with the Queen and her family, and the Monty Roberts who came afterward.

With horses, there was my life before and after Johnny Tivio: I have never gotten close to another horse with a brain like his; he trained me, not I him.

My experience with a horse called Lomitas in 1991 must be counted as the most recent landmark event in my life.

Owned by Walther J. Jacobs of Bremen, Germany, and placed in training there with the gifted Andreas Wohler, Lomitas was a good-looking chestnut colt that would race in the colors of Gestut Fahrhof, the Jacobs stud farm. Lomitas's sire is Nininski and his dam is La Colorada, by Surumu.

By early 1990 Lomitas began to show potential by turning in speedy workout times, and by early that summer he looked to be a fine prospect. Lomitas won both of his starts in 1990, and that year was the highest-rated two-year-old in Germany. Gestut Fahrhof was no stranger to top horses, but it is always an honor to have a champion two-year-old. The Kentucky Derby and other classic races for three-year-olds present themselves as exciting targets. This was the kind of horse Lomitas was.

The first sign of trouble came in April 1991. Lomitas was prepped and ready for his debut as a three-year-old, but he initially balked at loading in the van to go to the race. At the track, there was a bigger problem: the starting gate. The horse repeatedly refused to go inside, threw his head up, sidestepped, and pulled back. Other horses and their jockeys were in their stalls, awaiting Lomitas. No one likes this situation, least of all the jockeys, for whom sitting in the starting gate is always a nerve-racking time.

After close to twenty minutes of struggle, the race began and Lomitas won. But imagine the apprehension in the Gestut Fahrhof camp when their champion came so close to being disqualified. After two weeks of more schooling and tests before race stewards—who warned that a similar episode would result in a life ban—Lomitas was entered in a race on a turf course in Cologne. Once more it proved difficult to load him into the van—but what happened on the track that day defies belief.

Lomitas was the last horse brought to the starting gate, and again he refused to enter. As they had on the previous occasion, the other horses stood and waited for twenty minutes while track officials literally wrestled with Lomitas. They put a hood on to blindfold him, they yanked his tail up over his back and even the jockey's shoulder. (Perhaps they thought the tail was a lever they could use to pry him into the gate.) A dozen men, some in front, some behind, alternately pulled and pushed the horse, trying to force him forward and into the gate.

At that point, Lomitas became vicious, attacked the men, and caused injuries. He ended up lying on the ground, exhausted from the fight. The race finally started, but without Lomitas. He lay behind the starting gate like a fallen athlete, immobile, on his side. Immediately after the race, the stewards carried through with their threat. The owners, the Jacobses, left the track in despair. Their young champion horse was not only a nonperformer, but a convicted criminal who would never race again.

By this time, I had a reputation for successfully treating remedial Thoroughbred racehorses. Andreas Wohler, Lomitas's trainer, asked me if I would set the horse straight. So on June 12, 1991, I put my life aside and left for Germany.

At the airport, I saw a young man in riding breeches, perhaps a Wohler stable hand sent to meet me. "Do you know Andreas Wohler?" I asked him. He smiled. "I am Andreas Wohler."

We drove immediately to the Bremen Racecourse (where Andreas and others lease facilities for training and stabling their strings of horses). There I met the superstar, Lomitas. When I entered his box stall, he turned his head to look at me. Out loud, and full of awe, I said the single word "Gorgeous!" He was a registered Thoroughbred stallion, sixteen hands high, 1,150 pounds, chestnut in color. He had a white pastern on the off-hind leg and a star between his eyes with an elongated strip that widened and ended between his nostrils. I could see every point of his skeletal frame hitting its mark: he had a near-perfect Thoroughbred racehorse conformation. "Correct of limb, in every way," I said.

I walked over to where he was munching hay, standing against the back of his stall, and greeted him with a stroke on his neck. "Hello, Lomitas, you're a fine man, eh?" I proceeded to move my hands back along his body, and I felt that he wanted to move into my hands, away from the wall. I held out against the pressure, and he immediately kicked out behind. I logged this as a possible response to any number of things, and continued making his acquaintance. He struck me as a breathtaking animal, with a look in his eye that spoke of very high intelligence. I had traveled a long way to be standing here, and suddenly I was pleased to have made the journey.

My task was specific: cure this horse of his starting-gate terror. After discussing it on the phone beforehand, Andreas had constructed for our mission a solid-wall, permanent training gate, which was much safer than the conventional kind. I would work with Lomitas in the center of a riding hall on the Bremen Racecourse where the footing was secure and the facilities are first-class.

I would need an assistant, someone who could speak English and who knew horses as well. With remedial horses, the people are as important to the success of the project as the horse. Andreas introduced me to a young man by the name of Simon Stokes. Talented and courteous, Simon Stokes is a former champion jump jockey from Chichester whose nose had been broken many times from pushing fences over with his head. He also rode on the flat and helped Andreas train horses; after living in Germany for eleven years, he spoke fluent German. With Simon and Andreas I had expert help.

On June 13, I set about trying to get to know Lomitas a little better. I took him into the covered riding hall—a small track 200 yards in circumference and sixteen feet wide. Standing there with him, I moved to the end of the rope and asked him to step toward me. He seemed reluctant to step into my space. I raised one arm sharply above my head, then the other. He did not seem unduly alarmed, which told me that he had not been abused by punishments that come from a raised hand. I stood next to him and lifted my knee and leg under his keel. Again, there was no discernible tightening of the abdominal muscles, no sudden grunt or lifting of the thorax. Plainly, he had not been abused in that area either. Then I took a short length of rope and swung it near his head. He paused and looked at me, then moved sideways and paused again. In his own intelligent fashion, he was struggling to understand me, but his lack of panic told me he had not been whipped.

Finally, I led him closer to the wall and placed my hands along his side, as if to hold him closer against the wall. Immediately, he kicked out and plunged forward, showing classic signs of claustrophobia.

This much was clear: Although his relationship with humans was obviously a good one, he was prepared to blame us for placing him inside enclosed structures such as starting gates and vans. And he was perfectly happy to express that discomfort to his handlers. As Lomitas saw it, people were treating him unfairly.

I stopped to allow the pair of us a breather. Looking at his fine build and marking the extraordinary intelligence in his eye, I thought, I am in the presence of greatness. I had better do my job with patience, diligence, and competence.

If I tested Lomitas for signs of abuse, it was not because I distrusted Andreas and Simon. I always accord my horses the respect of asking them to speak for themselves. I have been lied to by humans but never by a horse; it's not within his scope. And unlike a green horse (who is more like a blank slate), any horse ever handled by humans comes with stories, perhaps baggage and sometimes terrible events etched on their psyches. Lomitas was telling me, "I have been treated unfairly and I fear it's going to get worse."

When Andreas and Simon returned to the stable from their other duties, I was back near Lomitas's stall, leading him around. I asked, "Can we use a round pen or lunging ring somewhere nearby, so I can work him?"

"Hmmm ... that might be difficult," said Andreas.

"I need to turn him loose, to let him go on his own and win his trust."

I felt that if I could join up with Lomitas he might accept the confined positions we asked him to walk into. "Well," said Andreas after giving the matter some thought, "there's a show-jumping ring about ten miles away, but we'd need to get him into a transport truck to take him there, which counts that out."

"No," I replied, "hang on, we can do the van, I'm sure we can." Andreas and Simon were both nervous about this, but clearly it had to be done. So they ordered a van. When it arrived, Andreas suggested backing the van into the barn: with the ramp in the center aisle, Lomitas would be less able to slip around the side.

"He's going to have to learn to enter the van like a gentleman one day," I replied, "and we might as well start as we mean to go on. Let's deal with this in the middle of the yard and do it properly from the outset."

With the van parked there, the ramp down and waiting, I attached a long lead rope to his halter (a come-along) and schooled him for about half an hour. During the schooling process he was obedient, hard-working and well-mannered. Until he showed me a problem, I was going to treat him like a normal horse, and that meant loading him into the van.

I walked up the ramp and he willingly followed me into the van. The instant he was inside, the helpers standing by ran to lift the ramp. "No," I told them, "leave the ramp down. I'm going to walk him off and on several times." The Irish exercise riders who were there warned me: "If you bring him off, you'll never get him back on again."

Have a little faith, I suggested. I walked Lomitas off and on the van without incident fifteen to twenty times before we closed it up and made our trip to the show-jumping yard. The building offered good footing, but it was too big: 150 feet long and 100 feet wide. Ideally I needed a fifty-foot round pen.

With jump poles and standards, I fashioned a round pen, built it, in fact, around Lomitas while he stood there watching me. Then I went to work.

Free of any rope on his head, he went into flight immediately when I pressed him away from me. He cantered steadily around the perimeter, with one ear already locked on to me. Within a minute or two, he understood what I was doing and I began to observe some licking and chewing. He was such an intelligent horse that in less than fifteen minutes he was in full conversation with me. I quickly had a good join-up; he trusted me.

Now I wanted to take this trust a bit further. I dismantled the jump poles, so that we now occupied the main arena. It took a few minutes. He ran away from me for a while and thought he was going to take charge, but as soon as I told him to go away, farther away, he was pressing to come back. I would go anywhere in the building, and he was right there with me, his nose to my shoulder.

When that happened, I felt confident we could work through the problems with the starting gate. Going home, he entered the van like an old horse who had never had a problem with vans. Back at the stables in Bremen, we put him away, fed him, and left him to have a good night's rest.

On June 15, 1991, I started to work Lomitas in the permanent training gate. I was banking on his trust, on taking it one step at a time, and on creating within him a desire to enter the gate. Within a short period, he was going in and out with no problems. Later that morning, Simon put some tack on him and sat on his back while I led him in and out. We were able to close the gate behind him and initiate the process of letting him walk out in a very relaxed manner. This took us through the morning.

In the afternoon, Andreas had invited the head starter from the Bremen Racecourse to watch Lomitas walking in and out of the training gate. He spent about an hour with me that day and was impressed by what he saw. The starter would recommend that the stewards reassess the situation and give Lomitas another chance—if he could pass all the necessary tests.

During the first test the next morning in proper racing gates at the Bremen Racecourse, Lomitas was troubled and a bit difficult at times, but he was trying hard for me, and before the morning was over he was going in and out of the gates easily. The stewards then set up another test on June 18. They would want to see Lomitas exhibit the same steady behavior, but this time with other horses in the starting gate. Lomitas passed that test with flying colors, but it was still not the way I wanted it. He was a little tentative entering and a little nervous while in there.

Andreas wanted to run Lomitas at Bremen on June 23. The stewards, though, would require yet another test—and this time they would want him to be nearly perfect. Only then would they consider reinstating him.

On the morning of June 20 we all assembled in front of the Bremen grandstand. With three horses for company in the starting gate, Lomitas was close to perfect. The stewards said they would reinstate the horse for one race and then reassess. They added a proviso that I come with him, and that nobody from the track handle him. To avoid him standing in there for a long period, it was also suggested that Lomitas be the last horse to enter the starting gate.

The morning of the race I was tense. I felt the gaze of all 20,000 people in the stands. Lomitas had become something of a legend among German racing fans. A national hero with an immense follow-ing, he was the gifted horse who had fought with his trainers and re-fused to race. As I walked Lomitas around behind the starting gates, parents were holding little children over the fence and calling out, "Oh, Lomi, Lomi, Lomi."

We walked around behind those stalls for what seemed an inter-minable length of time. Finally, I realized that something was wrong. All the other horses in the race were gathered to one side of the track and the jockeys were deep in conversation. Andreas was huddling with the head starter and other officials.

Finally, Andreas came to me with the news that the jockeys would boycott the race unless Lomitas entered the gate first. They said they were tired of being put in the gates and waiting for Lomitas to have it out with the starting-gate crew.

I said it made no difference to me. I walked Lomitas right in: he was good as gold. As I stood there with him, thanking him for giving us a good result on this important occasion, a starting-gate attendant opened the gate in front of us, then—with me directly in Lomitas's path—he went around behind and closed the back gate. Normally this is never done: I could have been severely trampled.

Then it hit me: perhaps the starting-gate crew did not *want* this to work. With their straps and ropes and blindfolds, they would brush Lomitas as they went behind him. Accidental or intentional, I cannot say, but the horse never did misbehave. If they were surly then, the crew would have been more so later: the burden of the coverage in the sports pages that evening was that the German starting-gate attendants had been put to shame by a Californian.

Lomitas stood there calmly while they loaded the other horses. And, in a delicious bit of irony, track officials had considerable diffi-culties with some of the *other* horses. Finally, all were loaded. Lomitas broke well. He stayed in third or fourth position for much of the race and, with his great talent, simply overwhelmed the field in the last quarter mile. It was an undiluted pleasure to see that horse take his rightful place in the winner's enclosure.

This triumph was the first in a series of victories for Lomitas. Later that year, he would be named Germany's champion three-year-old and Horse of the Year. His earnings climbed to 1,600,000 deutsch marks ($1.1 million U.S.).

Such an experience with a horse of this quality bonds man and beast in a way not easy to describe. In just a short time, I felt the same degree of love for Lomitas as I had for Johnny Tivio, Brownie, and Ginger. Lomitas finished his year with three Group I victories in succession, the highest-rated German racehorse in the history of the country.

Andreas gave Lomitas an easy time through the winter of 1991 in order to prepare for the 1992 racing season. Hopes were high for another outstanding year, but then the story took a strange, dark twist. Lomitas was owned by Walther Jacobs, a man I came to know and admire, and one of the finest owners in the racing industry. In 1991, he was eighty-four years old, and his courage and determination would be tested as the Lomitas story unfolded.

Early in 1992, before the racing season began, Mr. Jacobs received a blackmail letter demanding 400,000 deutsch marks, or Lomitas would be harmed or killed. He told me they were taking special precautions with security, and naturally he was concerned. It occurred to me that Mr. Jacobs might simply want to back away from the whole situation and retire Lomitas from racing. He was, however, determined to meet it head on.

I went to Hamburg in June 1992 and watched Simon, who was now handling Lomitas in the starting gate. Lomitas had no problems and won the race. Everything seemed fine. But blackmail letters were still coming and still threatening harm to the horse if the extortionist was not paid. To signal his intent, the letter-writer burned down a hay barn on the Gestut Fahrhof stud farm.

Guards with dogs were deployed around the clock, and additional security was arranged. In late July 1992 Lomitas made the trip to Düsseldorf. He entered the gate without incident and ran in the race, but his performance was lackluster and he finished fifth. He was clearly not himself, and a new letter from the blackmailer pointed to the reason: "We only gave him enough to make him sick," it read. This was simply a warning shot across the bow—to demonstrate that someone had access to the horse and the will to harm him.

Now events took on a new momentum: Lomitas would go into hiding when he was well enough to travel. He would be quarantined in England, then travel to the United States, where he would race in California. I was amazed at the strength and tenacity of Mr. Jacobs through all of this. Another owner might have hidden from the blackmailer, but Mr. Jacobs, in essence, said, "This man will not stop me from racing my horse if I want to race him."

We had to wait fifteen days before moving Lomitas because he became very ill. The letter indicated he had been given a heavy metals poison, which affected his liver and other vital organs. He was a cruel sight. The beautiful horse hung his head, and his eye was dull; he was turned in on himself, concentrating on the illness and the pain. We all felt great anger and incomprehension that anyone could be capable of doing this.

Lomitas fought off the poison within ten days. His head came up, he began to eat a little. A measure of interest returned to his expression. As quickly as possible, he was shipped in secret to Newmarket. Only an inner circle of high-ranking police officers, Lufthansa officials, and people in Mr. Jacobs's office knew of the plan. Simon had once ridden a horse called Pirelli, and that was the name we gave him. In England, we hid him in Susan Piggot's yard.

During the four-week quarantine period, Simon gradually put Lomitas back to work. In mid-September, he was placed in training with Ron McAnally at Santa Anita, California. Lomitas trained well through October and November, and looked to be ready to start racing at Santa Anita after Christmas.

But unexpectedly, in mid-December, Lomitas developed a quarter crack on the off-fore foot. This was a blow to me, for Lomitas never had a foot problem the whole time he trained and raced in Germany. A patch was applied to the crack and training continued. Soon other cracks showed up, on a rear foot, then on the near-fore foot. All this within a three-week period.

Ron McAnally knew of a good quarter-crack specialist in New York by the name of Ian McKinley. We had him flown out and at a roundtable discussion at the track with the veterinarians and other farriers, McKinley asked, "What happened to this horse about five months ago?" At that moment the connection became clear. "He was poisoned," I replied.

McKinley showed me a band of disconnected foot wall about half an inch wide right around all four feet on Lomitas. I had not made the connection until Ian asked the question. The band of tissue had darkened around the entire foot, and the foot had grown down, this separated area had been taxed and the cracks resulted.

McKinley used a substance called Equilox on each foot, whether it had cracks or not. He was strengthening the wall artificially by laying this space-age polymer over the top. We were then able to train Lomitas without further cracks developing, but it was February before he could race.

In his first race, the horse who crossed the line before Lomitas had interfered with him, and Lomitas was named the winner. His next race was in April at Hollywood Park. Distracted just as the gates opened, he got off to a terrible start and began nine lengths behind the leader. Even as the field turned for home, he was probably twelve to fifteen lengths behind.

Then he made a blinding run at the leaders. He ran the fastest last quarter ever undertaken at Hollywood Park. As far as we could tell, had he broken with the pack at the beginning he would have been only two-fifths of a second off the world record for that distance.

But his feet continued to plague him, and it was decided to retire him to stud. He left the United States in 1994 to stand at Gestut Fahrhof for the breeding season of 1995. While his American initiative fell short of my goals, Lomitas earned approximately $100,000 and served notice that he was a formidable competitor on the American race scene.

The German breeders have responded strongly to Lomitas as a breeding prospect, and he was booked to sixty mares in 1996 and sixty more in 1997. Like a true champion, he does this job well, too. He has a conception rate in the ninety-percentile range. It will be interesting to see if Lomitas can pass along his talents to the next generation. My hope is that his story is just beginning.

As for the extortion attempt, no one was ever arrested, but the police did confront a likely suspect and the letters ceased.

———

Plainly, horses and starting gates sometimes mix like oil and water, and if Lomitas presented a great challenge in that regard, so did a horse with the imposing name, Prince of Darkness.

In 1990, I was staying in an English country house. It was the dead of night, but sleep would not come. Prince of Darkness was the source of my insomnia, and I could not stop thinking about him. Getting out of bed, I began to pace up and down the upstairs landing. What could I do with this horse? Where was the gap in my understanding of this big, highly charged animal?

Then I heard footsteps. A door opened and my host, Sir Mark Prescott, appeared, likewise in his robe. The two of us blinked at each other.

"I'm sorry if I disturbed you," I said "but I couldn't sleep. I can't seem to get my brain to stop working."

Sympathizing, Sir Mark took up a position at the window, his face cast in moonlight. Suddenly, his expression sharpened. "Well, I'll be," he muttered softly. "Come and see."

I went and stood next to him. From the window, we could see over the sloping roof of the house to the stable yard. In the moonlight we could clearly make out Prince of Darkness, his head appearing first at the window of his stall and then at the door as he walked around. He was as awake as we were.

Sir Mark sighed. "That's three of us trying to work out what's wrong, then."

Prince of Darkness had been trained by Sir Mark in Newmarket, and was owned by Pin Oak Stables of Kentucky, along with English partners. He was a large-framed dark bay standing about 16.3 hands high, very muscular and long in the body.

He must have weighed 1,400 pounds, but he was no big clod of a horse: he was bright in his eyes, with alert ears, well-balanced and well-proportioned. They called him Prince of Darkness because he had once killed a steer in the paddock, perhaps not viciously but after rough play. He would have been like a cat playing with a mouse. This horse was on fire all the time but nothing set him off more than starting gates.

Starting gates were not built for a horse his size: he was so long that his nose touched the front gate and his hindquarters pressed into the rear gate, and so broad that the rails touched him on either side.

Typically of horses who learn to hate starting gates, his first few entries had been trouble-free. Then one day they were loading him during a training session on the heath in Newmarket, and he failed to step in fully. An attendant slapped him on the outer thigh with his hand and the horse kicked out, hitting the side of the starting gate. He subsequently developed a negative attitude toward all gates—while walking toward them, entering them, or standing inside.

I had come to England to work with him once already and thought the job had been done, but I was not back in California three days before I got a call from Sir Mark. I was disappointed, but I also stand behind my work and I returned immediately on a no-fee basis.

What had happened was this: They had apparently gone to the gates on the heath and Prince of Darkness had been upset from the time he arrived. They got him in, but once there he had tried to kick the gate to pieces. Now he would go nowhere near one.

What had changed him so much? I had had him going in and out of starting gates like a dream. And now the three of us—the horse, Sir Mark, and me—were bedeviled by it all and sleepless to boot.

That night, over dinner, I asked Sir Mark what it was like to transport Prince of Darkness in a van. The horse was no problem, he said, whether the stalls were narrow or wide. This was hard to believe, given what I had been through all that day in the starting gates. Sir Mark suggested that we book a van with adjustable partitions so I could see for myself.

My plan was to load the horse and give him a wide stall while we drove slowly around. Then we would narrow the partition and subsequently increase the van's speed. I would stand inside the van at the horse's head so I could both observe him and instruct the driver. The aim was to identify the source of the horse's deep-seated claustrophobia.

We loaded Prince of Darkness and started a tour of Newmarket, driving slowly and making careful turns. He was completely at ease in his stall, so we stopped and narrowed the partition. Still, he seemed comfortable. When I asked the driver to increase his speed and make more aggressive turns, the engine note rose an octave. In front of me, Prince of Darkness seemed unconcerned. He braced himself against the corners and took no notice when any part of the van touched his body. Now we were sailing around the town. Anyone following us must have thought crooks had stolen the van as we squealed around corners and took roundabouts at stomach-turning speed. The horse and I were rolling around like a ship's cargo in a storm.

Prince of Darkness was in the narrowest possible stall and the driver was risking his license to give us all the ride of a lifetime. For all that, the horse did not kick or lean, and offered not the slightest resistance or anger. A far cry from what I had seen the previous day in the starting gate.

What distinguished the stall in the van (which he abided agreeably), and the starting gate (which he kicked to bits)? Back at the yard, I stared hard at both of them. Where was this horse's fear coming from? Clearly it was not claustrophobia, because he had been content in the van. Something about the starting gate spooked him. But what?

That night, after three days of futility, I wanted to quit and offer Sir Mark a refund, but those words just would not come. All my life I had found ways to win, and I could not bear the thought of losing this contest. I decided to give it one more try.

The following day was the toughest of them all: nine demanding and dangerous hours. Geraldine Rees, a friend of Sir Mark's, came along and patiently watched the proceedings. As Prince of Darkness was led riderless into the starting gate, I stood in front of him, just as I had in the van. I wanted to observe every nuance of behavior as he went in.

He walked in, crashing and banging. No sooner was he in than he lunged forward, charging from that gate as if men with lances were arranged along the sides and poking him. He had no concern for me being in his way at all and galloped right through me, knocking me to the ground.

I stood up and wiped the dust off. This was a problem, because I needed to get even closer. The next time he blasted from the stall in a flurry, he knocked me down again, and still I was no wiser about his terror. This was no game for a man of my age and with part of his spinal column missing, but I was determined to go in yet a little closer.

Once again he jumped forward and bowled me over, stepping on my leg, side, and ear. Then he ran to the end of my come-along, turned, and stood there looking at me from twenty feet away. I was hurting badly, but in a flash, it came to me. Though my brain was muddled by this time, I had noticed something: just before he jumped up and ran over the top of me, Prince of Darkness had rolled his eye back to look at his off flank and his attention seemed to be focused on the off-side rail.

I stood there, bruised, battered, with a trickle of blood running into my collar, but I had found the source of his fear. The rail itself, of course! A van has smooth sides whereas starting gates have rails on each side. I could have kicked myself for not realizing sooner, but I felt a surge of excitement. After a few tests, I knew I was right.

That evening, Sir Mark and I discussed the situation. With mounting anticipation, he phoned various racing officials to investigate the possibility of removing the rails from inside a given starting gate. No luck: because of the way they are constructed, when you remove the rail from one horse's stall, you also remove it from the next.

Early next morning, I outlined another idea. If we could create something similar to what a picador's horse wears in the bull ring—a drape made of heavy leather to go over his rear quarters—perhaps we could convince Prince of Darkness that he had enough protection from those evil rails.

It was a wild thought, and I had grave doubts about its practicality. Many years beforehand, I had draped a leather cape over a horse's rear quarters and attached it to my Western saddle. When I then asked the horse to make a sliding stop from extreme speed, it encouraged him to drop his hips. He had to in order to hold his rear feet in the ground and support the weight of the cape.

If I could use something like this to protect Prince of Darkness's sides from those rails, he might accept the starting gate.

"What if we used carpet?" asked Geraldine Rees. *Yes.* We drove to Newmarket and bought a roll of remnant carpet. Then we went to Gibson's Saddlery, and I started to design the kind of thing I thought might work. The prototype, no more than carpet sewn onto both sides of a stable blanket, was finished in just a few hours and we raced back to the stables to try it out.

When I put the Prince in the starting stalls with his special blanket on, I immediately knew we were on the right track. I gave Geraldine Rees a congratulatory pat on the back. "Look, he's still frightened and not very confident, but he's staying in there, isn't he?"

It felt good to stand in front of that huge animal and know that I might at last stay on my feet. The more he rubbed against the sides of the stall, stepping backward and forward, the more Prince of Darkness realized that he had protection from the rails. He relaxed and calmed down. We were making progress.

We raced back to Gibson's Saddlery, fearful that the shop would be closed. The next day was Good Friday, with the Easter holiday period to follow. But Gibson's staff were good enough to work that evening and the next morning to further develop the prototype.

The blanket would fit only the horse's hindquarters and would be held in place by straps. A ring sewn onto the blanket near the tail offered a place where a rope could be fastened: the idea was that the horse would actually break from the stall and run out from under the blanket. The horse races on, the blanket stays behind.

Sunday afternoon we tried it. We took Prince of Darkness, with other horses for company, to the starting gates. I did my routine of letting him break slowly, using the blanket for protection. He responded very well. We schooled him again the following day, and that evening I told Sir Mark—then in France on business—that I thought the horse would make a good start at Warwick on the following day.

George Duffield, the jockey, was game to try this invention, but a little embarrassed.

"Carpet? He's wearing a carpet?"

"That's what it's made of, sure."

"Is it patterned carpet or plain?"

"It has a slight pattern, I suppose you'd say."

"Oh no," he groaned.

"Don't you like patterned carpet?"

He held his hands up in the air in mock surrender. "No—it's fine, I don't mind looking like an idiot. Maybe I ought to wear the same pattern. The same color. Let's go for it. Trade in the silks. Can we stop at the carpet store on the way and measure me up for a tufted Wilton?"

I assured him that Prince of Darkness had to have his magic carpet or he would refuse to start. The head starter was similarly apprehensive about the blanket, but he had given Sir Mark permission to use this unconventional apparatus and he could not back down now.

When I put the contraption up behind George in the starting gate, it drew a lot of comments from the other jockeys. In truth, it was a touch ignoble to have someone holding on to the rear of your horse with a piece of rope when you were hoping to run a race in a few seconds' time. I hoped the invention would work the first time. Inventions seldom do.

Now they were under starter's orders. I dug my heel in, grasped the rope firmly, ready to take the strain as Prince of Darkness left the stall. "And they're off!" the announcer called. There was a terrific kick on the rope and then it went dead as Prince of Darkness broke from underneath his blanket with perfect timing. The carpet lay there on the bottom of the gate. Success!

There were eighteen horses in the race, and at Warwick they run about seven furlongs and make a hard left. When they made the turn, Prince of Darkness was the clear leader. He did not win that day, but he made the best start and he went on to be a winner.

Since that time, Gibson's Saddlery has gone on to make many more blankets like the one that Prince of Darkness wore. On Thoroughbred racetracks all over the world, they call horses who need the security of such a device "blanket horses," and more than 1,000 such horses have used it successfully.

I'll take some credit for the invention, but it was Prince of Darkness who made me see the light.

———

To understand how Greg Ward became the best breeder and trainer of cow horses in North America, you must know something of his first horse—a fat little creature called Blackie. He was bought for

$350, saddle included. When I met Greg and heard the story, I thought the saddle was worth more than the horse.

Greg was born in 1935, the same year I was, in Bakersfield, California, and we were to become good friends. He seemed destined for a brilliant career in sports, but at the age of seventeen those dreams ended. To earn money to buy a horse, Greg was on a neighbor's farm driving a tractor when it rolled on a hillside; metal driven into his head left him unconscious and blind. After numerous operations, one to insert a plate in his head, his sight returned—but his peripheral vision was all but gone, and with it his future in athletics.

His parents later helped him to buy his first horse, the eight-year-old Blackie. When Greg went to California Polytechnic State University, San Luis Obispo, he took Blackie with him. Ahead of me by two years, he had been asking questions and watching riders in competition: all in an attempt to make the college rodeo team. He did make it, and contributed to national championships we won in 1958 and 1959.

I recall watching Greg ride Blackie and thinking, "Why is he wasting his time? What will that horse ever be?" I was young, wore championship buckles, and had no time for an ordinary horse like Blackie. I now realize how wrong, how pompous I was to laugh at that horse. Blackie gave Greg everything he had and forgave him his mistakes. A classier, more sensitive horse might have been less sympathetic to him. Blackie, it turns out, mattered a great deal to the Western horse industry—because he was teaching one of the greatest horsemen who ever lived. I should have known better about Blackie, because my Brownie had been important to me.

Greg later bought forty-three acres near Tulare, California, where he built the training establishment he still owns. It now includes two covered arenas and a half-mile track. Horses trained at the Ward Ranch, either by Greg or his son John, have for the past thirty or more years amassed an enviable record. Their horses have won twelve world championships in cutting and reined cow-horse events, along with millions of dollars in prize money. Young horses bred on the Ward Ranch—including Dual Pep, the most popular stallion in their industry—have sold for millions of dollars and won that amount in the showring. Valued at $2 million, Dual Pep has won more than

$300,000 in prize money and has a breeding income of $500,000 per year. Where cow horses are concerned, the Ward Ranch is the class of the continent.

Economics alone requires that his horses perform extremely well in competition to earn back their high value. His training methods, plainly, are not the result of vague notions about kindness to animals—though Greg would never be anything but kind and respectful of them. As proven against the toughest competition, his methods are both the best *and* the kindest.

I once saw something at his ranch that thrilled me. "Monty," he said, "come and have a look at my new babies." Five handlers led the young horses in from the field without so much as pulling on their lead ropes. The horses were then saddled up and the riders carefully mounted. Out on the track, the gates were closed but the horses were otherwise free to wander. A sixth person on an experienced saddle horse carried a long wand with a plastic flag at the end—used if needed to keep horses from endangering one another. "During the first twenty days of riding," said Greg, "we allow them to do whatever they want. There's no tension on the reins whatsoever."

If a horse wanted to graze along the fence line, to canter, simply stand, or even lie down and roll, that was all fine: to grant this last wish, the rider dismounted and watched, unconcerned. I marveled at the correct thinking behind this approach. The horses were learning to carry the riders' weight and had no suspicion that they might ever be punished for anything. There was no chance to cultivate resentment or aggressive tendencies toward their human partners.

The success of these methods and others outlined in this book point to a new beginning in the relationship between man and horse, and it has been my privilege to make a contribution to this spirit of understanding.

———

In England recently, I received an invitation to meet with the Queen to bring her up to date on my work and to discuss views on the world of horses in general. Corporal Major Terry Pendry drove me through the now-familiar grounds of Windsor Castle. "You'll be meeting Her

Majesty outside," he said, as he briefed me for the upcoming meeting. Outside? Were we going to stroll around the grounds together, or meet in the mews and look over some of her horses? Terry parked to one side of the lawn that sweeps down in front of the castle.

In the middle of this huge expanse of perfectly manicured green lawn sat a figure at a small table. A white cable snaked from the table to the castle and disappeared inside. I began the long trek over the lawn, and as I drew near I recognized Her Majesty sitting there. The corners of the snowy-white tablecloth flapped idly in the breeze. The bone china and silverware stood ready for our tea.

The Queen greeted me in a very informal way, and I sat down at the table. She poured tea from a pot attached to that long white cord. We enjoyed finger sandwiches and tea as we began to talk. It was a perfect occasion in a perfect setting. We talked about horses, and once again she proved to be an interesting and informed owner. I felt thoroughly privileged to have met this woman whom history has placed in a unique position.

I brought her up to date on the course offered at West Oxfordshire College under the directorship of Kelly Marks. The course offers my training methods—the first time that a course of this nature has been specifically designed and built into the curriculum. I told her of my recent experiences over starting gates. I said I looked forward to the future, when students of my methodology would advance to such an extent that my current practices would be dismissed as archaic. Even as I write *The Man Who Listens to Horses,* veterinarians are developing the ability to "listen" to horses to determine which part of the animal's gut hurts—the duodenum loop, the small or the large intestine.

Long after the tea party was scheduled to end, the Queen and I rose to our feet. Our parting was genuinely warm. I had a vision of what this scene would look like from the ramparts of the castle: the white square of the table amid the green expanse of lawn, the remains of our tea, the chairs askew, the Queen of England strolling in the direction of the castle, and heading toward a parked car, the California cowboy, shaking his head in disbelief at the curious circumstances in which he found himself.

Nearly 800 years ago, a very different ruler, a conqueror named

Temujin, had a very different attitude to horses. His Mongol empire grew to encompass the shores of the Pacific and the northern stretches of the Black Sea. Standing astride a quarter of the world's surface, he changed his name to Genghis Khan, meaning "master of all." Deservedly, that name now conjures unimaginable cruelty, an iron will, and an inflexible resolve.

His chief ally in the remarkable expansion of his power and influence was the horse. Using ropes and whips, Genghis Khan harnessed the horse's strength, stamina, and speed. Like many who profess to love the horse and *do* love the horse, the Mongols broke their young horses in the cruel, conventional way. They cherished the string of horses they took to war, but inevitably some were ridden to death.

Horses had no answer to the Khan's cruelty, had no voice. But they did have a language. No one saw it, no one tried to see it, but that language has probably existed for 45 million years, virtually unchanged. We should put this into perspective: Humankind has been on this planet for only a few hundred thousand years, and already human language has fragmented into thousands of different tongues.

The absence of communication between human and horse has led to a disastrous history of cruelty and abuse. As a result, we did not gain the willing cooperation of the horse nearly as much as we might have done. Our loss has been considerable—the emotional connection with the horse has been diminished, but so has the performance and work we might have gained.

It is a balance I have tried to redress during a lifetime's work with horses. Happily, that work continues.

CHAPTER 9

Full Circle

All my life, since I was sixteen, I always wanted to join up with a mustang in the wild.

Everyone told me I was crazy. It was too dangerous. Impossible. No one could do this. It was asking to be killed.

Nonetheless, for forty-five years, in the back of my mind, I had the desire to prove myself on a particular point: that join-up is a moment of genuine trust and communication between a man and a wild horse—and would happen just the same with no round pen, no sash line, just a man, a horse, and a wide open space.

As I grew older, I told myself no, it wouldn't happen, half my back was drilled out, I could never do it now anyway.

Yet, it gnawed away at me.

This book was first published in the autumn of 1996. In February 1997, at the age of sixty-two, I was offered the chance to try to achieve my long-held ambition.

It all started with the BBC documentary television program *Q.E.D.* They'd already made a half hour program about join-up some three years before. Then they offered to provide me with the resources necessary to attempt join-up in the wild.

By the time they came forward, however, we were already on a short fuse. Time was running out if they wanted to shoot the program the same year; the rattlesnakes come out of hibernation in April, so we'd have to shoot in March. Also, I had to plot for some moonlight so I could have night vision.

We squeezed the schedule into the last days of March 1997, and everyone scrambled to organize.

Not the least of our problems was the question of the mustang. A lot of things have changed since my trips out to Nevada in the 1950s. Now mustangs are a species protected by federal law, and an act of Congress forbids interfering with them in any way. They are owned by a federal body called the Bureau of Land Management, and it's illegal to go near them in their wild state. I told the BLM what I proposed to do, but it was out of the question. They saw the importance of what I was doing, but if they were to allow it, they'd have to break the law for others, too. They turned me down flat.

No, the only way I could get near a mustang was to adopt one. This is a system of herd management whereby a certain number are run off the open range—using helicopters—and, still with branded numbers on their necks, are offered for adoption to approved homes. The mustangs aren't sold, but names are put into a hat, and if you're lucky, if your name comes up, you can adopt maybe up to four at a time.

A mustang caught in this way is no less wild. It's like capturing a lion, darting him, hauling him to London, and then letting him go in Trafalgar Square. His adrenaline will be sky-high, the whole experience will have him at full flight, and he won't be easy to settle. If anything, he'll be more wild.

But first I had to enter a lottery—and this lottery doesn't happen every week; it's an occasional event. And we were already well into February.

However, just after I got the go-ahead from *Q.E.D.* that funds were available, as God is my judge, a student came up to me at Flag Is Up Farms and told me there would be an adoption event in Paso Robles the next day!

So off we went.

I needed males, not females, because the females might be pregnant. I wanted the mustangs to be between three and five years old. Among the 220 head up for adoption, only 20 fit into this category.

We put our names into a hat. There were only fifty-two people who were going to be lucky enough that day to be offered the chance to adopt.

I waited while the names were called.

After forty-nine, mine hadn't come up. I was going to have to give up on the whole idea and go home. Fifty-one, and I still wasn't mentioned. I was just about ready to dial *Q.E.D.* in England, to tell them to cancel the shoot.

Then they drew number fifty-two. I was the last name out of the hat.

This was meant to happen, wasn't it?

I needed three horses. A first choice—as good-looking as possible for the film cameras—and then a backup, plus a second backup.

I needed the backups because a number of things outside of my control might go wrong. The mustang might run lame halfway through the shoot. He might be struck by a rattlesnake. With the resources that were being made available for this attempt, it was wise to plan it effectively. We would have a second chance only if that possibility were built into the system.

Looking around the wild mustangs corralled there in Paso Robles, I wrote down three numbers, taken from the brands on the mustangs' necks. After everyone else had chosen, my three numbers were still available. Yes, it was meant to happen.

My three youngsters were run down the chute, unknowingly adopted for this unique project.

Now, an adopted mustang can't be returned to its former environment. No one is allowed on these lands owned by the BLM. Part of the adoption charter requires them to be kept on private lands.

I had to take them to a ranch, but one that resembled their natural habitat as near as possible. The ranches up there on the high desert are more than 40,000 acres. The only reminder that it isn't wild virgin territory is a fence every twelve miles or so....

And the fences wouldn't be making it any easier; they'd be making it worse. Fences would be my most horrible fear. Mustangs have no knowledge of fences, so they don't respect them.

Again, it might be said that if I couldn't perform join-up in the wild, I was somehow accepting the next best scenario by working within what was technically an enclosed area, however big and untamed. In fact, the opposite was the case. I was inundated with problems and had to work harder to avoid them.

At this point, I took care to hire a woman from Santa Barbara Wildwatch as a referee. When the three mustangs were taken to open land and integrated with the semi-feral ranch herds, she would drive around twice a week to ensure they hadn't been handled, they were still wild.

I had a base ranch for my primary mustang—Pat Russell's place, the Chimeneas Ranch. Then, from there, I found a second and third ranch to look after the backup mustangs.

Q.E.D. also hired an animal behaviorist, Dr. Bob Miller, to observe and comment on what I was doing for the cameras. He also verified that the mustangs were completely wild.

Then we had a warning—the rattlesnakes had come out three weeks early. They killed two horses before the shoot even began. They strike at body heat, and when they first emerge from their dark winter dens, they're cranky and unpredictable—a disaster waiting to happen. A struck mustang and we might get by with our backup number one or two. A saddle horse struck and it might be replaced. But myself struck—that would be the end of it.

But we couldn't very well tell them, "Go back inside! Hibernate a while longer!"

We pressed ahead.

On Saturday, March 29, the crew and myself met in the Maverick Saloon in Santa Ynez. Art Green's band was playing and there was line dancing. The film crew were happy to find old-timer Dutch Wilson telling anyone who'd listen, "Maauun-tee's absolutely crazee. He stands as good a chance as any of bein' killed outright.... So who is it wants to go with 'im?"

That evening, I felt relaxed and as ready as I ever would be. If I were to fail to accomplish my dream now, it wouldn't be because I'd never had a crack at it.

I was prepared for a long ride, maybe for as long as two days, nonstop. I'd discovered some stuff made by the company 3M; it's like a patch you put on, and an hour later you can't find it, it's like another skin. It's used for marathon runners' heels, for triathlon athletes and so on. With this tape, half long johns, elastic socks, pants, and chaps, I hoped to minimize the amount of broken skin I'd have to suffer during what would probably be a day, a night, and another day's continuous riding, nonstop wear and tear.

For my bad back, I was on anti-inflammatories, and I had a back brace ready.

So, at around nine-thirty that Saturday night, I got into my trailer and drove off with my three horses—Dually, Big Red Fox, and The Cadet—up to the primary ranch and shoot headquarters, the Chimeneas.

The enterprise started for real on Easter Sunday at daybreak, after a cold night spent sleeping in the truck.

This is big country, in every sense of the word. It's where they come to make the Marlboro ads. The early sun brought the place alive: I noticed the white hives for the bees that feed off sage. Sycamores lined the dry riverbeds in the valleys; yucca and cactus grew in the dust.

Sometimes, around here, the bees hit the windshield of your car like hail, and tarantulas are so great in number they cover the roads.

I can see only in black and white, but for those who can see colors, I'm told there's a mixture of ochre, burnt orange, slate gray, chalk, and cream.

The first task of the day was to cut the mustang out of the herd. To this end I had five wranglers helping me: Pat Russell, Cathy Twisselman and her son Caleb, Barney Skelton, and Scott Silvera.

The aim was to drive the herd west while picking out the mustang and sending him in the opposite direction, due east, into open country.

Cathy Twisselman, an old student of mine from years before, saved the shoot right there and then when she was quick enough to stop the mustang from running toward a fence.

Then it was done. The herd was off one way and I was driving the mustang, in full flight, over the high desert. The film taken from the helicopter shows a sleek, fast mustang, fluent and youthful, followed by a well-padded-out old cowboy galloping along behind him.

In terms of the round pen, this would be the equivalent of sending the horse around the ring with the use of the light sash line. In terms of the psychology of the wild herd, I was the dominant mare running at the adolescent, driving it away to show I was displeased, and asking for it to show me some recognition and respect.

Except, instead of taking ten minutes, this flight would go on all day.

I hadn't reckoned on the level of panic caused by the helicopter. In retrospect, I should have asked that it follow us only for the first twenty minutes and then back off, so we could have regrouped, read the situation as it developed.

Instead, the helicopter ran us to death. We covered nearly one hundred miles in that first day, the mustang in full gallop for an hour and a half. It was an unforgettable ride.

I was waving the helicopter back, trying to shout into the two-way radio while running full tilt, but communications weren't as effective as we'd thought; the radio was bumping all over the place, and although I had a white shirt tucked into my jacket to wave at them, they couldn't see it. I could hardly hear them either, because of the engine noise.

It was killing to stay at a full gallop for an hour and a half, and a lot of the time I had to be up out of the saddle to spare the horse's back. I was unsure of the ground, and one stumble at that speed could have been fatal. I was just praying for the sun to go down.

So that day was traumatic—I practically ran my first horse, The Cadet, into the ground. He ended up with swollen legs but thankfully wasn't injured.

And the fences were a horrible worry, as I'd predicted—but here the helicopter came into its own, overhauling the mustang and containing him. There were twelve miles between fences, but mustangs don't know barbed wire—they don't see it.

I kept going during that long first day with beef jerky from my saddle bag and water from the canteen. The only respite I had was to step off one horse and onto another. It was one hell of a run.

Then at last it got dark and the helicopter went home.

Now another thing happened that told me this project was meant to succeed—I made the decision to ride through the night on the horse called Big Red Fox.

Big Red Fox was a thoroughbred, retired from the racetrack and kept in shape on Flag Is Up for his owners, who every now and again would come and ride him. He was not a pretty horse, so he wasn't to be used in daylight, on camera.

He saved the whole shoot during the night.

It was dark, but the half-moon showed us the mustang up ahead. It was a minefield of badger holes, but we didn't fall into any of those.

The mustang slowed right down.

I allowed him to rest, to eat and drink, but kept on him. I needed to maintain pressure on him, just as in the round pen when I keep driving the wild horse away, until he shows signs of wanting to join up with me.

So I was letting him know I was there, gently moving him on, keeping tabs on him by moonlight... and now my black and white vision gave me an advantage because—so I'm told—at night I can see better than normally-sighted people.

Then, around midnight, in came a fog and shut the moon off. It was pitch-black.

And I couldn't see the mustang at all.

I was in desperate trouble, because if I lost him, I'd have to start the whole thing over.

Yet this horse, Big Red Fox, kept me on him. He'd stop himself, start himself, take me right, take me left. Big Red Fox was on him like the mustang was wearing a tracking device. I could have been a blind man and not lost the mustang in the pitch-dark.

I dropped the reins and let Big Red Fox do his thing. We'd stop, and I'd be looking around, staring into the fog, and then suddenly I'd see the mustang five feet away from me. It was magic. It raised the hairs on the back of my neck. Big Red Fox was right on him, every time. I'd see a shadow, he'd take me through it, and it'd turn out to be the mustang's.

We passed the whole night in this way—it was like a spell had been cast over the landscape.

Then, around four in the morning, there was a glow in the east and Big Red Fox picked up speed. We were in a long trot, and as the glow increased, we moved into a canter.

The mustang was reading the daylight; he was having one last shot at getting away.

Right at daybreak, at around four-thirty, he took me on a high-speed chase for fifteen miles. It was as harrowing a ride as I'd ever had.

There were no cameras. I'd been in the saddle for nearly twenty-four hours nonstop, but I kept on him.

Around five in the morning, apparently Pat Russell—occupying a patch of high ground—spotted me through his binoculars going hell for leather, aiming to hit the top of a valley.

At the same time, as luck would have it, he saw the camera crew coming in from the northeast. He rode back down and told them where to intersect with me.

So at around five forty-five the 4WD and ATV vehicles came in, the video camera was fitted up, and they started filming from half a mile away, just as I was coming down this valley, with treacherous ravines and boulders troubling us in the bottom of it.

Then we ran out of the valley into a flatter, more open area. Suddenly the ground was easier. The mustang slowed down.

This area of flat ground at the foot of the valley turned out to be the mustang's comfort zone, a place where the grass was tall, where he could graze without bending his head too much, without stopping. Also, there was water. Mustangs are survivors; they know a good place when they find one.

And then he was beginning to look at me. I was acknowledged. Flight wasn't working, so he needed to ask for my help. It would be up to me to recognize the language and signal back to him that I was his helper, I was on his side.

I felt the time had come to attempt join-up.

I had a powerful flashlight that I could use to signal my position even during daylight hours, so now I called for a change of horse—and for this task, it had to be Dually.

Caleb Twisselman brought up Dually for me, and I changed over.

Now I could talk the language of Equus.

This mustang could put an ear on me, lower his nose, and in the same instant I'd have Dually break away, relieve the pressure on him, let him off the hook. But when the mustang started going away, *whoof!* Dually was on him, driving him farther off, letting him know we were the surrogate matriarch.

In the same way as in the round pen, Dually and I were communicating with this wild horse in the language it understands, its mother tongue, Equus.

On a horse as highly schooled as Dually, I could use these delicate, interpretive movements—and so I could reach out to this mustang, let him know we could be trusted.

Dually was part of my body; the speed and delicacy of his responses made it possible. I can get a quarter of an inch out of Dually; he's that accurate when he answers to my commands.

Tentatively, this mustang began to follow us around. He was reading the situation. This was a whole different thing for him, but he was prepared to accept Dually and me.

We had join-up.

It was magic as, together with Caleb Twisselman, we stood close enough, for long enough, to allow us to touch him. Without ropes, without penalties. He was fidgety, liable to go into flight at any moment, but he trusted us enough. It was truly remarkable.

Dr. Bob Miller, the animal behaviorist, agreed. As he said, this was an animal that could "kick a fly off a wall at fifteen feet." He was explosive, wild. Yet, of his own free will, he was accepting a human touch. It was a privilege.

Now I had a name for him—Shy Boy.

And moreover, I knew it was done, there was no chance of failure now, barring a strike from a rattlesnake. I'd joined up with wild horses enough times within the confines of the round pen, all over the world, to know we'd achieved the same thing here, but in a round pen ten miles in diameter.

There was also this sense of my life coming around full circle. As a teenager, I'd observed these horses in the wild, and seen things I believed no one else knew about, things that led me to develop my techniques in secret. Now a television crew was watching this mustang's every move.

By now, Dually was getting tired of carrying my weight, and I changed to my fourth horse in thirty-six hours: He wasn't one of mine, but a ranch horse called George.

This ranch horse made a difference instantly. Dr. Bob Miller also noticed the same thing, that the mustang could identify this as a local horse, even though he'd never seen George before. From what George had eaten and drunk, from his scent and his presence, the mustang knew that whereas Dually was not from around here, George shared the same lifestyle as him.

So the mustang trusted George noticeably more than Dually. He let me get closer.

Very gently, I dropped a rope onto his mane. I caught the other side of it and tied it around in a loose boland knot.

He upped and slapped me in the hand, once, but after this nervous reaction, I had him leading and resting comfortably.

And this was enough, for his first day. Shy Boy could rest, catch up on his new experiences, take in food and water.

I, too, was happy to go to the Buckhorn Hotel, eat a full meal, and celebrate!

I'd ridden nonstop for thirty-six hours, but I was OK. My back never said a word! The half-emptied vertebrae held up the whole way through, and I never needed the back brace.

In addition, when I peeled off my layers of clothes, I found I hadn't suffered any broken skin, because of this miraculous tape made by the 3M company.

That night in the Buckhorn Hotel, I slept like a log.

Meanwhile, Shy Boy rested up, still on this flat piece of ground, his comfort zone. The wranglers' horses weren't far off, and he was happy to stay within range of them. He was checked overnight but wouldn't stray far, I was sure.

The next morning, I turned up to be informed that Shy Boy had broken away, run onto the highway, and been hit by a car. I went cold, frozen on the spot, before I realized what day it was.

April fool...

Then it was back to work: time for the surcingle.

I dismounted and approached Shy Boy on foot—and this was a crucial moment. Not only was I more vulnerable, but I was a different entity from the man-and-horse that he'd learned to trust.

But it went smoothly, by the book. I used a four-foot wire with a little hook on the end to catch the buckle from underneath his belly, and he had to learn this wasn't a snake.

Again, the saddle was a whole new thing. We started off with a baby saddle, but still, as I walked toward him with it hanging off my arm, Shy Boy was pretty sure it was a predator, that there was a whole lot of trouble connected with it.

Dr. Bob Miller agreed, "He'd have had a fit" if I'd put the big stock saddle on him right away.

We were building trust all the time. As we worked through that day, Shy Boy learned the saddle wasn't a big cat; he learned we weren't going to hurt him or restrain him in any way.

It took three saddles—a small one, a medium one, and then the stock saddle. Each step was taken with great care. The trust was like a thread of cotton between us—I had to make sure it was never broken.

That second day passed in arduous, patient work: the surcingle, the first saddle, the second, the third. The running—the flight—was over, but the tension, if anything, was greater.

By the next day, April 2, I'd learned a few things about Shy Boy. He was intelligent, and tolerant to a degree. But he didn't like being outside his own language.

On this third day, we worked to consolidate what we'd achieved with the saddle, and we introduced him to a bridle.

Then it was time to find out how dangerous he remained. Scott Silvera was going to ride him.

I wished it could have been me who'd be on him for the first time, but I couldn't put myself in that position. Quite apart from the fact that I weighed more than the average young man, there was the question of my age, and the danger to me and to the horse.

Again, with Scott Silvera approaching him and asking to put his toe in the stirrup, we were asking Shy Boy to take a whole lot more on trust. A new person, a new smell. This was a whole new pressure on him: a live person on his back.

The first time Scott approached him, Shy Boy jumped back and struck out with his front foot.

It was necessary for all of us to keep uppermost in our minds a sense of calmness, an utter lack of urgency. These horses need patience. If you act like you've got only fifteen minutes, it'll take all day. If you act like you've got all day, it'll take fifteen minutes.

Then Scott had his foot in the stirrup. He lifted himself up very carefully, and his rear touched the saddle as light as a feather.

This was a very emotional moment for me.

The desire to see this happen was buried deep, and experiencing it was like an explosion. The reality was like a gift of great happiness and a sense of closure. I knew we'd achieved something.

For an hour and a half, Scott Silvera gently schooled this mustang. He walked him, turned, rose to a trot. He reined him back a step after each maneuver.

Then Scott Silvera rode Shy Boy back to Pat Russell's ranch house at the Chimeneas—just as I'd returned to a different ranch house after my expeditions in Nevada forty-five years earlier.

Back then I'd been greeted with outright disbelief when I'd described to my father and the other horsemen what I'd found out from observing the wild herds; this time we arrived back to cheers of congratulation from our friends and colleagues, with the whole event recorded by a British documentary film crew. It was an incredible sensation.

They even managed to get on film the two old cynics from the Maverick Saloon in Santa Ynez, on seeing the successful party come riding home. "Well, if they can put a man on the moon, I guess he can bring back a mustang."

Appendix

Join-up: A Step-by-Step Guide

The Man Who Listens to Horses sets out to tell the reader something of my life and how my ideas on starting horses were shaped. This appendix constitutes the how-to section of the book.

It should be plain that starting horses gently is easy, efficient, and systematic: it is freely available to anyone with a positive attitude who is not frightened of horses. The first requirement is that you discard all preconceived notions about starting the young horse. Do retain, however, all your experiences with the horse that have taught you not to fear him and that enable you to move around him safely and effectively.

Hold in your mind the idea that the horse can do no wrong; that any action taken by the horse—especially the young unstarted horse—was most likely influenced by you. We can do little to teach the horse; we can only create an environment in which he can learn. Likewise with people: the student who has knowledge pushed into his brain learns little, but he can absorb a great deal when he chooses to learn.

Actions speak louder than words. We say it but too rarely live by it. The horse uses a predictable, discernible, and effective language, one that requires no interpreters. Like any form of communication, Equus, as I call it, requires some effort to master. If we refuse to believe that the horse can communicate, pain can be used to train him somewhat effectively. But pain is needless and terribly limiting.

What if, on your first day of school, your teacher put a chain through your mouth or over your nose, gave it a jerk, and then took a whip to you when you tried to get away. What would your relationship with that teacher be like? How would you view school from that point on? While the horse's brain is not as complex as the human's, our response to cruelty is similar. The point of my method is to create a relationship based on trust and confidence.

Most conventionally started horses form an adversarial relationship with the humans who employ them. If they agree to perform, it is with a reluctant attitude. The first rule of starting a fresh horse, then, is *no pain*. You the trainer will not hit, kick, jerk, pull, tie, or restrain. If you are forced to use some restraint, it should be of the mildest nature and without the feeling of *you must* communicated to the horse. Suggest to the horse that *you would rather he did* but not that *he must*.

The horse is the quintessential flight animal. When pressure is applied to the relationship, he will almost always choose to leave rather than fight. The phenomenon that I call Advance and Retreat is evident throughout the animal kingdom—between animals of the same and different species and even between humans. Consider, for example, the fourteen-year-old boy in high school who is attracted to a girl in his class and follows her incessantly. She wants nothing to do with him. He may persist for several months, and then give up. Only at this point does she show interest. Advance. Retreat. It's a useful tool in both human and equine psychology.

In starting the young horse—I never use the term *breaking*—the intention is to cause this animal to accept without trauma the saddle, bridle, and rider. In my demonstrations we accomplish that in about thirty minutes. I am suggesting, however, that with completely green horses it is best before the starting procedure to take a few days to accustom them to the bit and to a small measure of communication through long-lines and the mouth of the horse.

In starting the horse, the aim is to achieve a number of related aims: you want to join up with the horse and convince the horse to follow you. You want to be able to touch his vulnerable areas and pick up his feet. You want to put on him saddle pad, saddle, bit, and bridle. Attach long-lines. Get the rider on. Move a full circle right, one step back, a full circle left and, again, one step back.

You will need the following equipment:

- two long lines thirty feet long
- one snaffle bit, fully equipped
- one saddle (your preference)
- one saddle pad
- one stirrup leather
- a halter on the horse

I use a round pen in my operation, and while not absolutely necessary, it does make the job easier. My pen is fifty feet in diameter (16 meters) with a solid wall eight feet high (2.4 meters) and roofed over. Its sand surface has a two-inch cushion. I have, however, started horses in the wild with no fences, riding a horse to aid in travel. A square pen can be used, but it is much better if you can panel the corners out. Fifty feet in diameter is optimum for mid-sized horses. Good footing is important for the safety of horses and people.

Bring the horse, with his halter on, into the pen and have with you one long-line, preferably a light sash thirty feet long (nine meters). Stand near the center of the pen and introduce yourself by rubbing with the flat of your hand (no patting) the horse's forehead, even if you are already acquainted. Now move away and toward the rear of the horse, staying out of the kick zone.

When you are behind the animal or when he flees—whichever comes first—pitch the line toward his rear quarters. This light sash (long-line) cannot hurt him in any way. At this point, almost all young horses will take flight and proceed around the pen. The horse is retreating so you must advance. Keep the pressure on. Pitch the line about two times per revolution or whatever it takes to keep your subject retreating.

Maintain an aggressive mode: Your eyes drilled on his eyes, your shoulder axis square with his head. Maintain forward movement as much as possible, but do not enter his kick zone. Try to get the horse to canter five or six revolutions one way; then reverse and repeat, except that this time you are readying the horse for a message: Would he like to stop all this work?

Particularly watch the inside ear (the ear, that is, closest to you in the center of the pen). That ear will slow up its movement or stop moving altogether, while the outside ear will continue to monitor his surroundings. The head will begin to tip, ears to inside, and the neck will bend slightly to bring the head closer to the center of the circle. He will probably lick and chew, running his tongue outside the mouth.

Finally, he should crane his head down near the ground. The ear gives you respect. Coming closer means just that. Licking and chewing says, "I am a flight animal, and I'm eating so I can't fear you." Craning the head down means, "If we could have a meeting to rene-gotiate, I would let you be the chairman." Experience will sharpen your senses to this communication, but essentially when you observe the horse in this mode, he is asking you to take the pressure off. He wants to stop.

Now coil the line and assume a submissive mode, with your eyes down. Do not look at his eyes. Bring your shoulder axis to a forty-five degree position. This is an invitation for him to come to you, or at least look your way and stop retreating. If he will come to you, this is good! If he stands and faces you but does not move forward, then start to move closer to him, but do it in arcs or semicircles, not straight at him.

If he leaves you, put him back to work for a few more laps. Then repeat the process. As you move closer, do it with your shoulder axis at forty-five degree angles to his body axis. For the most part, show your back to him. He should voluntarily move toward you and reach out with his nose to your shoulders. This is *join-up*.

When you can approach his head, give him a good rub between the eyes and then walk away, moving in circles. I like to start by circling on the right hand about ten feet in diameter. After the right is accom-plished, circle left and repeat several times. He should follow you or at least move to maintain his head in your direction. This I call *follow up*. If he does not follow you, then you will find yourself facing his rear and you should put him back to work. Again, stay clear of the kick zone.

Once *follow up* is evident, the horse should follow you to the center of the pen and stand comfortably for the next step, which is to enter his vulnerable areas. Starting on the near side (the side you mount and dismount on), use both hands to massage neck, withers, back, hips, fore flanks, and rear flanks. Once you have done the same on the off side, you are ready to pick up the feet. Do this using the normal safe procedures.

You are now ready to bring the balance of your equipment into the pen and place it on the ground near the center. Allow the horse time to look the equipment over. Move between the equipment and the horse several times in both directions until your subject prefers to follow you instead of examining the tack. Once you have his attention, snap one line to the halter, placing the line over your left arm about three feet from the snap.

Gently place the saddle pad on his back, first ahead of the withers and then sliding it back in place. If he walks away, do not punish him; just ease him around, cause him to *join up,* and repeat the process (though you should not have to). Once the pad is in place, pick up the saddle (with the irons up and the girth over the seat). Slide your body along the near side of the neck to the point of the shoulder.

With the saddle resting on your right hip, gently place the saddle on his back and move past his head giving him a rub on the off side. Without hesitation, take the girth down slowly and smoothly, adjust the girth to reach approximately to the mid-fetlock joint and move smoothly back to the near side, giving the head a rub on the way by.

Stand near the fore leg and bring the girth up and place the front buckle on the front billot, draw it snug, reading your horse all the way. Do not make it too tight, but tight enough that it will not turn if he bucks. Next, place the back buckle on the back billot and snug it up a bit tighter than the front one.

Go back to the front one and level the two up. Unsnap the line and step back cautiously, line in hand, moving backward away from your horse. Favor the rear portion, staying out of the kick zone. Send him away with the line and be careful not to encourage joining up and bucking at the same time.

Above all, *stay calm*. Your horse must believe that he is the only one bothered by this saddle, or he will be more inclined to buck. Watch for signs that he once again wants to *join up* but only allow it when he is traveling comfortably with the saddle.

As soon as he is back with you, put the bridle on and place the reins under the rear of the saddle or some other place of safe attachment. Leave plenty of slack in the reins. Now, take your extra stirrup leather and drop it through the off-stirrup iron so that it hangs half-way through. Then move to the near side and carefully pick up both ends of the leather and buckle it through the near iron. The stirrups are thus buckled together under the horse.

Take both lines at the snap end and place one over the seat of the saddle, allowing the snap to just reach the ground on the off side. Then place the second snap through the near iron (back to front) and snap it on the near-side bit ring. Move to the off side and repeat.

Move back to the near side. Pick up the two lines at the side of the horse and move backward and laterally—outside the kick zone—toward the rear of the horse. You are now justified in moving him forward and swinging the right rein over his hips to the long-lines.

If you are not experienced with long-lines, move slowly. You want to accomplish a little communication through the mouth, but do it cautiously. Practice this process with older, more experienced horses for a significant period of time before you try it with a first-timer. You could hurt your horse or yourself.

If you are experienced with lines, ask your horse to circle at the canter and then trot both ways. Ask him to negotiate turns and stops. Finally, stop him, facing away from the center and ask him to rein back one step.

At this point, most horses I start are ready to be ridden. You may elect to ride him yourself or have another person do so; either way is fine. Make sure the saddle is adjusted properly and the girth is tight enough to prevent the saddle from turning. If you are using a rider, bring in that rider (wearing, of course, all proper safety equipment).

Snap a line on the near-side bit ring. Give your rider a minute or two to get acquainted with the horse. Have the rider rub both sides of the horse and treat him as you have. I then leg my rider up. First, I ask the rider to just "belly over," so that the rider's belt buckle lies against the pommel.

Then I move the horse carefully, first in two or three left circles and then to the right two or three times. If the horse is happy and accepting the rider lying over him, guide the rider's foot into the near iron as he mounts. Repeat the circles.

If your horse is relaxed and accepting the seated rider, make larger circles that lead the horse nearer the perimeter. Carefully unsnap the line and help the rider accomplish a circle of the pen in each direction. No cantering; walk and trot will suffice. After each revolution, I like my rider to rein back one step.

Do not rush matters. If your horse is not ready to be mounted, do it another day. Remember that my demonstrations must be done in one session so that viewers can see the entire procedure. This does not mean that you must do the same.

This system of starting horses will save so much time that even moving slowly and cautiously, you will still be well ahead. It is the quality of your work that matters, not how fast you accomplish it. We all want the well-behaved, happy, and willing horse at the conclusion. It is on this result that you will be judged.

When the horse has accepted saddle, bridle, and rider, he should *not* be traumatized and should elect to stay with you rather than go away. Remember, let your animal be free. *Do not restrict.* Make it pleasant for him to be near you, and put him to work if he wants to be away from you. *No pain.*

If you can accomplish this process, then you have helped to make the world a better place for the horse.

Afterword

Another Life

The Man Who Listens to Horses was first published in 1996, when I was sixty-one years of age. This is a time when most men are contemplating spending more time at activities such as fishing and golf.

Dry-fly-fishing has been a favorite hobby of mine since childhood, but since this book came out, it has become more firmly placed on the back burner of my life than ever before. I was off and running on a second lifetime I never could have dreamed of. The richness of this second life significantly overshadows what I believed was a very full existence in the first sixty-one years.

Since 1996 I have engaged in a wider array of activities, accomplished more, and met more wonderful people than in all the years before. While it's true that my mission to leave the world a better place than I found it, for horses and for people, has become an obsession, the gratification I feel for what's actually occurring is well worth the work and lifestyle changes required to accomplish this goal. The way that humans interact with horses has changed more since this book came out a decade ago than in the previous 8,000 years, since the domestication of the horse.

These changes toward training horses without using force or violence are happening on a global scale. This second life of mine has taken me to more than thirty countries, and this book has been translated into fourteen languages. While I would like to see still further changes and a still better existence for these wonderful partners of ours, I could never have dreamed that so much could have been accomplished in such a short period of time.

It has been my great good fortune to remain healthy enough to spend approximately 300 days each year traveling to distant locations in an effort to bring my concepts to as many people as possible. Obviously, no one knows how long I can continue to do the kind of work required to demonstrate my principles, but as time goes by, I am working hard to encourage and train students who will eventually take the baton from me. Courses in my methods are well established now in the United Kingdom, in the United States, and in Germany.

When I look back on my life, it seems that the workload I face now is far greater than the one I considered demanding when I was thirty years old, and I could write a whole book about the challenges I've faced on the road. I take inspiration from the fact that England's Queen Mother continued with royal engagements well into her nineties. If I could carry on with my work for that length of time, I would consider it a fantastic gift!

The four years following the publication of *The Man Who Listens to Horses* were absolutely packed with demonstration engagements and television, print, and radio interviews. I gradually learned the most effective way to demonstrate my methods and that I should include showing "remedial" work—dealing with deep-seated phobias, bucking, rearing, refusing to load, for example—alongside a demonstration of persuading an unbroken horse to accept a saddle, bridle, and rider without fear or restraint.

It was in 1997 that Kelly Marks, who teaches my U.K. courses, and her team of students came to me with a suggestion for something quite new. "We think we have sufficient public interest to make an evening at the London Arena, Docklands, work. We'd have to bring in soil and create a space for you to work comfortably with the horses, but I think we can do it." Up to that point all my demonstrations had been in equestrian centers of some kind, each with a capacity of a thousand people or so. The London Arena was a huge space often used for pop concerts, in a totally urban environment. With some trepidation I agreed to try it.

More than 5,000 people turned up on a very rainy evening, muddy old Land Rovers full of enthusiastic horse lovers chugging into the concrete jungle. I remember well the feeling of walking to the center of my round pen and seeing tiny people who appeared to be a mile away. They reached higher than I imagined possible, and the sound of their applause is something I'll never forget.

Nobody could have been certain that it was possible to work with totally untrained horses, or ones with remedial problems, in a place like that. Remaining a horseman and considerate of the needs of these animals who had trained me was my great concern. The skills being applauded should never overshadow my work with the horse.

Later I would come to know that *Equus* is a genus of incredible tolerance. It is amazing how, when you get your work right, horses will shut out unnatural scenes and allow you to work with them under what I had up to that point considered impossible circumstances. These tours, and all that have come with them, have taught me so much, and I admire horses more and more each day.

Germany was the next country to request these big events. In Cologne, we had 7,500 people on one night, 8,000 in Essen, 6,500 in Hamburg, and so on and so on across Germany's cities. Each time I entered one of those monster arenas, my system would vibrate with the enthusiasm of those massive audiences. Many said to me that it was like meeting a rock star, and as time went on, I suppose that began to concern me.

In Australia, I was taken to Olympic villages in both Sydney and Melbourne, as well as to huge arenas in Brisbane, Adelaide, and Townsville. It was commonplace to have 3,000 to 6,000 at our demonstrations up and down the east coast of Australia. In the United States and Canada I also demonstrated at many huge venues. I suppose the most memorable one was the Cow Palace in San Francisco. It has a seating capacity of 7,000, and every seat was occupied for my evening in that city. The Cow Palace is where I won many championships as a child and as a young professional with horses. Little did I realize that I was preparing for this, my second life.

Listening closely to those I respect most in the horse industry, I have concluded that people who attend my events seem to get most out of them when audiences are limited to fewer than 2,000. It is important that each person who sees me is informed and entertained. Informed because it is the only way we learn, and entertained because many simply won't continue to be interested if it's viewed only as hard work. I know that this decision means more work for me and the people who assist me, but I believe the results are more gratifying than going down the "rock star" route, and I feel much more comfortable now that we have returned to these more intimate venues.

There is no question in my mind that if I had not enjoyed the endorsement of England's Queen Elizabeth II, I would have at best published my work as a how-to manual. It might have been important to some in the horse industry, but in no way would it have ever reached the level of importance that it has throughout our society.

With all thirty countries and fourteen languages tallied, it is probable that more than five million copies of *The Man Who Listens to Horses* have found their way into homes. (The first publisher I visited in the U.K. predicted that the book could hope to sell only 3,000 to 5,000 copies in total. We ended up selling that number in the U.K. in the first week alone.) After speaking to publishing people, I find it likely that each copy is read by 3.2 people. Experts in this area believe this book has been read by at least fifteen million people.

If these numbers are anywhere near accurate, it means that this book has had a greater impact on the world than any other book in its category. As a nonfiction work by a horseman about his life and work, it stands alone.

When *The Man Who Listens to Horses* was accepted for publication in the United States by Random House, New York, the publishers were very concerned that it should appeal to the general reader. The fact that it appeared on *The New York Times* bestseller list almost immediately after the launch in August 1997 certainly qualified it as a book that was going into homes that didn't have horses—and it stayed on the list for fifty-eight weeks! My English agent, Jane Turnbull, was proud of being able to take such a book to New York and see it work so well there.

Thousands of horses have benefited from my work subsequent to this first book: Prince of Darkness, Lomitas, Song of Africa, and many others perhaps less famous but no less important to the individuals who cared for them. Those thousands of horses were the recipients of violence-free training, to be sure, but the true importance of the work was for the people who needed to learn the principles of training without violence.

Not one horse has ever read *The Man Who Listens to Horses*. My mission has not been to train horses at my demonstrations, but to bring an alternative mind-set to people, as it is they who make the decisions that affect the lives of the horses we work with.

For More Information

My goal is to leave the world a better place, for horses and people, than I found it.

In that effort I invite you to call for further information regarding clinics, conferences, educational videos, or other educational material at:

phone	1-805-688-6288
online	www.MontyRoberts.com
E-mail	info@montyroberts.com

Thank you,
Monty Roberts